Exploring
1 & 2 Peter:

Suffering, Certainty and Hope

RICH CASTRO

DayOne

ISBN 978-1-84625-736-0
Unless otherwise indicated, Scripture quotations are from The Holy
Bible, English Standard Version (ESV), copyright © 2001 by Crossway
Bibles, a division of Good News Publishers. Used by permission. All
rights reserved.

British Library Cataloguing in Publication Data available

Published by Day One Publications
Ryelands Road, Leominster, HR6 8NZ
Telephone 01568 613 740 FAX 01568 611 473
Email—sales@dayone.co.uk
Website—www.dayone.co.uk

Cover design by Kathryn Chedgzoy
Printed by 4edge

CONTENTS

Introduction   5

1 Peter: Suffering and glory   7

Chapter 1:   *Destined for better*   9

Chapter 2:   *Security in suffering*   29

Chapter 3:   *Suffering first, glory later*   49

Chapter 4:   *Live in the light of your salvation*   67

Chapter 5:   *How do you fall?*   85

Chapter 6:   *Suffering in submission*   103

Chapter 7:   *Submitting to Christ*   115

Chapter 8:   *Suffering and love*   129

Chapter 9:   *Deep waters*   143

Chapter 10:   *A theology of suffering*   161

Chapter 11:   *A pastoral conclusion*   175

2 Peter: Suffering and certainty   189

Chapter 12:   *Salvation belongs to our God*   191

Chapter 13:   *Bible bedrock*   213

Chapter 14:   *Charlatans in the church*   233

Chapter 15:   *Passion and purpose*   253

Chapter 16:   *Now and then*   271

Introduction

Despite the huge advances in medical science in the past half-century, medical killers remain. One of our friends died from cancer two days before Christmas. A close friend suffered a stroke on Christmas Eve. Other friends have suffered great injustices in the church; injustices which seem highly unlikely ever to be resolved in this life. Another friend continues to suffer with daily pain and has done for decades. One friend is struggling with job insecurity; others have been made redundant. Many people lie in intensive care units struggling to recover from Covid-19. Loneliness and isolation are causing a big rise in mental health issues across our nation (and across the world), especially among young people and older singles. Personal addictions are becoming entrenched. At the height of Covid-19, schools were running online only, churches were unable to meet in person and families were separated from one another for six weeks or more. Many Christians around the world also suffer regular persecution for their faith, some even to the point of death. In short, our world is full of suffering.

Peter writes to a suffering church and brings an eternal perspective to the age-old question about suffering. It is a message that is full both of challenge and of comfort. Peter, like the Psalmist, pushes us to raise our sights from the here and now to the glory of heaven (See Psalm 121:1–2). He reminds us that God will bring us one day to a glorious inheritance where there will be no more death or mourning or crying or pain—an inheritance which is 'imperishable, undefiled and unfading, kept in heaven for you, who by God's power are being guarded through faith for a salvation ready to be revealed in the last time' (1 Peter 1:4–5). Peter urges us to see the depth and the breadth of the love of God as he brings us closer and closer to himself even amid our pain.

My prayer in writing this book is that God's word will bring you great comfort and joy amid your suffering, and that, as you study 1 and 2 Peter, so God will shine his light into the darkness. For our good, and for his great glory.

Rich Castro

January 2020

1 Peter
SUFFERING AND GLORY

1 Destined for better

1 Peter 1:1–2

Introduction

In a larger family, the washing machine is rarely off, the schedule is never blank, and the house is usually noisy. Every day is filled with eating, working, cleaning, cooking, clubs, preparing, planning, running errands, shopping, and so on and so on. It feels sometimes as though life goes round and round and round with no let up. Is this how life is meant to be, or are we missing something? Are we destined for better?

For Peter, he also had a daily grind. He had long shifts through the night at work, out on the lake whatever the weather, trying to make a living from fishing. Perhaps he was concerned about the need to provide for his wife, concerned over the health of his in-laws, or struggling through the aridity of the dry season. In all of this, perhaps Peter wondered whether there might be something more to life, too. Then one day, on the beach by the boats, he met Jesus for the first time. He got out of his boat and into belief—he became fully convinced that he *had* missed something all this time. He had missed the most important thing of all, in fact. Peter now knew; he was destined for better.

Peter is a complex character. On the one hand, he is a towering New Testament figure, providing key leadership in the fledgling church. On the other hand, he fails repeatedly. He is a follower of Jesus who declares loudly and boldly that we have no hope outside of Jesus. 'Repent and be baptized every one of you ... for the forgiveness of your sins' (Acts 2:38). He tries to walk to Jesus across the water, but collapses into the waves, due to fear of the wind, moments after Jesus told him: 'Take heart, it is I. Do not be afraid!' (Matthew 14:27). He confuses Jesus' mission to die on our behalf right after he has declared Jesus as divine. He cowers before servant girls right after he has drawn his sword before an arresting army. He compromises his faith in the book of Galatians right after he has planted numerous churches. Peter is such a comforting figure in the New Testament because he is just like us. His progress through life is not a carefully drawn straight line towards heaven. Rather, his life story is mixed. He is a 'two-steps-forward and one-step-back' kind of person—a contradiction at times. In life, Peter struggles.

As he writes his first letter to a new but growing church facing increasing resistance and persecution, Peter writes for one simple reason: *encouragement*. In these first two verses of 1 Peter 1, his primary point is a simple one: Christians are destined for something better.

He begins with two major and connected truths. Firstly, election is eternal. Secondly, suffering confirms citizenship. But before we unpack those two interconnected things, we need to deal briefly with two other things. We must remind ourselves of Peter's resumé—his qualifications for writing. We need also to remind ourselves of Peter's reason—why does he write at all?

Peter's resume

When I receive a letter from the local council, I open it worriedly, mostly because I'm expecting a bill. There is the official county council stamp on the envelope, and the letter inside carries governmental authority. Perhaps it says I am behind in paying my council tax and I have fourteen days to pay up or face prosecution. When I receive a letter like that, I take notice and get my affairs in order.

Notice here how Peter begins his letter. He writes, 'Peter, an apostle of Jesus Christ.' That is his official stamp, if you like. An apostle is a person who has met the risen Jesus, has been trained by Jesus, and has been commissioned by Jesus. Peter witnessed the resurrected Jesus on a number of occasions. He trained as a disciple under Jesus for three years. He was commissioned and sent by Jesus, not just in the 'Great Commission' of Matthew 28, but also in his own personal commissioning in John 21:15–18.

These three qualifications hold true for all the apostles. Even Paul fulfils them after a fashion.

He met the risen Jesus on the road to Damascus. He spent three years in training, it would seem, in Arabia (Galatians 1:17–18). He was commissioned and sent by Jesus as a missionary (primarily, as it turned out, to the Gentiles). We read in 1 Corinthians 15 that Jesus appeared 'last of all' to Paul (v. 8). Because he was somewhat late to the party, Paul described himself as an apostle only 'as one abnormally born'. Paul was the last apostle; so contrary to some ideas around, there are no apostles today.

Back here in 1 Peter 1, Peter gives his resumé—his official stamp: he is an apostle of Jesus Christ. He wants his readers to sit up and take notice when they receive this letter. It would be foolish to ignore its contents. What he writes here is directly *for* his readers, and we need to take it in and respond appropriately.

The writings of the apostles are authoritative because letters which carry apostolic authority are, above everything else, letters from God himself. The words we read, in their original form, are completely and perfectly true. They are words to be pondered, learned, digested and loved. They are words that will transform us. Like reading the letter from the county council, only far more serious and important, the words, 'Peter—an apostle of Jesus Christ …' should make us sit up and get our affairs in order. Peter needs no more for his resumé than to say: 'I am an apostle of Jesus Christ.'

His reason

In verse 1, we notice that Peter is writing to a specific group of churches in Asia Minor, namely Pontus, Galatia, Cappadocia, Asia and Bithynia. It is helpful to understand why Peter writes to these Christians in particular.

At Pentecost, in Acts 2, a huge crowd from all over the known world heard Peter preaching about Jesus—his death and resurrection. They were confronted with their rebellion against God ('sin') and they were 'cut to the heart.' They realized they were guilty, so they cried out to the apostles: 'What shall we do?' (v. 37).

It is the same for us, too—when we are confronted with our sin, we should realize that we are guilty. We cannot stand before God and claim innocence and perfection. We have all gone against him— each of us, like sheep, have turned astray; everyone to his own way (Isaiah 53:6). We, too, should cry out: 'How can we be rescued and freed from our guilt? How can we gain eternal life?'

Peter responded to their question with utter clarity: 'Repent and be baptized every one of you in the name of Jesus Christ for the forgiveness of your sins, and you will receive the gift of the Holy

Spirit' (Acts 2:38). Three thousand people were obedient to his call, became Christians and were baptized.

It is those events in Acts 2 that Peter has in mind as he writes this letter to the churches of Asia Minor. How do we know that? Because the people to whom Peter preached in Acts 2 were, 'Parthians and Medes and Elamites and residents of Mesopotamia, Judea and *Cappadocia, Pontus* and *Asia*, Phrygia and Pamphylia ...' (vv. 9–11) [emphasis mine]. In Acts 2, Jews had come to Jerusalem from all over the Roman world to celebrate the festival of Pentecost. Peter preached and 3000 of them become Christians. After this, the people from those disparate places returned to their hometowns. The now-converted Jews (as a result of Peter's preaching) were instrumental in starting up churches in all those new places.

Thus, Peter writes to those particular churches named in 1 Peter 1:1 because those churches were planted and grew as a direct result of his own preaching and the persecution that followed. These are his spiritual children and grandchildren, if you will. He has a special affinity with them. Even as Peter suffers, he writes to encourage them in the midst of their own suffering, because his heart aches for his children. His desperation for them to keep on with God, despite their suffering, compels him to write.

The prime purpose of his writing is simple. He wants to remind them that, despite their suffering, they are destined for something better. Look how he begins his letter to them. He produces perhaps the most encouraging description it is ever possible to give any Christian anywhere, especially in the midst of persecution. He uses just two words, side by side in the Greek, which he then goes on to expound in verse 2 and beyond. He describes them as 'elect exiles'.

These two words emphasize two central ideas in Peter's first letter, so we will study each in turn. Firstly, Peter believes that election is eternal. For this reason, the Christians to whom he is writing can have assurance of their eternal destination. Secondly, suffering confirms citizenship. Because they are suffering, they can be confident of their position as children of God and citizens of God's eternal kingdom.

Election is eternal

What does Peter mean by, 'elect'? There is a great deal packed into this small word. Peter is asserting that before the foundation of the world, before Genesis 1, God chose these people for salvation, not because of anything they did or would do, but because of his own infinite mercy and grace. Many struggle with this doctrine of *election*, and they make two primary objections. Firstly, they feel that it removes humankind's freewill. Secondly, they feel it is unfair of God to choose to save some and not others. Let us think about these two objections for a few minutes.

Freewill

In trying to solve these problems, people look to what Peter says here and argue that God's election of Christians is based on his foreknowledge of their response to the gospel. After all, we read right here in vv. 1–2: 'To those who are elect ... according to the foreknowledge of God the Father ...'. So, the argument goes, God foresees whether or not a person is going to respond to the gospel, and if they repent and submit to him then he elects them—predestines them—to eternal life. They are chosen on the basis of their response to the gospel. God is a gentleman, people say—he does not force his way in. We have free choice, they argue—we can accept him or reject him. God is not unfair—we all have a chance of salvation. God's choice of us is dependent upon our response to Jesus.

I am not convinced that this argument helps us with the question of freewill, however. If God foresees that we will respond positively and then elects us before the foundation of the world, then his foresight is absolute. What he sees happening in the future will definitely happen. It cannot fail to happen. Thus, when it comes to us living our lives, either we will respond positively to the gospel and cannot fail to repent because God has foreseen that. Or we will not repent and we never will repent, because God foresaw that before the foundation of the world and therefore did not choose us. In other words, irrespective of what we do, God foresaw it and his choice is set in stone before we are ever born. If God knew, before the foundation of the world, how many people would get to heaven and how many would not, then those facts were determined before any of us were ever conceived. There is nothing you or I can possibly do to change it.

There is a deeper reason why this argument does not wash, too. It relies on a faulty understanding of the word *foreknew*. To say that the words, 'God foreknew' simply means he knew what people would do, is really to say very little indeed. The Biblical view of God is that he is eternal, all-powerful, all-loving and all-knowing. Therefore, he knows everything that was and is and is to come, and he knew all of it before any of it happened. If this is the true meaning of *foreknew*, then to say, 'God foreknew', is simply to state the obvious—it is to say, 'God is God'. Of course he knew, otherwise he would not be God.

But in fact, foreknowledge is not knowledge *about* something. It is not knowledge regarding something we will decide. Rather, God's foreknowledge is about us being intimately *known* before the foundation of the world. It is deeply personal knowledge, like when a man *knows* a woman. It is not knowledge *about* a person, but rather knowledge *of* a person.

God does elect those of us who are Christians on the basis of his foreknowledge. But his foreknowledge is not data. It is not, 'I know that this person will do this or do that,' or, 'I know that this person is like this or that.' Rather, his foreknowledge is about his love. It is not that he knew what we would do and say and think before we came to exist, although of course he did. Instead, it is that he *loved* us before we came to exist—before the foundation of the world. *Because* he loved us, he chose us to be conformed to the likeness of his Son. He first loved us, and the result of this love is to elect us to eternal life. We might even say that 'foreknown' could be equally well translated, 'foreloved'.

To say that God chose on the basis of his seeing whether or not we would respond to the gospel, is simply to say that God's election and choice is dependent upon our choice of him. But when Jesus speaks to his disciples, what does he say? He says, 'You did not choose me but I chose you ...' (John 15:16). And in his first epistle, John wrote, 'We love because he first loved us' (1 John 4:19). This leads us to the heart of the issue.

Either salvation is ultimately rooted in a human decision, or it is ultimately rooted in God's decision. Either it is as a result of a personal choice by a human being—our response to the gospel—or it is the result of a personal choice by a Sovereign God. Either salvation is because of something *I* have done, or it is the result of something God has done. How do we know which of these two Peter means?

He gives it away in verse 3. 'According to his great mercy, he *has caused us* to be born again to a living hope ...'. Did you respond to the call to repent and turn to God for your salvation? If you are a Christian, then yes—you did. But Peter writes that it is God who *caused you* to repent and believe. 'He *caused us* to be born again to a living hope.' Who is the ultimate cause of your salvation and mine? According to Peter, it is God himself.

Salvation is by grace alone, through faith alone, in Christ alone, to the glory of God alone, not by works—not by anything a human being has done or said or thought—so that no one can boast. That was the heart of Reformation theology, because it was the heart of early church theology, because it *is* the heart of Biblical theology. I am not a Christian ultimately because I responded to the gospel call, although I did. I am a Christian because I was chosen before the foundation of the world on the basis of the love of the eternal Father. From a human perspective, it is nothing to do with me. I do not deserve it; I did not earn it; and I could not earn it. In him alone can I boast.

Is it not unfair to save some and not others

This leads us to the second objection: is God unfair in electing some to salvation but not others? We have said that God's election to salvation is based solely on his mercy and grace and love. As a

Christian, I am not elect because of anything in me. Rather, I am elect because of God alone. But for someone who never comes to trust in Jesus and thus faces eternal punishment, that punishment is because of their rebellion against and rejection of God.

To put it another way, there is asymmetry in this doctrine of election. Person A deserves hell, but is chosen and heads for heaven because God, in love, chose them. Person B heads for hell because of their rebellion against God. They get what they deserve. If justice were meted out in a human way, every human being would stand condemned and have no hope of eternal life. We would all head for hell with no recourse. But God, in his mercy and love, chose some for heaven. The unchosen get what they deserve—there is nothing unfair in that. The chosen get what they do not deserve—if there is any unfairness, then this is where the unfairness lies.

In the current climate which prizes human autonomy above everything else, those of us who are Christians must be careful not to put human autonomy above the eternal God. We must remember that human freedom is limited, or secondary. None of us has unfettered freedom. I cannot hop onto an aeroplane and fly around the world each month because of the financial constraints I live under (and, currently, because of the lockdown restrictions due to Covid-19). I cannot play football for a premier league football club (or indeed for any other club) because I am too old (and have zero soccer skills). I cannot break the law repeatedly and expect to avoid punishment. My freedom is limited. These Christians, to whom Peter writes, *did* choose to follow Jesus, yes. When they cried out to Peter in Acts 2, 'What shall we do?', Peter does not respond, 'Some of you are elect and others are not, so it doesn't really matter what you choose because it has been decided from before the dawn of time anyway!' No! Peter pleads with them, 'Repent and be baptized every one of you for the forgiveness of your sins ...'. It is because they responded to the gospel that these churches to whom Peter writes are founded. Jesus himself cries out to all of us, 'Come to me all who labour and are heavy laden and I will give you rest' (Matthew 11:28). There is a required response to the gospel, and the New Testament calls to you and to me that we would respond. That call comes to you even today as you read this, if you are not yet a Christian.

But our decision to follow Jesus is the secondary cause, not the primary cause of our salvation. The ultimate decision for our conversion—our resurrection from spiritual death to life—lies in the electing mercy, grace and love of God before the foundation of the world. It is because he chose you, Christian, that you repented and turned to him. We were 'dead in ... [our] trespasses and sins,' but God 'made us alive' (Ephesians 2:1–5). When Jesus called Lazarus to 'come out' (John 11:43), Lazarus was dead. The only reason he came out was that Jesus brought him life and enabled him to do as he had been commanded. Likewise, our salvation does not depend on us. The only reason we could respond to the gospel call was because Jesus gave us life and enabled us to do so. Our salvation depends on him, not on us. That is a huge comfort!

George Whitefield, a preacher from the 18th century, was utterly convinced of this divine election, rooted in the heart of God before the foundation of the world. The conviction of its truth drove Whitefield to proclaim the gospel as powerfully and effectively as he knew how, urging people to repent and believe the good news.

Likewise, Peter, even in the very first introductory sentence of his letter, shouts from the rooftops this towering doctrine of election. 'You are chosen by God,' he tells them. If you are a Christian today, then you also are chosen by God. You are destined for something better than this life.

Many of us have a tendency to hide this doctrine of election a bit. We think it is something we need to feel a bit wary of and a bit embarrassed about. Many churches go light on doctrine, because they think it is not that important—not something to worry about too much. The important thing is to love Jesus and love one another, they say. Doctrine is less important. Peter disagrees. Paul disagrees. John disagrees. God disagrees. These believers are facing some persecution and soon will face far more. They are struggling through life and wondering if it is worth it. Peter decides that the primary thing these believers need is good doctrine. He begins by reminding them of their divine election.

We may wonder why he does this. And the reason is wonderful— we will come to it in a moment. But first, we need to explore Peter's second idea. He describes his readers not just as 'elect' but as 'elect *exiles*'.

Suffering confirms citizenship

An exile is someone whose home is elsewhere. After becoming Christians following Peter's sermon in Acts 2, many returned to their hometowns all over the Roman Empire and began churches there. For those who lived more locally, many had to leave their homes and were dispersed as a result of persecution. At the very start of his letter, though, Peter is very clear—no Christian is living in their true home because Christians are citizens of heaven. On earth, in this life, we are only sojourning here—home is where we are headed.

Back in 2012, our family moved to live in a different country. One of the songs we found very helpful contained the lines, 'All I know is I'm not home yet. This is not where I belong.'[1] The truth of it helped us as we tried to adjust to a different culture. As Christians, Peter is telling us here, we are citizens of heaven.

A great American theologian once told the story of when he and his wife were travelling in Europe behind the iron curtain. They had been instructed to be very careful at the country border crossings and try to keep a low profile—Westerners had disappeared while travelling. They reached one particular border crossing and two beefy, stern-looking guards moved towards them down the carriage. They wanted paperwork and credentials. 'Who are you? Where are you from?' they wanted to know. Then one of them spotted that the theologian had a Bible on his lap—a great felony indeed. Suddenly this guard relaxed slightly and said, in heavily accented English, 'Leave these two alone. They are citizens of a great country.' It turned out that the guard was a Christian and had found a way to let them go. They were not, ultimately, citizens of the United States, and therefore to be detained. They were citizens of heaven—a very great country indeed—and therefore should be freed!

We may think of ourselves as citizens of this country but, in reality, we are citizens of a greater country. Here, Peter reminds his readers, 'You are exiles.'

Now we return to our earlier question: Why did Peter think it good to remind these suffering Christians of their divine election and their status as exiles? How does my earthly exile and my current suffering move me to recognise God's love?

Our tendency is to think that, because we are experiencing hardship or suffering, God must have forgotten us for a bit, or perhaps does not love us as much as we had hoped. But Peter is arguing from the outset that the opposite is true. These Christians experience the pain of being exiles in the world. They are refugees. They experience physical, emotional, mental and social pain as a direct result of being exiles. They suffer because they trust in Jesus. They are overlooked for promotion. They are looked down on because of their out-dated views. They are ridiculed for believing what many see as unbelievable. They are pushed aside, dragged to the courts, shut up, shut out and shut off because they trust in Jesus. They struggle against sin because they are exiles. They struggle to pray because they are exiles. They struggle to read the Bible because they are exiles. They walk differently from the world. Therein lies the pain of being an exile.

They and we experience such things not because God has rejected us, but because God has chosen us! We are citizens of heaven, and therefore we are aliens in this fallen world. We struggle to pray and read the Bible because we are exiles. If we were not exiles, we would not struggle—we simply would not bother to try! Our struggle with sin, hard though it is, is an encouragement—it means we are God's chosen people. If we were not chosen, we would not bother to struggle! The fact of our repeated repentance and reconciliation and falling and repentance and so on and so on, is a potent reminder that we are God's chosen people.

We see this in Peter's own life, as we said earlier. 'You are the

Christ!' he proclaims, and Jesus affirms this fact. And then, just a few verses later, he is rebuked sternly by Jesus: 'Get behind me, Satan!' (Mark 8:29,33). Peter denied Jesus before the crucifixion, and then after the resurrection, he is restored. He proclaims Christ and thousands are converted, but then he wavers and is rebuked by the apostle Paul. Peter had his ups and downs, just like we all do.

But his point here is a simple one and a glorious one. The elect will struggle. The elect will face hardship and nakedness and danger and sword. The elect will wrestle. The very fact of the struggle proves our election.

This is why Peter puts these two words together: *elect exiles*. The fact of suffering proves they are chosen. Remember Paul's words from Philippians: 'I want to know Christ and the power of his resurrection and *the fellowship of sharing in his sufferings*, becoming like him in his *death* ...' (Philippians 3:10, NIV). There is joy in the struggle. It is because God has chosen you before the foundation of the world that you suffer as exiles. Suffering, while very hard, should also be a huge encouragement. Election is not some doctrine to be hidden under the carpet. It is precisely the encouragement we need as people living in our broken world. If you are a Christian, then you are chosen by God. You are an *elect exile*.

It is according to the love of God that you are chosen. It is according to the love of God that you are exiles. It is because God loved us before the dawn of time that we are exiles, strangers in the world. We are destined for something better.

Our present struggle

We may be destined for better, but how does that work itself out in the here and now? Peter moves to answer this question as he continues his thought in this first sentence: 'To those who are elect exiles of the Dispersion ... according to the foreknowledge of God the Father, in the sanctification of the Spirit, for obedience to Jesus Christ and for sprinkling with his blood ...'.

In the midst of all their troubles, Peter is reminding us that they are embraced by the Sovereign Triune God: Father, Son and Holy Spirit. We are elect according to the foreknowledge—the *first-loving-ness* of God the Father. We are elect in the sanctification of the Spirit. We are elect for obedience to Jesus Christ and sprinkling with his blood.

For the Jews of the Old Testament and of Jesus' day, when a priest ministered in the temple, he would sprinkle the blood of a sacrifice as he stood in front of the curtain. Behind the curtain was the Ark of the Covenant and the mercy seat on the ark, representing the presence of God the Father. To his right was the table on which sat the bread of the presence—representing the Messiah (we know that to be Jesus), the bread of life. To his left was the golden lampstand with its tongues of fire, burning oil day and night, representing the Holy Spirit. In effect, then, as you stood there at the altar of incense, you were surrounded by the Triune God—the Father before you, Jesus to your right and the Holy Spirit to your left. In the midst of sacrifice, the Triune God embraced you because of the blood being sprinkled.

So here, Peter reminds Christians—you are surrounded and enfolded and embraced in the arms of the Trinity. Once chosen by the Father, now being sanctified by the Spirit, and one day finally fully obedient to Jesus and sprinkled by his blood. All of this was made possible because of Jesus' sacrificial death on the cross.

These Christians are suffering, and for some of them, their blood is being shed. But Jesus has already suffered and paid the ultimate price on their behalf. They are privileged to walk in the footsteps of their Lord, who has gone before them. They have the fellowship of sharing in his sufferings, becoming like him in his death, even. Jesus died to pay for their sin—to make salvation possible—to bring them to the door of heaven. Their own suffering is momentary compared to the suffering they have been saved from. All of this is because they are chosen by God and declared *his*. They are destined for something better.

If you are not a Christian, then recognise here, in 1 Peter 1, the three reasons Peter gives for being a Christian:

1. Christians are elect according to God's foreknowledge—his love,
2. Christians are sanctified in the Spirit,
3. Christians are to live for obedience to Jesus Christ.

These three reasons are undergirded by his final point: we are 'sprinkled with his blood'.

Being 'sprinkled with his blood' refers back to that aforementioned Old Testament picture of the priest in the Temple. Breaking God's law means we deserve for God to punish us. The punishment for sin—for our treason against the King who created us and sustains us—the punishment we all deserve is death. Thus, an animal was sacrificed in place of the person, as a sort of substitute for their death so that they did not have to die for their guilt. When the animal was killed, its blood was sprinkled to show that the price had really been paid. Now *that* animal sacrifice could not really pay for sin—going against God's law—because an animal is never a replacement for a human being. But the sacrifice the priest made pointed forwards to the time when Jesus—God as a human—was sacrificed on the cross as our substitute.

Peter is arguing that Jesus' sprinkled blood pays for our guilt and now we can be forgiven. If Jesus is my substitute, then I do not deserve death any longer. A key reason for being a Christian is that Jesus' death pays for what we deserve, and we are forgiven for our rebellion against God. We are declared 'not guilty' in the sight of God. Your guilt can be taken away, if you will only ask Jesus to be your substitute. That is what being 'sprinkled with his blood' is all about.

So, Peter's reasons for being a Christian are three-fold:

- Firstly, being a Christian means being chosen by God according to his great love. You do not have to be any better than you are now to be saved—'while we were still sinners, Christ died for us' (Romans 5:8). You do not need to be a better person before God will accept you. Come *now*, and his electing love will include you and his sprinkled blood will free you from guilt. Your sin is paid for.

- Secondly, Christians are sanctified in the Spirit—this means they are declared righteous. The cross is like some giant joyful mathematical wonder (I am a maths teacher, so I should be allowed to say this!). Our sin, our guilt, our shame, is taken away from us and put upon Jesus, so that he takes the punishment we deserve. At the same time, the perfect life that Jesus lived, his perfect character, is taken from him and given to us, so that we are declared righteous—holy—in the sight of God. You can be put right before God if you will only ask Jesus to be your substitute. Now, of course, this does not mean that Christians are perfect now—we are not. We are pretty much as imperfect as anyone else. But there is a huge difference: we are forgiven and we are declared right before God.

- Thirdly, the Christian's purpose in life is 'obedience to Jesus Christ'. The call of the Christian is not to live for himself or herself anymore, but to live for Jesus. Jesus is in charge of my life. If I am a Christian, then I am called to obedience. One day, we will be completely obedient—completely righteous— without spot or blemish, the Bible says. We will be living forever with Jesus and with his spiritual children. We are destined for something better.

So, if you're not a Christian—do you not think you need forgiveness? Do you not think you need your guilt taken away? Do you not think you need freedom from the way of life that entangles you? Do you not think you need God to change you from the inside out, by the power of his Holy Spirit, changed from glory into glory until at last you see Jesus' face? Then, if you will come, you will be lost in wonder, love and praise along with the rest of us as we contemplate his glory and majesty and power and authority and justice and mercy and love.

Peter finishes this introduction in verse 2 with a heartfelt prayer: '*May* grace and peace be multiplied to you.' In the midst of all of life, he is saying, 'know increasingly the grace of God in saving you and the peace of God in the storm'. Hold firm to the fact of your election as an exile here, but a citizen of that eternal city where one day you will dwell. Know deep within that you are destined for something better—something far, far better.

As a result, *grace and peace will be multiplied to you* as you hold on to these wonderful truths in the midst of the storm of life.

Notes

1 Building 429, 'Where I belong', from the album, *Listen to the Sound,* (Provident Music Group, 2011)

2 Security in suffering

1 Peter 1:3–7

In my job as a teacher, often I will begin the year laying the ground-rules for behaviour in the classroom. Once I have done that, I move into the meat of the subject material, assuming they remember the basics for how to conduct themselves in the classroom. Occasionally they need reminding (ok—for some it is rather more often than 'occasionally'!), but those rules are the groundwork upon which success in the classroom is built.

In the first two verses of his first letter, Peter has been reminding his readers of the 'ground-work' of their faith. He has explained that they are 'elect exiles'. For Christians, at the core of their being, they stand as God's children through the decision, work and seal of the Triune God: 'according to the foreknowledge of God the Father, in the sanctification of the Spirit, for obedience to Jesus Christ and for sprinkling with his blood'. Peter completed his introduction with an expressed desire for an abundance of grace and peace to these persecuted people.

In effect, Peter has marvelled: 'I was nothing. I was dead in my sin. I deserve nothing. I repeatedly fail to follow Jesus and go against him. I who have no claim on hope, help or happiness. I deserve punishment and hell. And yet, somehow, God chose me, fore-loved me, saved me, forgave me, rescued me, brought me to life, and sealed me!' It is an incredible truth, and it is true for all of us who are Christians.

After such a catalogue of wonders, it is hardly surprising that

Peter overflows in praise to God. Peter now cannot help himself. Verse 3: 'Blessed be [honour to—good words about—praise be to] the God and Father of our Lord Jesus Christ!' Would that God take our fallen hearts and transform them to effervesce with praise. Blessed be God!

As we turn to consider the next few verses, though, we might expect him to move on from the groundwork of salvation to the meat of Christian living. But Peter does not do this. Instead, he pushes relentlessly deeper, expounding further the doctrine of salvation. Why does he do that? He does it because the doctrine of salvation is not only the groundwork, it is also the meat of Christian living. It is not just unbelievers who need to explore the truth of the gospel. Christians need to do it also—to return to the cross of Jesus every day.

Firstly, in these verses, Peter considers God's work in our salvation, both in the past and for the future. Secondly, Peter outlines three of God's key purposes in our suffering. We will consider each one in turn.

Salvation is God's work in our past

In verse 2, Peter has reminded us that we are elect according to the foreknowledge, or *fore-loving-ness*, of God. Now Peter expands on that doctrine by describing how sovereign election is worked out. At the root, how does salvation come about? Peter answers that question right away: 'According to his great mercy, he *has caused us* to be born again ...' If you are a Christian, like the people to whom Peter is writing, then praise God, because according to his great mercy he *gave* you new birth. Your repentance and submission to

Jesus—your 'becoming a Christian'—was caused ultimately by God himself. It is *His* work, not your own.

Now, wait a minute, you might say. I am a Christian because I went forward at a youth meeting. Or perhaps you knelt by your bed and gave your life to Jesus. Perhaps you followed the ABC of becoming a Christian—you admitted that you are a sinner; you believed that Jesus died in your place; and you confessed your sin, asking for his forgiveness, and committing yourself to him from now on. This is how you were saved. This is how you were born again.

In one sense, that is true. Repentance before God is required for us to be saved. 'Repent, for the kingdom of heaven is at hand!' Jesus proclaimed through his ministry (Matthew 4:17). 'Godly grief produces a repentance that leads to salvation,' wrote the apostle Paul (2 Corinthians 7:10). Peter himself, who wrote today's text, cried out to the crowds at Pentecost: 'Repent and be baptized every one of you in the name of Jesus Christ for the forgiveness of your sins, and you will receive the gift of the Holy Spirit' (Acts 2:38). Then, in Acts 3:19, Peter declares, 'Repent, therefore, and turn back, that your sins may be blotted out.' Both repentance and trust in Jesus are necessary for salvation.

But underneath all that, Peter is saying here in 1 Peter 1:3, that if you are a Christian then you are saved because in God's great mercy, he saved you! Verse 3: God '*has caused us* to be born again'. You becoming a Christian is not something *you* have done—not in the end. It is something God has done.

Watch how Luke records early Christian convictions about the doctrine of divine election. In Acts 11:18, the Christians praise God because Gentiles have become Christians. They say, 'Then, to the

Gentiles also, God *has granted repentance* that leads to life.' They do not say, 'Praise you that these people repented and now you have saved them.' No, no. These Christians praise God because he has granted the Gentiles repentance unto life. In other words, why did those Gentiles repent? Because God granted repentance to them. He gave it to them—that is what the word *granted* means. They repented because God gave them the gift of repentance. They are not saved because of themselves—not because of their response to the gospel—not because they did something. They *did* respond, of course, but that is not the reason they are saved—not in the end. Rather, they were saved because God did something. They were saved because of God's great mercy in their past.

God, in his glory, chose to love them, and to give them repentance leading to salvation, forgiveness of sins, imputed righteousness, and eternal joy bringing glory through Jesus back to God. It is the same for you and me if we are Christians today. We are born again because God brought it about according to his great mercy (v. 3). It is God's work in our past.

Jesus declared to Nicodemus in John 3:7: 'You must be born again.' There is no other way to be saved. So, if you have not been born again, then you are not saved. You *must* be born again—a new birth which comes about through your repentance and trust in Christ. However, the root cause of your new birth is God himself. According to his great mercy, he has *granted* us new birth. According to his great mercy, he birthed us, not physically this time, but spiritually.

Some time ago, Meghan, Duchess of Sussex, gave birth to Archie Harrison Mountbatten-Windsor, the seventh heir to the throne in

Britain. Prince Archie did not work long and hard to get himself out of his mother's womb. No—of course not. Meghan, the Duchess, did all the hard work (it is not called 'labour' for nothing!). Furthermore, her hard work was not painless. New birth never is, even for royalty. But despite the labour and the pain, that new birth brought freedom and joy.

In a similar way, we were birthed as Christians. Our new birth was not pain free. Jesus was beaten, flogged and executed in agony—physical agony and spiritual agony—so that you and I may be freed from the sin that binds us, freed from the darkness that enfolded us, and released into the light of the glory of God. We did not birth ourselves into God's family, either. Our birth, of course, was brought about not by a duchess, but by the King of the Ages. God did the work through Jesus on the cross. Immediately before he died, Jesus cried out 'Tetelestai,' meaning 'It is finished.' You had to come down and out of the spiritual birth canal to get into God's Kingdom, of course, but it is God who did the work, not you. And he did it by means of the death and resurrection of Jesus.

Recently, our family enjoyed watching a documentary on the life of Billy Graham. Like Jesus and like the apostles who followed him, Graham repeatedly asked people one simple question: 'Have you been born again?' A woman once asked Graham, 'Why do you keep on saying, "you must be born again?"' In typical Billy Graham fashion, he responded, 'Because, dear lady, you *must* be born again!'

There is no hope outside of this new birth. You can go to church your whole life, do the Sunday Christian thing every week, dress nicely and pretend, and others may think that you are saved. But if you are not born again, then you remain shackled, bound by your sin, and still in darkness. Your only hope is Jesus. You *must* be born again. We must respond to the upward call of God. And ultimately, it is *God* who births us and brings us new life—he is the ultimate *cause*. It is God who paid the price and did the work—he is both the cause and the means. Our salvation is God's work in our past.

Salvation: God's work for our future

There is a flip side to this chronological coin. When Archie Mountbatten-Windsor was born, he was born *from* something. He was born from the darkness of the womb, from the constraints of the womb, and from his umbilical dependence upon his mother. But he was also born *to* something. He was born into the world, born into the light, and released to breathe and move and live in the world. His birth brought freedom and joy, both for himself, but also for his parents. Likewise, while we are born *from* something (from darkness, from the shackles of sin, from rebellion against our Creator), we are also born *to* something.

Peter tells us precisely what we are born *to*, in the same sentence: 'Born again to a *living* hope,' he writes. Notice that it is a living hope, not a dead hope. He explains that this living hope is through the resurrection of Jesus Christ from the dead. It is a living hope because Jesus is alive. He is risen from the dead. He broke out of the cold, dark tomb, defeating death, and now he lives eternally. We have a living hope because our hope is in a living Saviour. Christians know that eternal life is possible because, and only because, Jesus is alive.

In 1 Corinthians 15:17–19, Paul wrote, 'If Christ has not been raised, your faith is futile and you are still in your sins. Then those also who have fallen asleep in Christ have perished. If in Christ we have hope in this life only, we are of all people most to be pitied.' If Jesus is still dead then we have no hope at all, but because Jesus is alive again, we have a living hope.

This begs the question: 'What *is* this "living hope" to which Peter refers?' Again, in classic Peter style, he recognizes the likely question and then answers it in the next verse. This living hope is 'an inheritance that can never perish, spoil or fade' (v. 4, NIV).

In order to inherit something, two things are required of you. Firstly, you have to be part of the family in the first place. Secondly, the patriarch of the family has to die. This is one reason why the story of the *Prodigal Son* is so shocking. 'Dad, give me my inheritance,' said the prodigal son (See Luke 15:12). In other words, 'Dad—I want you dead so I can have your stuff.' It is an outrageous demand. A person comes into an inheritance only if they are a relative *and* if a person dies.

If we are Christians, then we are born again, born anew into the family of God. He is our Father, we are his adopted children, and Jesus is our adopted brother. Our inheritance is certain and fixed because we are not waiting for the patriarch to die and thus for us to receive it. No—our patriarch has died already. So, the inheritance is a certain, secure, immovable fact. As Paul writes in 2 Corinthians: No matter how many promises God has made, they are *yes* in Christ (2 Corinthians 1:19–20). Our inheritance is certain. Peter affirms it directly, so we would not miss it: 'born again to a living hope through the resurrection of Jesus Christ *from the dead* ...' The inheritance is assured because the benefactor has already died, and now lives and reigns. Our living hope, our inheritance, is guaranteed and assured and certain. You can bet your life on it.

So, as an adopted child of God, what is this inheritance that awaits? A person inherits that which is owned by their father. What does our Heavenly Father own? Everything! As a result, our inheritance is enormous in scope! 'All things are yours, whether Paul or Apollos or Cephas [Peter] or the world or life or death or the present or the future—all are yours, and you are Christ's and Christ is God's' (1 Corinthians 3:21–23). *All* things are yours. Our inheritance is all-expenses paid, all-inclusive and all-encompassing.

Before we run away with ourselves, we must grasp the truth that this is not a *prosperity gospel* kind of word. Peter is quick to explain the nature of our inheritance. It is an inheritance that can never perish, spoil or fade. In the ESV we read that it is 'imperishable, undefiled and unfading'.

- Firstly, it is imperishable—not liable to corruption or decay (unlike anything in this world).
- Secondly, it is undefiled—not touched by the fall (unlike anything in this world). Totally holy and pure and righteous and just and loving and joyful and peace-filled and good. Undefiled. Unspoilt.
- Thirdly, it is unfading—ever-strong, perennial, eternal.

An inheritance that will never perish, spoil or fade. None of these adjectives describe health or wealth or prosperity in this life—they are words describing the future.

Now beyond these three adjectives, Peter does not describe our inheritance in detail. We know very little of its content from what Peter writes. Instead of the substance of our inheritance, he focuses on its quality. On this earth, everything perishes, spoils and fades, but when Jesus returns in glory and raises us beyond judgement to live on a renewed earth with him, then he will wipe every tear from our eyes. There will be no more mourning or tears or crying or pain. Instead, there will be only joy and wonder at an inheritance that never perishes, spoils or fades, and joy and wonder at Jesus who reigns eternal. Our salvation is God's work for our future.

At this point, we may find ourselves asking, 'But what if we fail? What if we sin too much? Surely then we could lose this possible inheritance?' But to these sorts of questions, Peter responds with an emphatic. 'No!' He does not tell us that our inheritance is *possible*. Rather, he writes that it is *certain*. Your inheritance does not depend on you. It is not the case that if you mess up then you lose your inheritance. It is not that our human failings and weaknesses and consequent sinfulness might mean that God will renege on his promises and we will lose our inheritance. This would not fit with God's choosing of us from before the foundation of the world. This would not fit with God birthing us anew. This would not fit with God causing us to be born again. If we truly repented of our sin and trusted in Christ for our salvation, then we may be a wayward son or daughter of God, but we remain a son or daughter of God. We cannot negate God's work in our past. We are not disowned or disavowed by the one who brought us new life, because our inheritance does not depend on us.

Look at what Peter writes here: This inheritance is 'kept in heaven for you' (v. 4). He does not say that it is 'kept *by* you' but rather 'kept *for* you'. This word 'kept' in verse 4 can mean either kept, guarded or retained. It is a strong word. In the next verse, however, where the ESV translators have 'guarded', they are using a military word. It means *garrisoned*, *surrounded* and *guarded*. Notice, too, that this *guarding* is not being undertaken by a few soldiers. It is not even coming via a legion of angels. Instead, Peter writes profoundly, that you, '*by God's power* are being guarded'. The one who garrisons, surrounds and guards Christians is God himself. In other words, your inheritance is utterly secure. Our salvation is God's work for our future.

Reading forward from this point in our study, we may wonder whether we have, in fact, misunderstood the whole argument. Peter puts two words in verse 5 that seem to throw doubt on his whole discussion. This inheritance is 'kept in heaven for you, who by God's power are being guarded *through faith*'. Succinctly, we are kept 'through faith'.

The problem is that my faith is weak. What if it fails? Surely, if that happens, then my inheritance disappears. Does not the presence of these two words undermine the whole of Peter's argument? Peter, who is trying to encourage and reassure his people, has just pulled the rug from under his own feet, has he not?

No. First of all, this phrase cannot mean that we are guarded by dint of (as a result of) our own faith. How would you respond to the question, 'How do you know that you will still be a Christian tomorrow or the next day or the next day?' If we reply, 'Because of my faith,' then how do we know our faith will not fail? What guarantee do we have that we will continue to trust Jesus tomorrow? To put it another way, if my perseverance depends on me keeping faith, then, well—it depends on me! What has God done? *I* have kept me. *I* have guarded me until the end. My security depends upon me. What does God's 'keeping' achieve? Nothing at all. If I lose faith, then I am kept no longer, and this guarding means nothing.

As we have seen, however, the whole thrust of the text here is that Christians are kept and guarded not because of their own work, but by God himself. We *can* have assurance about our eternal security because it depends on God rather than on us. What, then, does Peter mean when he inserts the words 'through faith'?

Ephesians 2 is helpful here. In that text, Paul writes, 'For by grace you have been saved, *through faith*. And this is not your own doing; it is the gift of God ...' (v. 8). Paul is making the point that the faith you have, if you are a Christian, does not originate with you. Your faith is God's gift to you, and it is God's power that works that faith in you. It is not your own work, so that no one can boast.

Peter uses exactly the same words back in 1 Peter 1:5. Peter, like Paul, is explaining that a person does not remain a Christian because they hold on to their faith and manage to keep going whatever happens. Rather, they remain a Christian because God has caused them to be born again, to an inheritance that is imperishable, kept in heaven for them. God's faith-giving power keeps us / guards us / garrisons us about, for the salvation that is to be revealed in the last time. It is through the instrument of faith that God keeps us, and even the faith we have is actually God's gift to us, not our own invention. Faith itself is part of the gift.

So how can we know that we are eternally saved? Peter tells us: it is God who birthed us, keeps us, gives us faith, and keeps that faith in us. It is his work, not our own work. Your inheritance is more secure than anything else you know. Peter is not undermining his argument. He is strengthening it. If you are a Christian, then God chose you, God wrought faith in your heart, God birthed you, and you are His. Your salvation is God's work in your past, and God's work for your future.

We would do well to remember how relevant these truths would have been to Peter's audience. He is writing to a suffering church, and one of the greatest concerns for Christians facing suffering is this: 'What if, as I face torture or even execution, I renege on trusting in Jesus because of my weakness? What if, at that moment, I deny Jesus? Will I lose my salvation? I want to stand firm. I want to be true to him through all things. But I am not certain that I will manage to stand firm if the pain gets too great. If I fail to stand firm, perhaps I will be lost forever.'

Here, Peter is not engaged in a merely intellectual mental exercise. Rather, he is writing to an audience who need deeply practical help. More than this, Peter knows the problem intimately from his own personal experience. 'Even if I must die with you, I will not deny you!' he declared (Matthew 26:35). Then, within a few hours, he had denied Jesus three times and the rooster crowed. Peter knows this deep, deep worry, and he knows it personally. Can I lose my salvation?

Therefore, he writes here with an emphatic response. 'No!' Peter denied Jesus when it got too tough for him, but Peter did not lose his salvation. He lost his pride, his confidence in the flesh, and his dependence on his own ability to stand. He discovered that his own power to 'have faith' evaporated. Later, when faced with the truth of what he had done, what did he do next? He wept in repentance. We only have to note Jesus' response to the situation to know that Peter's salvation was not lost. Firstly, he died for Peter anyway.

Secondly, he reinstated him, instructing him to be a shepherd to God's people (John 21:15–17).

Here in 1 Peter, Peter is remembering again his own denial of Jesus. Yet, he says in the same breath, 'My inheritance is secure—not because of me, but because of the power of Almighty God.' To put it another way, if you are a Christian then God grasps you with an iron grip so strong that it almost hurts. He holds you and he will never let go. No one, Jesus cried, no one will be able to snatch you out of his hand (John 10:28–29). That includes you! Your power is nothing compared to the power of God, and it is God who guards your inheritance because you have trusted in Jesus. Your inheritance is kept in heaven for you. To put it Paul's way, our inheritance is laid up for us in heaven (Colossians 1:5; 2 Timothy 4:8). Your final salvation—your entry into eternity with God—is certain because God keeps it for you.

This is why Peter wrote, 'Blessed be the God and Father of our Lord Jesus Christ' (v. 3). God has done all of this for us, not because we are great, but because he is great. He has done it not because we are worthy, but because he is worthy. He has done it not because we chose him, but because he chose us. He has done it not because we have great faith and hold fast to him, but because we have a great God who holds fast to us. Therefore (v. 6, NIV), in all this we 'greatly rejoice'. How could we do otherwise? Salvation is God's work in our past, and it is God's work for our future.

Secondly, Peter turns to the crux of the purpose of his letter. He is writing to provide his readers with a deeper theology of suffering, and he outlines here the primary point of his whole letter. The obvious question that bubbles up when suffering comes our way is this: 'Why?' It is to this question that Peter turns now.

The purpose of suffering

Suffering proves faith

Peter provokes the 'Why do I suffer?' question by his use of a key little phrase in the midst of verse 6. '... for a little while, *if necessary*, you have been grieved by various trials.' How is it that our suffering is necessary? Who deems it necessary? For whom is it necessary? Even when it feels like perverse, pointless, pain, nevertheless Peter writes, 'It is necessary.'

God deems it necessary that we go through our trials. Of course, it is not necessary for him, but it *is* necessary for us. Why is it necessary? Again, Peter anticipates the question and then answers it. It is necessary '*so that* the tested genuineness of your faith—more precious than gold that perishes though it is tested by fire—may be found to result in praise and glory and honour at the revelation of Jesus Christ' (v. 7). According to Peter, the prime purpose of your trials is to test the genuineness of your faith.

Again, this test is not for God's benefit—it is for ours. God has birthed us into new life, flooded our hearts with faith, and he keeps us through faith until our inheritance comes. The faith we have is the gift of God. God knows we have genuine faith because he gave it to us. Suffering is not necessary in order for God to know the genuineness of our faith—he knows it already. Rather, suffering is necessary in order for *us* (and others) to know the genuineness of our faith.

How do you know you have genuine faith? You know because in

the midst of great trials, when you face losing your job, your thought is not to give up on God but to run to him for help. You know because when you face another day of pain, your thought is not to give up on God, to curse God and die, but to run to him seeking help. You know, because when you face another day of relationship turmoil, your thought is not to run away, but to run *to* God for help. The point Peter is making here is that pain proves your position before God.

In a similar vein, how do I know the faith of another is genuine? I know because they stand up under trial. If someone has remained steadfast 'under trial' (James 1:12) then I can have confidence that their faith is genuine. One vital question to ask any potential ministry candidate concerns whether or not their faith has been tested. Have they suffered? If they have not, it is much harder to know whether or not their faith is genuine. When we see people walking with God in the midst of the furnace, like Daniel's friends, then we know that their faith is genuine and that their God is genuine.

It is suffering that demonstrates to us and to others whether or not we are truly Christians. Remember Job's well-known words: 'Though he slay me, I will hope in him.' (Job 13:15). Job's faith was proven in spades. Peter is urging suffering Christians to take the long perspective. Our time in this world is only brief—eternity awaits. This is only for a little while. We are to live in the light of the eternal, not the temporal.

The most important decision you ever make is whether or not you are going to cling to Jesus, whatever the cost. If you think, 'I cannot. I can't do it. It's too hard. It's too painful. It's too difficult,' then you are absolutely right. No one can stand up under the trial if they try to do it alone. But if you are a Christian, then the Holy Spirit lives within you. Jesus, by his Spirit, walks alongside you, every step of the way. You can do *all* things through Christ who gives you strength (Philippians 4:13). You cannot do it in your own strength—no one can do that. But with the strength of God, you can walk on.

Live through the physical pain each day. Work through the relational mess hour by hour, day by day. Keep your promises, however hard it may be, month by month. Do what God calls you to do, whatever the cost. The result of living this way is not bitterness, but beauty. It is not misery but majesty. It is not resentment but rejoicing. It is not grudges but glory. Suffering proves the genuineness of your faith.

Suffering provides sanctification

In verse 8, Peter makes a second crucial point about suffering, namely that suffering grows our love for Jesus. Not only does suffering prove the genuineness of our faith but it also sanctifies us. In other words, God uses suffering to prepare us for eternity with Him. He will do whatever it takes, for however long is necessary, to make us holy and complete, ready for eternal joy.

Isn't it strange how the economy of God works? The world would suggest that if something gets us money, possessions, good relationships, enjoyable work, fun at play, etc., then we will love it more. That is the premise for the deeply flawed prosperity gospel movement across the world. Preachers cry out that if you become a Christian then God will supply health, wealth and prosperity.

In the economy of God, however, such things often dull our senses and drive us away from him. Most commonly it is suffering that grows our love for Jesus.

Consider King Solomon. It looked like God was his top priority early on in his life. Later, though, with the exponential increase in his wealth and material possessions and wives and concubines, he began to worship other gods. The increase of worldly things did not grow his love for God. Rather, such things weakened it and undermined it and unravelled it. Here, then, Peter is arguing that suffering drives us to love Jesus more.

I was chatting to someone the other day who was saying that his son had died 13 years ago—a hugely painful experience. But, he said, he is much closer to Jesus as a result than ever he had been before. Suffering drives us to love Jesus more. Somehow, we identify more with Jesus, the man of sorrows who is familiar with sufferings. So, we must pray for God to change our hearts, to have the strength to keep on keeping on. We must pray that God would grow our love for that person we do not really love anymore. We pray that God will deepen our desire for him, so that we may stand firm amid the pain, knowing that inexpressible joy awaits.

Thus, Peter has argued that pain proves our position before God, and sickness and stress are the engine of our sanctification.

Suffering promotes praise

Finally, though, Peter moves us to another glorious but counter-intuitive truth. Peter asserts that suffering promotes praise (v. 6). Before we are tempted to retort, 'You don't know what I'm going through,' we must not forget our early church history. In Acts 16, Paul and Silas are flogged and imprisoned and they are praying and singing songs of praise to God. In Acts 14, Paul is stoned nearly to death. In Acts 12, James is executed. In Acts 7, Stephen faces his martyrdom, looks up to heaven and is filled with the Holy Spirit. Hardly any of us are going through things of that nature.

We must not forget Peter's own experiences, either. In Acts 12, Peter is imprisoned by Agrippa I. More pertinent to our point here, though, is Acts 5. There, following a brutal Roman flogging which left his back in shreds, Peter left the Sanhedrin rejoicing (vv. 40–42, NIV)! Rejoicing, despite the fact that he would be in pain every time he moved, every time he put a shirt on, every time he tried to lie down. That pain would last for weeks, yet Peter is rejoicing. Peter knows what it is to suffer. We must not think that we are in a worse situation than those early church believers. Church history suggests that later on, Peter himself was martyred.

Notice, too, Peter's description of the timeframe for suffering. He writes, 'Now for a little while …' You may be in the midst of suffering that has been continuing for days, weeks, months, years, even decades. You may think, 'I need to give up, get out and move on before I can do any rejoicing.' But Peter says, 'No you don't—your suffering is just for a *little while*.'

You may had been in pain for thirty years or more. Perhaps you feel that your pain has to end before you can rejoice. Peter disagrees. Perhaps you feel a close relationship is dying, and you need to end it before you can rejoice. Peter disagrees. Our suffering, according to Peter, is just for a little while. We need to get our heads out of our small, short-term, self-centred world, and focus on the eternal God who is strong to save.[1]

We have a hope that is steadfast and certain, kept and guarded for us. Our hope is eternal. It goes on for ever and ever and ever and ever. Compared to the joy and wonder of that, your suffering is just for a little while. That is the heavenly perspective we need, and that is the way God sees things.

Suffering promotes praise because it reminds us of two fundamental things. Firstly, our inheritance is being kept and garrisoned by the mighty hand of God. Secondly, we are being prepared for the future. Our inheritance is spectacular, and rests with God himself.

Conclusion

Overall, then, Peter's argument here has been two-fold. Firstly, he has urged each and every Christian to delve deep into the glory of the gospel, and supremely the glory of the cross of Jesus through which we have been given life. He refuses to *move on* from the doctrine of salvation to more important things, for the simple reason that nothing is more important. The cross of Jesus is and always must be central.

Secondly, Peter has reminded us that suffering proves to us (and to others) our faith. It provides sanctification, driving us to be more and more as God created us to be, living God's way in God's world. Peter finishes by urging that suffering promotes praise. In the midst of trials, Paul and Silas could sing songs in prison. Peter could rejoice. The church to whom he writes can be filled with joy. So can we.

Note

1 I need to make the pastoral point that for those suffering under domestic abuse, God does not call you to remain and continue to suffer. Those who

perpetrate that abuse must not be allowed to continue to do so. Such abuse is terrible for those who suffer under it, and they need release, relief, freedom and the opportunity for restoration. Abusers should be confronted with their sin and face the consequences thereof. As Christians, while our prayer is that an abuser would repent of their sin and come to faith, such a result is highly unlikely to happen until the abuser is confronted and prevented from continuing in their sin. There is no place in the Christian faith for enabling those who inflict abuse to continue to do so.

3 Suffering first, glory later

1 Peter 1:8–13

B ack in the 1990s at Exeter University, three of the halls of residence were named, 'Hope', 'Lopez', and 'Kilmorie'. There was a student from East Asia who introduced himself by the name 'Keen', and we found it hilarious that he could introduce himself by saying: 'Hello—I'm Keen and I live in Hope.'

1 Peter 1:7 concludes with the words, 'at the revelation of Jesus Christ,' and verse 13 does exactly the same thing,[1] so it is clear that Peter wrote verses 8 to 13 as a cohesive unit. These six verses are a separate section in his mind and the focus is obvious. Peter is encouraging all Christians not just to be keen, but to *live in hope*.

We have noted that verses 3 to 7 expound the twin themes of salvation and suffering. Peter has explained that salvation is God's work both in our past and for our future, and he has asserted that our future is *certain*—guaranteed and garrisoned by God. Following this, Peter demonstrated that suffering provides sanctification for us, proves faith in us, and promotes praise from us.

Now, Peter continues on the theme of suffering to expose one primary truth: suffering comes first, glory comes later. Christians can live in hope, Peter argues, because this *suffering first, glory later* motif is exactly the experience of Jesus himself. His suffering gave way to glory. Likewise, for us, suffering comes first, but glory awaits. We can be confident this is true, Peter argues, because the Bible tells us so. God says it, so we can trust it.

You may know that old chorus, 'Jesus loves me, this I know, for the

Bible tells me so.' In these few verses, Peter writes in effect: 'Suffering leads to glory, this we know, for the Bible tells us so.' In fact, if we are going to be at all useful as Christians, then our mantra should always be like this:

> My sin is paid for and forgiven, this I know, for the Bible tells me so. God is sovereignly in control, even amidst the horror of my present circumstances, this I know, for the Bible tells me so.

> Because I have turned from my sin and I'm trusting in Jesus, I am going to escape hell and spend eternity with Jesus—this I know, for the Bible tells me so.

> I must submit to those in authority over me, under God—this I know, for the Bible tells me so. One day everyone who has ever lived will bow the knee before Jesus—this I know, for the Bible tells me so.

> Here in 1 Peter 1, then, suffering leads to glory—this I know, for the Bible tells me so.

It seems to me that these six verses are structured in a typically Hebrew manner. In the Western World, we tend to arrange things in an ascending pattern, with arguments building from the lesser to the greater. We like to conclude with a powerful punchline; the final blow to slay any opposing arguments. In the ancient Near East, however, they were less concerned about linearity, one-way arguments or strict chronology. They were more concerned with circularity and multi-directional argument, and structuring things in a way that was easy to remember. As a result, often an argument for something is shaped with the punchline at the very centre, rather like the bullseye in the middle of a dartboard. From each side of the bullseye come two directly supporting arguments, and each side of those come another two arguments, and so on.

To change the metaphor, it is a little like an old stone-built, arch bridge. The centre-stone at the top of the arch is the knock-out punchline. It is supported by one stone each side, complementing each other, and each of those arguments are supported by another stone, and so on down to the ground. This target or bridge pattern is known as a *chiasm* (from the Greek letter *chi* which forms a cross) and can be seen as a sort of *a-b-c-b-a* arrangement. Such linguistic structures are extremely common in the ancient Near East, so it should be no surprise that we find Peter using it here.

This structure was also used as a memory device—if we can remember the centre point, then that will help us remember the supporting arguments. Conversely, if we remember the supporting arguments, that will help us to remember the central point.

These six verses in 1 Peter reflect this classic chiasm pattern. It is not the only time Peter uses a chiasm—we will meet at least two more as we read on through the book. For this section, though, let me try to demonstrate the structure here.

A. vv. 8–9. Faith for the future.

   B. vv. 10–11a. Reliable revelation.

      C. v. 11b. Suffering first, glory later.

   B. v. 12. Reliable revelation.

A. v. 13. Faith for the future.

Because of the way the text is structured, we are going to examine it through these three parts, working from the outside to the inside. We will begin with 'Faith for the Future'. Next, we will consider 'Reliable Revelation'. Finally, we will conclude with Peter's focus: 'Suffering First, Glory Later.'

Faith for the future

It is important to notice that Peter makes a distinction between himself and his readers in these verses. Back in verse 3, Peter included himself in the argument: 'Blessed be the God and Father of *our* Lord Jesus Christ. According to his great mercy he has caused *us* to be born again ...' But then he moves from first person plural to second person plural. In verse 4 we read, 'kept in heaven for *you* ...'. In verse 6: 'In this *you* rejoice, though now for a little while, if necessary, *you* have been grieved by various trials so that the tested genuineness of *your* faith ...' Why does he change tack and move from first person to second person? Clearly verses 4–7 apply to Peter just as much as they do to his readers (including us), so precisely what distinction *is* he making, and for what reason?

Verse 8 provides the answer: 'Though *you* have not seen him, *you* love him,' he writes. Peter's original readers had not seen Jesus physically, and neither have we. But Peter himself *had* seen Jesus physically. Not only that, but he had also spent three years training under him. So, Peter has seen Jesus, and we have not.

Peter wants to highlight the fact that whether or not a person has *seen* Jesus, they may still love him and believe in him. One commentator helpfully describes four stages in seeing Jesus:

Stage 1: In the Old Testament, the prophets 'saw' him. Jesus himself makes this point: 'Your father Abraham rejoiced that he would see my day; he saw it and was glad' (John 8:56).

Stage 2 is the people who lived through Jesus' earthly life, death and resurrection—people like Peter as he writes this letter. Such people have seen Jesus in the flesh.

Stage 3 is all those who have not seen Jesus physically but have seen (and do see) Jesus through the eye of faith. This includes all of us who are Christians. Perhaps in these verses Peter has in mind the time when Thomas finally saw Jesus after the resurrection. At that moment, Jesus said, 'Have you believed because you have seen me? Blessed are those who have not seen and yet have believed' (John 20:29).

Finally, **stage 4** is when we will all see him face to face. This is what Paul describes: 'Now we see in a mirror dimly, but then face to face' (1 Corinthians 13:12).[2]

Peter writes here that although his readers have not seen Jesus, nevertheless they love him. Though they still do not see Jesus (except with the 'eye of faith'), nevertheless they believe in him and rejoice with inexpressible joy that is filled with glory.

I dislike the common phrase, 'Christianity is caught more than taught,' because it appears to suggest that when it comes to Christian faith, teaching is secondary. After all, if we are not taught, then we have no idea in whom we are to have faith; what our world is like; how God views us; our need for regular repentance; the commands of God in terms of how we are to live in response to his work in us; and so on and so forth. Teaching is vital and it is central— without teaching, no one would understand anything.

For many of us, our method for evangelism is that we try to explain everything we can about Jesus in the hope that someone will believe in him. We have the notion that as people believe in Jesus more and more, so they will begin to love him more and more.

But it seems that Peter might be suggesting this is not always how it works. Unexpectedly, he describes people's response to Jesus as love first, trust second. Although we have not seen him, nevertheless we love him—this is first. Then, second, although we do not see him, nevertheless we believe in him. Love first, trust second. Perhaps it was this way with the very first disciples, too. They spent three years with him, friends from early on, but became true believers somewhat late in the day.

It makes sense with our own experience as well. We tend to trust the people we love, and the people closest to us. Sometimes at least, trust follows love. So perhaps our evangelism could be rooted first in exuding our love *for* Jesus, before it is filled with our reasons for trusting *in* Jesus. More succinctly, perhaps we trust Jesus because we love Jesus and not the other way around.

As we love Jesus more, so other people begin to love him too, and the consequence is simple: the more they love him, the more they believe. At the least, I know that I love Jesus more now than I did before. Perhaps it is as a result that I trust in him more now than I did before. The more we love, the more we believe.

According to Peter, the result of loving him and believing in him is that we rejoice with inexpressible joy and we are filled with glory. He is not writing about being filled with our glory, of course, but rather about being filled with *his* glory. Our joyful hearts well up in praise not of ourselves but of Jesus and his glory. This joy comes naturally, Peter writes, because we are obtaining the outcome of our faith—the salvation of our souls.

To be clear, Christians are saved when they first turn from their sin and trust in Jesus, asking him to be King from now on. That is the moment of their salvation, and the future of all Christians is utterly secure, as Peter has already pointed out. In this sense, salvation is a past completed action with a future assured outcome. For

Christians, salvation is completely and utterly certain. You can bet your life on it.

But here, Peter uses the present tense, explaining that Christians are obtaining the salvation of their souls. He does it because salvation is also an ongoing event. Paul writes, 'For the word of the cross is folly to those who are perishing, but to us *who are being saved* it is the power of God' (1 Corinthians 1:18). Later, he writes, 'For we are the aroma of Christ to God among those *who are being saved ...*' (2 Corinthians 2:15). Then, in Philippians, he writes: 'Work out your own salvation with fear and trembling, for it is God who works in you, both to will and to work for his good pleasure' (Philippians 2:12–13). In other words, your salvation is worked out in the present. If you are not walking with the Lord, then perhaps you never belonged to the Lord. It is this present aspect of salvation to which Peter refers in these verses in 1 Peter—we *are obtaining* the salvation of our souls.

The Bible teaches that if we are Christians then we have been saved, and also that we are being saved. And it does not stop there. Look forward to the end of this chiasm, to verse 13. Here, Peter writes, 'Set your hope fully on the grace that *will be* brought to you at the revelation of Jesus Christ.' He is describing the fact that we *will be* saved at some future time. He is not alone in this. Paul makes the same point in Romans 5: 'Since, therefore, we have now been justified by his blood' [note: salvation in the past], 'much more shall we be saved,' [note: salvation in the future], 'by him from the wrath of God.' (Romans 5:9). One day, finally, we *will be saved*. We will be saved out of the turmoil and trouble and pain and despair of this world. We will be saved out of the soiling and stress and suffering and sin of this world. We will be saved into eternity with Jesus, into an inheritance that is imperishable, undefiled and unfading—to return to Peter's language back in verse 4. We will be saved to a pain-free, sin-free, stress-free, death-free, joy-filled, glory-filled, love-filled, Jesus-filled life. We have been saved, we are being saved and we will be saved. Peter covers all three facets of salvation in this first part of his letter.

Overall, recognizing this threefold nature of salvation, Peter urges that we set our hope fully on this grace Jesus offers us. We love, we believe, and we have great joy, *because* we set our hearts on Jesus. We set our compass by Jesus. We plot our course for Jesus. We live our lives anchored to Jesus, whom we do not see now, but whom we love and trust and one day will see face to face.

Peter anticipates an obvious question at this point: 'How we can be certain of these things?' So now he provides an answer to that question.

Reliable revelation

In the next section of this chiasm, Peter discusses the authenticity of the Bible. 'Concerning this salvation, the prophets who prophesied about the grace that was to be yours searched and inquired carefully, inquiring what person or time the Spirit of Christ in them was indicating when he predicted the sufferings of Christ and the subsequent glories' (vv. 10–11). Peter is writing about the Old Testament prophets and reminding his readers that they did not prophesy about 'salvation' as some kind of intellectual idea. Instead, it concerns a person. They prophesied about a Saviour—the coming Messiah. The prophet Isaiah wrote simply, 'God is my salvation' (Isaiah 12:2).

However, the question is: 'Is the Old Testament trustworthy?' Peter provides a clear two-fold answer. Firstly, the prophets 'searched and inquired carefully'. Secondly, the Spirit of Christ is the one who made the predictions about Christ. In other words, the prophets worked hard *and* the Holy Spirit is the one who did the work. It is the same for us, too. 'Work out your own salvation with fear and trembling, *for* it is God who works in you, both to will and to work for his good pleasure' (Philippians 2:12–13). Elsewhere, 'If by the Spirit you put to death the deeds of the body, you will live. *For* all who are led by the Spirit of God are sons of God' (Romans 3:13–14). In other words, if we work hard to defeat sin in our lives then it is the Holy Spirit who leads us to put those deeds to death. We work hard and God works in us.

The Old Testament prophets worked hard to make their predictions. They 'searched and inquired carefully'. This must refer to a searching and inquiring of the Scriptures that they had. After Moses, they had at the very least Genesis through to Deuteronomy. Later prophets had more Scripture than earlier ones, of course. They studied carefully God's word and prophesied on the basis of that. In the New Testament, Luke collected together eye-witness testimonies and thus wrote an orderly account for Theophilus. In a similar way, many of the prophets were eyewitnesses or spoke to eyewitnesses, and then wrote an orderly account of what was observed. The historical narrative of the Old Testament is mainly eyewitness testimony, whether direct (such as Moses describing the not-burning bush or Elijah describing the showdown on Mount

Carmel), or indirect (such as eyewitness accounts handed down from one generation to the next). The testimony of those eyewitnesses is reliable. For example, when Moses wrote an account of the exodus and the desert wanderings, he was surrounded by eyewitnesses to verify his story, and no one complained of any inaccuracy. When Joshua wrote his account of entering the Promised Land, his account is reliable. None of the thousands of people who experienced it alongside him, called his account into question. Again, the centuries-long history of the kings of Israel and Judah was recorded by various different writers, but no one disputed what was written. The accounts are reliable.

It is worth noting, too, that the Old Testament does not just point towards the coming Messiah by the words the prophets used. It also includes many instances of what I would describe as prophetic history. When Abraham nearly sacrificed Isaac up Mount Moriah, it is an event that happened in history. Abraham was a real person, with a son called Isaac. They climbed the hill with Isaac carrying the wood on his back. They built the altar and Abraham prepared to slay Isaac, but then a ram, caught in a thornbush by the horns, was sacrificed as a substitute. That account is true. But the historical event is also prophetic, as later prophets came to realize, and as we see when we look at it in light of Jesus' death. God prepared to sacrifice his only Son Jesus also up Mount Moriah. Jesus carried the wood of the cross on his back up the hill. Jesus wears the thorns around his head. Jesus, too, is the substitute lamb of God who dies in our place.

Furthermore, consider the Israelites enslaved in Egypt under Pharaoh. The ten plagues were real events happening to real people in Egypt. In the final plague, the first-born, male child died in every household, unless the blood of a first-born lamb was daubed at the entrance to the house, in which case the angel passed over that house and the family were spared. As a result, freedom came for God's people as they headed towards the Promised Land. This is historically reliable truth. But it is also prophetic truth. We, too, were enslaved to our sin, unable to rescue ourselves. Jesus, the first-born lamb, died on behalf of God's household and the angel now passes over and we are spared. The result is freedom for God's people as we head towards the Promised Land.

Returning to Peter's point, Peter explains that the prophets 'searched and inquired carefully' into this prophetic history, in order to interpret and prophesy about the coming Saviour. They worked hard. As we highlighted above, though, Peter is keen to point out that this work was not done in isolation. They did not just sit down, study the text, and then write their thoughts down. He explains that the source of their understanding is the Holy Spirit. He makes the same point in his second letter: 'Men spoke from God as they were carried along by the Holy Spirit' (2 Peter 1:21).

The point, then, is that the prophets had both God's inerrant word and God's inerrant Spirit.[3] Thus, they wrote of the salvation that was to come, the salvation to be found in Christ alone. They predicted the sufferings of Christ and the subsequent glories. The Old Testament is reliable. For the sake of completeness, it is worth mentioning that Jesus accepted all of the Old Testament as we have it today, and nothing more, as God's inspired written Word. To put it crudely, if it was good enough for Jesus, it should be good enough for us.

On the other side of the chiasm, Peter again begins with the prophets in verse 12: 'It was revealed to them that they were serving not themselves but you ...'. The prophets knew that their writings had a very limited readership in their own day. Furthermore, for most of those who did hear their message, it had little effect. Jeremiah prophesied for forty years and you could count the number of converts he saw on the fingers of no hands. Clearly, these prophets did not prophesy for their own benefit. Indeed, many of them led very difficult lives *because* they prophesied as God directed. Jeremiah was not serving himself. In his day, they had a very limited understanding of the coming Messiah, how sin would be dealt with, how the human heart could be changed, and so on. So, when Jeremiah wrote about these things, while he was seeking to encourage those around him that the Messiah would come, primarily it is *we* who are the beneficiaries of his writings. He was serving Peter's readership, and he was serving us today. We look at his prophecies and then we see them fulfilled in Jesus, and this provides proof that Jesus alone is indeed the Messiah, the only one able to save us. The prophets of the Old Testament prophesied primarily to serve not their contemporaries, but us.

From here, though, Peter's argument moves naturally into discussing the New Testament church era. The Old Testament writers were serving us, he explains, and what they wrote (and the implication of those writings) has now been 'announced to you through those who preached the good news to you,' (that is, through the apostles). Peter has shown that we can trust the Old Testament. Now he argues that we can trust the New Testament as well, since it records the words of the apostles. Like the Old Testament prophets, the apostles also 'searched and inquired carefully'. They had the whole of the Old Testament to study, so that helped, and they were also eyewitnesses of Jesus' life, death and resurrection. As a result, as Luke pointed out, they wrote an orderly account of the historical events of the life of Jesus. They wrote theological truth because they were eyewitnesses and they were taught by Jesus. We can depend on that writing not only because the apostles were eyewitnesses, but also because they had the Holy Spirit, given fully at Pentecost. Perhaps Pentecost is the event Peter had in mind when he writes in verse 12, 'the Holy Spirit sent from heaven'. The apostles' words are trustworthy because, like the Old Testament prophets, their words are the words of Almighty God.

In addition, like the Old Testament prophets, the apostles wrote not for their own benefit, but for *our* benefit. Peter is writing this letter to the suffering church not because he expects to gain anything from writing, but rather in order to bring encouragement, help and challenge to those to whom he is writing—his contemporaries and everyone who followed from then until now. We benefit greatly from the words of the prophets (Old Testament) and the apostles (New Testament) because they teach us about our Saviour. The Word of God is reliable—completely trustworthy. Jesus is our Saviour, this we know, for the Bible tells us so.

Let me provide a few examples of the way in which the Scriptures demonstrate that Jesus is the promised Messiah, come to save his people.

- Micah prophesied that the Messiah would be born in Bethlehem (Micah 5:2). The gospel writers tell us that Jesus was born in Bethlehem (Matthew 2:1; Luke 2:4). In other words, Jesus fulfilled the prophecies and thus is the Messiah.

- Zechariah prophesied that the Messiah would ride into Jerusalem on a donkey's colt (Zechariah 9:9). The gospel writers tell us that his words were fulfilled at the beginning of Jesus' final week before his death (Matthew 21:7; Mark 11:7; Luke 19:35; John 12:14). Jesus fulfilled the prophecies and thus is the Messiah.

- The psalmist wrote that the Messiah would heal the broken-hearted and bind up their wounds (Psalm 147:3; Isaiah 61:1)). The gospel writers give evidence of this in myriad ways, such as when they describe the widow whose son had died (Luke 7:11–15), or the woman who had been bleeding for 12 years (Luke 8:43–48). Jesus fulfilled the prophecies and thus is the Messiah.

- David wrote that the Messiah would be betrayed by one of his closest friends (Psalm 41:9). The gospel writers tell us that Jesus was betrayed by one of his twelve disciples, Judas (Matthew 26:15–16; Mark 14:10–11; Luke 22:3–6; John 13:11,26; 18:2–3). Jesus fulfilled the prophecies and thus is the Messiah.

- The prophets foretold that the Messiah would be a man of sorrows and familiar with suffering (Isaiah 53:3). The gospel writers tell us in detail about Jesus' arrest, beating, flogging and crucifixion. Jesus fulfilled the prophecies and thus is the Messiah.

- Isaiah wrote that the Messiah himself would be a sin offering on behalf of his people (Isaiah 53:3–11). The New Testament writers tell us that Jesus offered himself on our behalf, that we would be forgiven (Romans 8:3–4). Jesus fulfilled the prophecy and thus *is* the Messiah.

Thus, Jesus is the one, the only one, who makes salvation possible. There is no way you can be forgiven and your relationship with God restored unless Jesus died in your place. There is no hope, no life, no peace, no reconciliation, no joy, no future and no life outside of the death and resurrection of Jesus Christ. The prophets prophesied it. The apostles recorded it. Jesus fulfilled it. Now, because of the words of the prophets and apostles, we can be certain of it, and we can come to know this Jesus.

Notice how Peter finished this little section of the chiasm. He writes that these things are, 'things into which angels long to look' (v. 12). Isn't that a tantalizing little phrase? Does he mean that angels long to look into these things but cannot? Or does he mean that they look into them and always long to do so? Whichever it is, this phrase certainly expresses the idea that these things are incredible things. The unfolding revelation of Jesus the Messiah through the Bible is astounding, Even the angels of heaven long to look into them. How much more should we!

Peter's point in this section, then, is that revelation is utterly reliable. God's Word can be trusted, not only because it is the words of the prophets and the apostles, but even more because the Holy Spirit was speaking through those prophets and apostles.

Peter moves finally from the reliability of the Scriptures to his central point about suffering, namely that suffering comes first but glory comes later.

Suffering first, glory later

In verse 11, the centre of the chiasm, Peter writes about 'the sufferings of Christ and the subsequent glories'. That is the heart of his writing. It is the focal point of his argument. In v. 6, Peter wrote, 'Now for a little while, if necessary, you have been grieved by various trials ... so that the tested genuineness of your faith ... may be found to result in praise and glory.' In other words, 'suffering first, glory later'.

I suspect that as Peter wrote these few verses, he had in mind the words of Jesus on the road to Emmaus, where Luke uses that little word 'necessary' in a similar way. 'Was it not necessary that the Christ should suffer these things and enter into his glory?' (Luke 24:26). There it is again—suffering first, glory later. It was necessary for Christ to suffer, and Peter has suggested that it is necessary for us as well. For Jesus, suffering gave way to glory, and Peter now is arguing that the same is true for us. He links the idea of our own suffering and subsequent glorying *in* Christ, with the suffering and subsequent glory *of* Christ. Suffering is a privilege; we get to experience a little of what Jesus experienced. We become a little more like him. More than that, though, suffering reminds us that glory is coming.

Paul connects suffering and glory in a similar way in Romans 8. 'The Spirit himself bears witness with our spirit that we are children of God, and if children, then heirs—heirs of God and fellow heirs with Christ, provided we *suffer* with him in order that we may also be *glorified* with him' (8:16–17). Suffering first, glory later. Paul goes on, 'For I consider that the sufferings of this present time are not worth comparing with the glory that is to be revealed to us'(Romans 8:18). Again, suffering comes first, glory comes later.

Thus, the crux of this whole section, the centre-point of Peter's careful structure, is the sufferings of Christ and the subsequent glories.

Notice both the plurality and the asymmetry here. First, the sufferings (plural) of Christ are mentioned. Jesus suffered throughout his earthly life—temptation, neglect, rejection by his family, abuse, mockery, allegation, accusation, betrayal, denial, exposure, public humiliation, injustice, false witness, physical agony, execution, abandonment, death. Great and all-encompassing were his sufferings. But the glories then came later—the glory of his resurrection, his ascension, his being crowned with glory and honour.

I suspect that Peter is not limiting the 'subsequent glories' described here to the glories of Jesus. I think there is asymmetry. The sufferings are specifically *of Christ*—those are centre-stage. But the designation of the glories that follow is a-specific, perhaps referring both to Jesus' glories and to our glories. *Because* of the sufferings of Jesus, not only did his resurrection and ascension result (his glories), but also our own salvation and eventual resurrection result (our glories). We recognise Jesus as Messiah, and we see his sufferings and subsequent glories. As a result, we can rejoice in our own suffering because just as Jesus rose again to eternal, resurrection life, so we can be certain of our eventual resurrection life.

In essence, then, the focus of this chiasm is profoundly simple. It aims to bring comfort to suffering Christians, because while suffering comes now, glory comes later. Why are we filled with joy inexpressible? Because we are obtaining the outcome of our faith, the salvation of our souls (v. 9).

Peter's centre-point for these verses is that, ultimately, our salvation is the suffering of Jesus. If we are submitted to him, then his suffering and his eventual death is the very thing that saves us. Not only is it the case, then, that Peter has grounds for urging us to rejoice in our sufferings, but Jesus himself has grounds for urging us to rejoice in our sufferings, because his suffering made our salvation possible.

Conclusion

Peter is urging us to be keen and live in hope. If we are Christians, then the crux of our lives is the Lord Jesus himself. We know him through the Scriptures which are completely trustworthy, both Old and New Testaments. We can rejoice even in our sufferings now because we know that glory comes later. So, we wait eagerly and set our hope fully on the coming grace when Jesus returns. Christians, then, are to be keen and living in hope, because amid the myriad trials of this life, we know that glory awaits.

Notes

1 In the original Greek language, the phrase is identical in both verses, too.

2 Selwyn, E.G., quoted in: *Barclay's Daily Study Bible on 1 Peter*, https://www. studylight.org/commentaries/eng/dsb/1-peter-1.html

3 Note that the Holy Spirit here in v. 11 is called the Spirit of Christ, reminding us that the second person of the Trinity existed prior to his conception as a human being. If Christ did not exist, then the Spirit of Christ did not exist either. But the Trinity goes back to before the dawn of time, and Peter makes a brief reference to this fact here.

4 Live in the light of your salvation

1 Peter 1:13–25

In 2002 at White Hart Lane, Tottenham Hotspur led Manchester United 3–0 at the break, but they ended up losing the game 3–5. One commentator's words have now gone down in history: 'This really was a game of two halves.'

The same could be said of Peter's writing in the second half of 1 Peter 1. It is a text of two halves, asserting firstly that Christians are ransomed for holiness, and secondly that they are reborn to love. In the first half, Peter explains that the reason Jesus paid for your sin with his precious blood was so that you might sin less and less. The result of our ransom was that we would live holy lives, in obedience to God. In the second half, Peter emphasizes that Christians are born again into God's family. Therefore, we should love God's family. It is a text in two halves.

As usual, Peter is rooted in the Old Testament. In the previous few verses, Peter has answered the question, 'Is the Bible reliable?' with a resounding 'yes'. He showed that both the Old Testament and the New Testament are reliable revelation—they can be utterly depended upon. In this final part of chapter 1, Peter investigates another key question for his readers, many of whom would have been Gentiles. They knew the Scriptures were sacred Jewish texts, and they now know the texts are reliable and useful for Jews. But what about for them? As non-Jews, are the Scriptures for their benefit as well?

In fact, Peter has been driving at the answer to this question from the very beginning. Right back in verse 1, he takes an Old Testament phrase about Jewish believers, 'chosen by God' (See Isaiah 41:8) and applies it to his Gentile readers. He describes them as 'elect'—a word which means the same thing: 'chosen by God'. Furthermore, he takes a verse about Abraham from Genesis 23, in which Abraham describes himself as an exile or foreigner (he came from Ur of the Chaldeans (Genesis 15:7), and the Jews, descended from him, spent 400 years as exiles in Egypt), and then applies that same verse *to* these Gentile believers. 'Elect *exiles*', he writes. He is telling the Gentile Christians that they, too, are God's chosen people and thus foreigners on this earth. *All* Christians, whether Jews or Gentiles, are part of the family of God.

Now he reiterates the point in these verses at the end of the chapter. Written in the Law of Moses, originally for the Jews, we read, 'You shall therefore be holy, for I am holy' (Leviticus 11:45). But Peter applies those words to his *Gentile* readers (v. 16). Again, 'All flesh is like grass …' was written for Jews by the prophet Isaiah (40:6,8)—a text Peter quotes in verses 24–25. But Peter applies those words to *Gentile* believers.

Peter is making a clear point: 'both the Old Testament and the New Testament Scriptures are *your* Scriptures, Gentiles, because you are part of God's chosen family.' The same is true for us today. Do not think that the Bible is for Jews and not for us—that would be wrong thinking. A more common mistake is to consider the Old Testament as somehow not for us because we live in New Testament, post-resurrection times. The whole of Scripture is for all Christian believers, whether Jew or Gentile.

In Exodus 12, the exiled Israelites are preparing to leave slavery in Egypt, and they are instructed, in verse 11, to eat the Passover meal 'with your loins girded' (KJV). That phrase meant, 'tuck your cloak into your belt,' and was a metaphor for *getting down to business*, rather like we might say, 'roll up your sleeves'. God tells the people to *gird up their loins* because they were leaving their slavery to the Egyptians behind and heading off to live God's way in the Promised Land. In 1 Peter 1 verse 13 (KJV), Peter writes literally, 'Gird up the loins of your mind.' It is exactly the same imagery. He is saying, 'Tuck your cloak into your belt because you're leaving your slavery to sin and heading off to live God's way in the Promised Land.' The Old Testament and the New Testament are both for Jews and Gentiles.

When Peter writes, 'Gird up the loins of your mind,' we might imagine he is saying, 'Think straight and hard about where you've come from and where you're going.' It is an instruction preparing for action. 'Gird up the loins of your mind, be sober, ...'—*do* something. What are they to do? Simple: 'Set your hope fully on the grace that will be brought to you at the revelation of Jesus Christ.' To put it another way, 'Think about your salvation in Christ and live in the light of it.' He returns to this idea a little later: 'He was foreknown before the foundation of the world but was made manifest in the last times for the sake of you who through him are believers in God, who raised him from the dead and gave him glory *so that* ...' So that what? '*So that* your faith and hope are in God' (vv. 20–21). Live in the light of your salvation, he is saying.

Peter answers the question, 'Is the Bible for me?' with an emphatic 'Yes!' Then he undergirds that 'yes' with the vital truth that all Christians, Jew or Gentile, are part of God's family. So, he says, 'Now live in the light of that!'

I want to demonstrate that these few verses do form two complementary halves. The same ideas in the first half are then revisited in the second half. I have tried to show this in the table below.

v. 14	As *obedient* children	v. 22	*Obedience* to the truth
v. 14	As obedient *children*	v. 23	*born again* (i.e., children of the promise)
v. 18	Not with *perishable* things	v. 23	Not of *perishable* seed
v. 17	Call on him as Father ...	v. 23	*born again* (i.e., you are now a son)

In the first half, the obedience demanded is given in the language of holiness, exercised in light of our ransom. In the second half, obedience is couched in the language of earnest love, exercised in light of our new birth. In the first half, the focus of our salvation is ransom through the imperishable and precious blood of Jesus. In the second half, the focus of our salvation is new birth through the imperishable and abiding word of God. In the first half, the outcome of our salvation is general holiness of conduct, because our faith and hope are in God. In the second half, the outcome of our salvation is love for fellow believers, because God's Word stands forever. It is, indeed, a text of two halves.

Ransomed for holiness

Paul writes, 'Do not be conformed to this world ...' (Romans 12:2). We find Peter forwarding a similar idea: 'As obedient children, do not be conformed to the passions of your former ignorance' (v. 14). The pattern of this world is to live according to the passions of the flesh. In fact, Peter writes in effect, 'Before you became Christians, you were driven by ignorant passions.' He is not using the word *ignorant* in a pejorative sense. Rather, he is explaining that, until you recognize your sinfulness and desperate need of rescue, you are living blind to the truth. You are dead to the reality of true life in God. You are ignorant of it, and when you are ignorant of God, what else would you do but live according to your passions? We see it in the world in technicolour.

The world's mantra is often, 'Love whomever you want,' 'If it feels good, do it,' or even, 'If it feels right, do it.' This kind of morality is rooted in an individual's desires and emotions. According to the Bible, however, unless our morality is rooted in the law of God then we are living according to our former ignorant passions.

Note, too, that Paul explained how our transformation from worldly living should occur. 'Do not be conformed to this world, but be transformed *by the renewal of your mind*' (Romans 12:2). Peter writes in a similar fashion here when he accompanies, 'Do not be conformed to the passions of your former ignorance,' with the explanation in verse 13 (KJV): 'Girding up the loins of your mind.'

If you are a Christian, then you live by the renewing of your mind—by 'gird[ing] up the loins of your mind.' Christians are to live according to passions that are wedded to Christ. 'As he who called you is holy, you also be holy in all your conduct' (verse 15).

Obedience is about doing what God says, not doing what we want. For we who are Christians, that is our calling—our wonderful and glorious calling—called to be *obedient* children.

At heart, holiness is about being different. The temple was holy because it was different from the buildings around it. The altar was holy because it was different from the altars of invented gods in the nations around Israel. The priests were holy because they had a different role from everyone else. More pointedly, Christians are holy because they are different from everyone else.

In fact, holiness has two aspects. Firstly, to be holy means to have a new identity—set apart for God's use alone. Secondly, to be holy means to have a new character—obedient to God's law.

From God's perspective, we are to behave in certain ways because we belong to him. Because we belong to him, we should reflect his character. In some ways, holiness is an almost forgotten doctrine in the western church. It is seen as outdated, archaic, or irrelevant. It is as if people think we have moved on from holiness. But we have not moved on. We have regressed. We have moved backwards. According to Peter, holiness is a central call to all Christians. God's demand is crystal clear: 'Be holy, for I am holy' (Leviticus 11:45). We are set apart for God's work and now we must live God's way.

Holiness of character is often to do with the way we treat other people. God honours people, so we are to honour our father and mother. God gives of himself to us, so we are to give of ourselves to others. We serve because he serves. We love because he loves. We seek to be good masters because he is a good master. We seek to be good servants because he is a good servant.

Our problem, though, is that we cannot do it. However hard we try, we fail. We sin. We do what we know we should not do. We say what we know we should not say. We think what we know we should not think. So how *can* we be holy?

In Jonty Alcock's book, *Impossible Commands*,[1] he provides a vital message for Christians today, especially in the affluent west. In so many sermons we are exhorted to *do* something, to better ourselves in some way, to be more loving, to be more forgiving, to be more generous, and so on. These so-called 'sermons' urge us to *do* something, as if we have the power to do those things ourselves. They are a sort of weekly spiritual pep-talk to help us help ourselves.

Alcock reminds us, in his book, that when Jesus stood at the tomb of Lazarus and commanded, 'Lazarus, come out!' (John 11:43), it was an impossible command. Lazarus was dead, and he had been dead for four days. Nevertheless, he came out. The power for the obedience to Jesus' command was not in Lazarus—he was dead. The power which enabled obedience came from Jesus. In other words, the command Jesus gave came with the power required for Lazarus to obey it. Jonty asks so helpfully, 'What if all God's commands worked that way?' What if all God's commands come with the power to bring about that which they command? 'O how I love your law' (Psalm 119:97), the psalmist writes. Why does he love God's law? Perhaps it is because God's law itself provides the power for us to obey it.

'Be holy because I am holy!' God cries. His command comes with the accompanying power to obey. Paul explains: 'Because you are sons, God has sent this Spirit of his Son into our hearts, crying "Abba! Father!"' (Galatians 4:6). Christians can be holy, not because we are able, but because God the *Holy* Spirit lives within us and empowers us to be holy.

As we have noted before, Peter is deeply rooted in the Scriptures. In verse 15, when he urges us in the light of God's holiness to be holy in all our conduct, he turns directly to the Scriptures. 'It is written,' he writes in verse 16. The Greek verb tense here is the perfect tense. The perfect tense, while relating to a past event, has its focus on the present implications of that event. For example, 'he has seen,' means *he has seen, and he can still visualize it now.* 'He has heard' means *he heard it and the words are still ringing in his ears.* Likewise, here in verse 16, we have, in the perfect tense, 'it is written'. My Greek professor at seminary argued that this could best be translated, 'it stands written'. In other words, it was written in the past, yes, but it remains written today. It is still relevant. It is still true. It still applies. This is a fantastic use of the perfect tense in relation to the Scriptures *because of* what we have just said about God's commands. The power to obey His commands accompanies the commands themselves.

'Be holy in all your conduct' (v. 15) is a command rooted in Scripture. But the *power* to be holy lies not in my own ability and strength (I am faced with my own inability and weakness), but rather, the power to be holy accompanies the command. If you are a Christian, then the Holy Spirit, who lives within you, enables and empowers you *through* the command to fulfil that command. Consider Paul's famous words, 'All Scripture is breathed out by God (the Greek word is really, 'God Spirit-ed') and profitable for teaching, for reproof, for correction and for training in righteousness, that the man of God may be complete, equipped for every good work' (2

Timothy 3:16). How do we get equipped for good work? We get equipped from the life-giving and obedience-enabling Scriptures through which the Holy Spirit works out our salvation in us.

So, what does it mean to 'be holy in all your conduct'? It means we are set apart for God's use, and it means our character and our conduct reflect our convictions about Christ.

Notice, too, that the calling is reflexive. In verse 15, God called us and we obeyed his call, though we were unable in ourselves to do so (like Lazarus). We obeyed his call and submitted to Jesus. Accompanying the command to repent and believe came the power to obey the command. But then, in verse 17, Peter writes that we call on God. He called us. Now we call on him—we pray. Our call on God does not have the power to make God do anything, of course, but James does tell us that the prayer of a righteous man is powerful and effective (James 5:16). Peter tells us here that our prayer is effective because God is our Father. If we call on him as Father, then we can be confident in our calling being answered by him because he is our Father. Perhaps the closer we are *to* God, the more effective our prayer is *toward* God.

It is interesting that Peter highlights God our Father as one 'who judges impartially according to each one's deeds' (v. 17). As a Christian, I thought I was going to be judged based on the substitutionary death of Jesus upon the cross. I thought my response to Jesus meant that my future is secure. I thought that if I submitted to Jesus and asked for his forgiveness, then I escape condemnation and my life now continues beyond death and into eternity with Him. So why does Peter highlight God as one who judges impartially according to our deeds? Why is conduct so important?

The answer to this question, like these verses, has two halves. Firstly, our conduct—our works if you like—indicate whether or not we are saved. If we are Christians, then we are saved 'by grace … through faith … it is the gift of God, *not* a result of works so that no one may boast' (Ephesians 2:8–9). At the final judgement, though, the course of a person's life indicates their condition. No one is saved because of their works, but our deeds are evidence of our salvation. If my life does not reflect my Lord, then he is probably not my Lord and, in fact, I do not have life. It can be expressed this way: 'The way we live is not the *foundation* of our salvation, but it is the *evidence* of it.' Jesus argued that we can tell the heart of a person by the fruit of their life (Matthew 7:16). This is James' point, too: 'Faith by itself, if it does not have works, is dead' (James 2:17). He is not saying that works save you. Rather, he is saying that if you have saving faith, then your life will reflect that faith through your conduct.

As Calvin wrote, 'It is therefore faith alone which justifies, and yet the faith which justifies is not alone.'[2] In other words, true faith is always worked out in the way we live.

A person who claims to have faith and yet walks in darkness, by their actions calls their claim into question. True faith results in right-living. Our deeds reflect our destiny. The first purpose of judgement is that it provides evidence to prove our faith is real. In that sense, we can be said to be judged according to what we have done.

Of course, it is not that you can only be certain of your salvation if you have not got too much wrong or done too many bad things. Not at all. Rather, if you are truly saved then the trajectory of your life—

the overall pattern—is that you are growing to be more like Jesus in the way you conduct yourself. The upward trajectory may be slow and it may be rocky, but it is there.

The second purpose of judgement, though, is that it decides the varying rewards Christians will receive for living obediently to God. Paul makes this point about leaders in 1 Corinthians 3. Each will receive his own reward according to his own work as a leader of those in the church. If the work that they have built on the foundation survives, they will receive a reward. Paul puts it a different way in Ephesians: 'Whatever good anyone does, this he will receive back from the Lord' (Ephesians 6:8). It is the same point that Jesus made through the parable of the talents (Matthew 25:14–30). Your rewards are commensurate with how you run.

God the Father judges impartially according to our deeds not because our deeds save us, but because our deeds are evidence of our destiny and our deeds are the basis for our rewards. 'Be holy,' Peter urges, because holiness evidences your destiny and is the basis of your reward.

Finally, Peter gives the most crucial reason for us to strive to be holy in our conduct. As always, he is rooted in the Scriptures here in verses 18–19. In Exodus, the Israelites left slavery in Egypt. They were ransomed 'not with ... silver or gold' but with the blood of the perfect sacrificial lamb, killed on their final night in Egypt, with its blood daubed over the entrance to their houses. Then they wandered through the desert, awaiting the Promised Land.

Now Peter uses these events as an analogy. He explains that, in a similar way, Christians have left slavery to sin and its consequences. They were ransomed from sin, 'not with ... silver or gold, but with the precious blood of Christ, like that of a lamb without blemish or spot,' with his blood daubed over their lives. Now we wander through the desert awaiting 'the grace that will be brought to you at the revelation of Jesus Christ,' verse 13. Conduct yourselves with fear throughout this time of your exile, Peter says, *because* you have been ransomed.

Be holy in all your conduct, however much that costs you (and he is writing to Christians under persecution, remember), because the cost of Jesus' sacrifice on our behalf is far greater. The cost of Jesus' death is incalculable, so express your gratitude for that by living holy lives.

Notice, also, the contrast Peter provides in these two verses. He contrasts the perishable things of limited value with the imperishable things of eternal value. We should be holy because Jesus paid not with silver and gold, which has value only in this world, but with his own blood, which has eternal value. The value of gold and silver is temporary—perishable. When we die, the value of our assets is zero to us. 'You can't take it with you,' as my dear Granny used to say. When we die, however, the value of our inheritance in Christ remains. It is imperishable. We can and we do take it with us.

The reason we can be holy is that Jesus paid everything for us. His sacrifice is the ultimate incentive for our saintliness. His humility is the basis of our holiness. His crucifixion is the root of our Christlikeness.

This call to holiness is not a temporary thing, either. Peter is clear in verse 17 that we are to be holy, 'throughout the time of your exile'. In other words, the call to holiness is a call that lasts our entire lives.

In this life, we have never arrived. We are never, *now right with God*. We never achieve perfection here. We are to conduct ourselves with fear throughout this life. This is not a fear of others or a fear of the future or a fear of failure, but fear of God. We must be holy because *he* is holy. Jesus ransomed us and now we revere him. We can never repay him, but we can rejoice in him. We are ransomed for holiness.

Reborn to love

The second half of this section contrasts with the previous one. The first section says, 'Live right because Jesus ransomed you.' The second section says, 'Love right because you're in God's family.'

Peter begins, in verse 22, with purification of the soul through obedience to the truth. Later in the letter, Peter makes it clear what he means by obedience to the truth. In Chapter 3, he describes unbelieving husbands as men who 'do not obey the word' (1 Peter 3:1). Then in chapter 4, he describes unbelievers generally as those who 'do not obey the gospel of God' (1 Peter 4:17). In other words, 'obedience to the truth', is about faith. The soul is purified (v. 22) through faith in Jesus. Peter is not alone in his understanding of the intimate connection between faith and obedience.

Paul makes the same point twice in Romans by using the phrase, 'the obedience of faith'. To translate it another way, he writes, 'the faith which is obedience'. He does so at the very beginning of his letter and again at the very end (Romans 1:5; 16:26). Paul brackets the greatest theological treatise in Scripture with the notion of equating faith and obedience. To have faith is to obey.

Jesus himself, in talking to Nicodemus, says: 'Whoever believes in him is not condemned, but whoever does not believe is condemned already, because he has not believed in the name of the only Son of God' (John 3:18). Failure to believe is disobedience. So here in verse 22, Peter writes that purification of our souls comes about through obedience to the truth, that is, through faith in Jesus Christ.

Peter also explains the purpose of this obedience, this submission to Christ and trusting in him for salvation. 'Having purified your souls by your obedience to the truth *for* a sincere brotherly love.' The purpose of the purification of your soul is to 'love one another earnestly,' Peter writes.

Just as the first half of today's text calls us to, 'live in the light of your salvation,' so the second half does the same thing. You have been purified to love earnestly, *so* love earnestly. *Live in the light of your salvation.* To love this way means to consider others and ask, 'If I were in their shoes, what would I need? What would I find helpful? What would bring me joy?' The answer to those questions sheds light on the way in which we are to love them.

Suppose a friend or relative is mourning after a sudden death. Loving them may mean simply sitting with them, or providing some food for the family, or helping them with the practical things such as organising a death certificate or a funeral home or finding a solicitor. Suppose someone has lost their job or is looking for work. Loving them well might involve helping with a Curriculum Vitae or helping them liaise with the benefits office, or taking them to Citizens Advice, or providing some of their basic needs or paying them to do some work for you.

Peter seems to be arguing here that one of the reasons you are saved is to love others. 'Having purified your souls by your obedience to the truth *for* a sincere brotherly love, love one another earnestly from a pure heart.'

Peter reminds us of the connection between our work and the work of God. God causes us to be born again (if you are a Christian, it is because *God* saved you) and now, because he saved you, you are to love one another earnestly from the heart. This is God's work—the Holy Spirit works in you, remember—but it is also your work. It is work you can do because, Peter writes, you are 'born again, not of perishable seed but of imperishable through the living and abiding word of God' (v. 23).

Peter goes on to quote some verses from Isaiah 40 which highlight that God's word stands forever. The Word of God—the command of God to love—comes accompanied with the power to fulfil that command. Isaiah 40 concludes in this way: 'He gives power to the faint, and to him who has no might he increases strength. Even youths shall faint and be weary, and young men shall fall exhausted' (vv. 29–30). The battle against sin is, indeed, exhausting. Isaiah goes on: '*But* they who wait on the Lord shall renew their strength; they shall mount up with wings like eagles; they shall run and not be weary; they shall walk and not faint.' God provides the power. It is not *their* power, but *his* power! 'Lazarus, come forth!'

I wonder whether there is someone reading these pages who does not yet trust in Jesus—who has not yet submitted to Jesus for salvation? Perhaps God's cry to you today is like that cry to Lazarus. 'Jonathan—come forth!' 'Susan—come forth!' God calls you out of your sin, out of your rebellion, out of your worry about what other people might think of you and out of your wonderings about whether or not the Bible is true. He calls, 'Come forth!' Peter himself cried out, 'Repent and be baptized every one of you in the name of Jesus Christ for the forgiveness of your sins. And you will receive the gift of the Holy Spirit' (Acts 2:38). So come to him for salvation— there is hope to be found in no one else and in nothing else.

As Peter writes, 'Love one another earnestly from a pure heart,' he has not forgotten that the Word of God is accompanied by the power to fulfil that command. We should not forget either.

The quotation from Isaiah finishes with: 'The word of the Lord remains forever.' So, in case we are wondering what this 'word of the Lord' is, Peter finishes by explaining that this word 'is the good news that was preached to you' (v. 25). Thus, we have come full circle.

Having purified yourself by obedience to the truth, love one another earnestly, because God's Word stands—the gospel which calls you to the obedience of faith. We love because he first loved us. We obey because he works in us. We proclaim that love and obedience to those who are not yet believers, so that they also may enter into the eternal life we share in Christ.

Conclusion

Thus, these verses answer the question, 'Are the Scriptures for me?' with a resounding 'yes!' If you are a Christian, then you are chosen by God, an exile in this world, heading towards a wonderful future, despite whatever suffering you face now.

Why should I be obedient? Why should I strive to be holy? For some very excellent reasons. Firstly, your deeds reflect your destiny. Secondly, you were ransomed by Jesus' precious blood. Thirdly, you were reborn, brought from death to life. Fourthly, you are part of God's family. Fifthly, you are an elect exile. Sixthly, you are heading for an inheritance that can never perish, spoil or fade—an inheritance that is imperishable, undefiled and unfading.

The future is certain and Christians are in it together. So, gird up the loins of your minds, Peter urges us. 'Set your hope fully on the grace that will be brought to you at the revelation of Jesus Christ' (v. 13). Live in the light of your salvation because the Promised Land lies just ahead. We are but exiles in a country not our own, but the Promised Land awaits.

Notes

1 Alcock, Jonty, *Impossible Commands*, (The Good Book Company, June 2019), p.32.
2 Calvin, John, *Acts of the Council of Trent with the Antidote*, 1547. https://www.monergism.com/thethreshold/sdg/calvin_trentantidote.html

5 How do you fall?

1 Peter 2:1–12

On 30 July 2016, of his own freewill, Luke Aikins jumped out of a perfectly good aircraft flying at 25000 feet. He had no parachute and no wingsuit, and he fell 25000 feet to earth. He landed in a carefully constructed net, around a third of the size of a football field. As he left the aircraft and began his fall to earth, only one question mattered. Would he fall into the net and survive, or would he fall to the ground and die? Personally, I think he is an idiot.

Peter begins the second chapter of his letter by suggesting that one thing matters in life infinitely more than anything else. The question he considers here is not 'How will you fall to earth?' but rather, 'How will you fall in relation to Jesus?' Will you fall *before* Jesus in submission, and so receive eternal life. Or will you fall *over* him and so experience judgement and eternal death? Will you bow before him or stumble over him? In other words, Peter's focus in the first half of chapter 2 is simple: 'What is your response to Jesus?'

Most of us would agree that jumping out of an airplane at 25000 feet without a parachute is foolhardy. However, making the wrong decision regarding our response to Jesus is far worse than foolish. From the plane, a wrong fall has momentary bad consequences—physical death. For our response to Jesus, the wrong fall has eternally bad consequences—eternal death.

As we move into Peter's argument we discover (like in chapter 1:8–13) that he structured his argument using a chiasm. The text is carefully organised, with the outer parts supporting the next parts which, in turn, support the centre-point, the crux of the whole argument. To put it plainly, the focal point in these verses is in the middle of them. The outer parts concern living God's way. The next sections concern God's choices. The hub, the centre-point, is Christ the Cornerstone.

Here it is laid out in the classic ABCBA format.

A. Verses 1–3: God's way—how Christians should be living in the light of their salvation.

    B. Verses 4–5: God's choice: God chose Jesus.

        C. Verses 6–8: Christ the Cornerstone: Falling before or falling over?

    B. Verses 9–10: God's choice: God chose Christians.

A. Verses 11–12: God's way—how Christians should be living in the light of their salvation.

Since Peter, under the tutelage of the Holy Spirit, has ordered the discussion in this way, it seems sensible for us to do the same. Thus, we will begin with the outer brackets about living God's way and work our way inwards, finishing at the central point regarding Jesus the Cornerstone. In these verses, everything points towards Christ, and with Christ at the centre, everything flows from Him as well.

God's way (2:1–3, 11–12)

In the previous chapter, Peter highlighted that if we are Christians, then we are ransomed for holiness and reborn to love. One of the prime results of being a Christian is that we express love to one another. Now he picks up the same point as he begins this chiasm in chapter 2. As Christians, we should live in the light of our salvation. Peter is saying: 'If you *are* a Christian, then live like one!'

For Peter, though, it is not so much: 'You've become a Christian, so now you must ...' Rather, his understanding is: 'You've become a Christian, so naturally you will ...' Let me explain. Peter writes literally, 'Laying aside all malice ...'(NKJV). Perhaps his train of thought is, these things being put aside, 'long for the pure spiritual milk, that by it you may grow up into salvation.' If you are a Christian—if you have come to trust in Jesus for your salvation—then malice, envy, and the rest are being put behind you *because* you are craving spiritual milk.

Our task as Christians is not primarily to stop being envious and malicious and so on. Rather, it is to long for pure spiritual milk so that we can grow up into the salvation we have. The result of that growth is that malice and envy increasingly are put behind us.

If I display malice and deceit and hypocrisy and envy and slander, then I am not reflecting the salvation that is mine in Christ—that is true. But living God's way is not rooted in stopping certain secondary behaviours (malice, envy, deceit) but in starting one primary behaviour, namely, drinking pure spiritual milk. We do not grow up into salvation by stopping being hypocritical. We grow up into salvation by starting on pure spiritual milk.

I think this makes sense when we consider the meaning of the five attitudes Peter highlights. He has argued in chapter 1 that Christians are reborn to love one another. A natural consequence of being truly converted is that we will love one another. So now, Peter exposes five attributes which reflect a lack of love for one another.

One commentator on this text writes that 'malice' is the

overriding attribute, and the other four are all forms of malice.[1] I think he could be right. Malice concerns desiring ill-will or injury to another person—it is the opposite of the brotherly love we are reborn to embody (1:22). Perhaps there are two ideas here, then, each of which reflect a heart of malice. There are two double-sided coins which each express malice to another believer.

The first coin is deceit and hypocrisy. Deceit is about misleading someone else—pretending something is true when it is not, or vice versa. Hypocrisy comes from the world of drama and concerns putting on a mask. It is also about deceit, but this time it concerns pretending and putting on an act about ourselves. We deceive others and we deceive ourselves. We pretend about others and we pretend about ourselves. Two sides of the same malicious coin designed not to build our brother up, but to tear him down.

The second malicious coin is envy and slander. Envy is about desiring what someone else has, rather than being thankful for the blessing they are enjoying. I want what you have to make me feel better about myself. Slander is a word that describes throwing dirt on someone else—telling untruths about another person, undermining their credibility, pulling them down. I slander you to make me feel better about myself. Envy is feeling pulled down by what someone else has. Slander is pulling someone else down because of what they have. They are two sides of a second malicious coin designed not to build up our brother, but to tear him down.

These five attributes reflect a heart devoid of love for another person. If we are reborn to love (chapter 1), i.e., if the natural result of our salvation is that we will love other Christians, then none of these attributes will be able to flourish. We will have 'laid aside' each of them.

It is straightforward to think of ways in which other people do these things, but sometimes we find ourselves blind to our own sin. When someone in the church hurts us (and they will), these five things often come tumbling from our hearts. We wish ill on that person. We hope their ministry fades. We do not quite tell the whole truth when others notice or ask us about it. We pretend. We are envious of their successes. We undermine them. According to Peter, though, if we are saved then we should love naturally, as a consequence of our salvation.

It is not necessarily when someone hurts us that we display these malicious character traits, though. Let me give you an example. For me, sung worship can be hard work. When Sunday church comes along, I stand along with everyone else, singing the song on the screen. I enjoy singing, as it happens. But at the same time, I might lament yet again that there are so many men in the church who do not even open their mouths for the songs. Running through my head are questions like, 'How can we teach our children to worship if we refuse to do it ourselves? Men are supposed to lead by example, not be passive and let "church" happen around them. Why won't they just sing? Are they really Christians? Maybe there are some deep issues that need attention?' My concerns filter through my brain as the song progresses. Then I realize that I am not worshipping, either—I am judging.

Worship is going on around me and I am singing, but I may not be worshipping. Sometimes I am working hard to focus on God and bringing him praise. Sometimes I am being put off by someone around me. Sometimes I am distracted by a minor mistake made by someone in the band. Sometimes I am just thinking about lunch.

My lamenting of other's failures to worship is deeply hypocritical. I want to worship, but I do not always manage it. Others will think I am worshipping, whether I am or not. Is that not far more hypocritical than someone who stands with their mouth shut without pretending to worship. So, for me, Peter comes along and speaks directly to my heart and says that I should be putting these things behind me and loving my fellow believers.

How, then, do I learn to love as I should? Thankfully, Peter explains: 'Like newborn infants, long for the pure spiritual milk.' That is how we grow up into salvation. That is how we love as we should. Consider how newborn babies crave milk. They cry loudly for it. They demand it with cries that are increasingly difficult to ignore. Only milk satisfies them. You can offer a finger to chew or a dummy or a toy to try to distract them, but, in the end, only milk will satisfy their craving.

Peter urges that we desire pure spiritual milk in precisely this way. The trinkets of the world, the pull of the screen, the volume of the music, the speed of the adrenaline rush—none of these should be able to drown our craving for pure spiritual milk. This begs the question: 'What is this 'pure spiritual milk' to which Peter refers?

A few verses earlier, Peter has written that Christians are born again *through* the living Word of God—the Word of the Lord which remains forever and which is the good news preached to you. Now, he is urging that Christians crave pure spiritual milk in order to grow up into salvation. John Piper puts it this way: 'Since you have been born again *by* the Word of God, now long *for* the Word of God.'[2]

The spiritual milk Peter is discussing is the Word of the Lord—the 'living' Word of God. If we have 'tasted that the Lord is good' (verse 3), then we must crave pure spiritual milk. We must crave the Word of God because it is through the Word of God that we grow up into salvation.

In chapter 1, Peter posed two vital questions. 'Are the Old and New Testaments reliable?' 'Is the Bible for me?' His answer to both questions was an emphatic 'yes!' Now he moves on from the reliability and applicability of Scripture to say very simply, 'Crave it!' (2:2, NIV). It is reliable and it is for you, so crave it.

We grow up into salvation—we live more and more the way God calls us to live—not because we try harder, or because we better ourselves, or because we have a new training regimen, or because we are more involved in church. Christianity is not some giant self-help movement. In fact, it is quite the opposite. It tells us that we cannot help ourselves but rather it is God who helps us. According to the Bible, before we become Christians we are lost, blind, poor, naked, enemies of God, without hope, helpless, and dead. Salvation occurs when God finds us, gives us sight, makes us rich, clothes us, becomes our friend, brings hope and raises us to life.

According to Peter, we grow up into salvation in one prime way. We grow up *because* we long for the Word of God; we eagerly desire the Word of God; we yearn for the Word of God; and we crave the Word of God. See how Peter explains it: 'Long for the pure spiritual milk, that by it you may grow up into salvation' (2:2). The only way to grow up into salvation is to read, mark, learn and inwardly digest the pure spiritual milk. There is no other way. You can go to conferences, hear great speakers, read books, watch sermons, and listen to podcasts, but the only sure-fire way to grow up into salvation is to read God's Word.

For some, it might be tempting to respond: 'But I'm not much of a reader.' Perhaps you find reading more difficult than others. Perhaps you suffer with dyslexia or dyspraxia. Nevertheless, Peter says, if you want to grow up into your salvation, God's Word is the only way you are going to do it.

Before you find that discouraging, remember Peter himself. He was a fisherman, one whom, in Acts 4, the religious leaders described as an 'uneducated and common man'. That word 'common' in the Greek is *idiotia*. Clearly, Peter was no intellectual! Regardless of this, however, Peter knew the Scriptures really well. Even in his first sermon at Pentecost he quotes from various parts of the Old Testament to make his argument. Here in this first letter, again he quotes from the Old Testament and applies it to the present. Peter is steeped in the Bible. He may not have had strong formal education. He may have struggled to read and write and do sums. But when it came to the Bible, he somehow managed to read it, learn it, and take it in.

So, if you struggle with reading, take heart, because reading the Bible is not like reading something else. God's Word is unique. There is nothing remotely like it. It grabs you. It satisfies you in ways nothing else can. God's power works through his Word by his Spirit in your heart to grow you into salvation. In essence, reading the Bible is different, because God himself works in you to help you read and understand.

When Peter writes about God's Word, he uses an imperative here: 'Long for!'. It is a command to be obeyed. He does not say, 'Getting into the Bible might help you, so why not have a go at that.' He does not say, 'My advice would be for you to read the Bible.' His words are far more direct: 'Crave pure spiritual milk.' It may help us to remember at this point that God's commands come accompanied with the power for us to fulfil them. Thus, when God commands us to crave, so He gives us the power to crave. As we read the Bible, so God grows in us a craving for the Bible.

This milk is described as 'pure' and 'spiritual'. It is unadulterated and untainted. It is God's Word not mediated through someone else's ideas or language, but directly from the page. Interestingly, the word 'spiritual' here is *logikon* rooted in the Greek noun *logos* which means 'word'. In other words, the verse reads literally, 'Long for pure of-the-word milk.' How are we to love the way God calls us to and avoid malice in all its forms? We can do it only by craving God's Word and letting it sink down deep into us.

Notice the other end of this chiasm structure. There, we find Peter urging believers to 'abstain from the passions of the flesh, which wage war against your soul,' and to 'keep your conduct among the Gentiles honourable, so that when they speak against you ... they may see your good deeds and glorify God on the day of visitation' (1 Peter 2:11–12).

Again, Peter is saying that we are to live God's way rather than the way of the world. How applicable Peter's words are to our modern culture. 'Abstain from the passions of the flesh ...' flies in the face of the way most people seem to approach life in the western world. In our culture, indulging the passions of the flesh is often seen as normal and right and good.

God's way is very different. Peter urges that we abstain from the passions of the flesh, because they 'wage war against your soul!' (v. 11). Living the Christian life is a battle—of that, there is no doubt. It is a battle to keep Jesus as our prime focus and the true love of our lives. This battle can be waged in one way only and that is by craving pure spiritual milk. The battle is fought as we read, study, learn, and imbibe the Word of God. The only weapon available to us to fight off the world, the devil and the passions of the flesh is the sword of the Spirit, which is the Word of God, according to Paul in Ephesians (Ephesians 6:17).

In our world today, it is so easy to indulge the passions of the flesh rather than abstain from them. Just a sneaky second peak at the scantily clad woman on the beach. Just one more click on the computer screen. Just one more chocolate bar. Just one more purchase. But we must make no mistake—those passions wage war against our souls, and we indulge them at our peril. We are called to abstain from them.

The purpose is clear in verse 12. In seeing the honourable way in which Christians live, those who are not yet believers give glory to God. Not only that, but Peter writes that we are to keep our conduct honourable so that 'when they speak against you', they may see your good deeds and give glory to God. Our response to verbal persecution should be a flashing neon arrow to the goodness of God.

Peter says that 'on the day of visitation' (i.e., when Jesus returns), even unbelievers will be bowing in awe, not only because of the majesty of Jesus himself, but also because they have seen the way Christians responded to the majestic King. With God's empowerment, we are to live God's way.

God chooses (2:4-5, 9-10)

The next bracket in the chiasm structure is about God's choosing—a subject to which Peter has already alluded in terms of how it applies to Christians. Back in chapter 1, he described Christians as God's 'elect'. He reminded us in 1:3 that God has 'caused us' to be born again—God did the work in you. Watch now as Peter explains in more detail here in chapter 2. He describes God the Father's *choosing* as an action relating not just to Christians, but also to God the Son. There is a parallel here from which we can learn. In verse 4, Peter writes that Jesus is 'chosen' by God the Father. He is contrasting people's rejection of Jesus by God's choice of Jesus. Jesus is precious *because* he is chosen by his Father. The Father *chose* the Son for his work in making salvation possible for humankind. The Son joyfully obeyed his Father in the power of the Spirit in doing that work for which he was chosen. Likewise, if we are Christians then God *chose* us. We, too, are joyfully to obey our Father in the power of the Spirit to do the work for which we were chosen.

In case you remain unconvinced of this parallel, on the corresponding side of the chiasm, Peter uses exactly the same word in the original to describe Christians as a 'chosen' race (1 Peter 2:9). If we are Christians, then God the Father *chose* us and then, in the fullness of time, 'caused us to be born again' (1:3). Jesus was chosen and we were chosen. Paul ties these things together in Ephesians, as well as providing us with a timescale: God 'chose us in [Christ] before the foundation of the world' (Ephesians 1:4). Before the world was ever created and, thus, before any people ever existed, God the Father chose God the Son to come in the power of God the Spirit, to live and die on our behalf and to be raised from death to glory. God's plan was made before Genesis 3 ever happened, rooted in himself—the sending of God the Son—in order to save Christians who, as yet, did not even exist. Therefore, if you are a Christian then God the Father's choice of you is as certain as his choice of God the Son to offer himself as a sacrifice on your behalf.

In time, Jesus was 'rejected' by people (1 Peter 2:4), but he was God's chosen and precious Son. We may experience rejection also, as we walk in the footsteps of our Lord, but just as Jesus was chosen, so we are a 'chosen race' (1 Peter 2:9). Look at the encouragement offered by Peter to the suffering Christians to whom he writes. Christians are chosen by God. We are royal—adopted brothers and sisters of the Prince of Peace. We are a priesthood—bringing praise and glory to God and bringing the Word of God to the world. We are a holy nation—set apart for God's work. God *owns* us—a people for his possession. Paul puts it this way: 'You are not your own ... you were bought at a price' (1 Corinthians 6:19–20).

Peter summarizes these ideas in verse 10. Before we came to faith, we were not a people—we were lost in darkness, stumbling about, blind to the truth, poor, wretched, naked, dead in our transgressions and sins. Now that we are saved, though, light has dawned, and we *are* God's people. This is nothing we can be proud of in ourselves— we are God's people not because we are good, or because we have some special qualities that entitle us to salvation. Rather, we are God's people because, very simply, we have received mercy. The chosen race, the royal priesthood, the holy nation—us. We are these things for one simple reason: we have received mercy. Therefore, day by day, we are to proclaim the 'excellencies of him who called [us] out of darkness into his marvellous light' (2:9).

The role of the priest in the Old Testament (remember, Peter is deeply rooted in his Jewish heritage) was to bring people to God and to bring God to the people. He was to bring praise and sacrifice to God as a pleasing aroma—telling God he is great. He was also to bring God to the people, telling them that God is great. The priest stood as a sort of intermediary between God and humankind, bringing glory to God and bringing God's glory to people. Now, in the new covenant era, we have direct access to God through Jesus, so no human priest is required. But as Christians we still have something of this dual function—to bring our praise and glory to God, and to bring the wonder of God to the world.

Notice that both aspects of the priestly function are in play here. The concept of priesthood appears on both sides of Peter's chiasm, too. In verse 5, we find we are 'being built up as a spiritual house to be a holy priesthood to offer spiritual sacrifices acceptable to God through Jesus Christ'. Then in verse 9 (as noted above) we find we are a 'royal priesthood' ... whose purpose is to 'proclaim the excellencies of him who called [us] out of darkness into his marvellous light.

This brings us, finally, to the centre-point of Peter's argument.

Christ the cornerstone: Falling before or falling over (2:6–8)

The midpoint of his chiasm, the pivot of his discussion, the keystone at the top of the chiastic arch, is Jesus himself. Here, Peter uses a building metaphor to establish a simple division. Remember, the outer part of the chiasm argues that if we live God's way then we point people to Jesus, and the next part explains that if we live as

God's priesthood then we bring our praise to Jesus. Right here in the centre, though, we have Jesus to whom the outer parts point.

On the other side of the chiasm, if we believe in Jesus then we are never put to shame. The result will be that we are God's priesthood bringing people to God's glory and bringing glory to God. The result of that will be that we live right.

Peter is keen that no one thinks he is inventing the necessity to submit to Jesus. It is not his own idea! While he was taught by Jesus himself, he does not simply go back to Jesus' words during his earthly lifetime. Instead, Peter returns to the Scriptures, written hundreds of years before—Scriptures which he knows well. Having urged these suffering Christians to crave God's Word, now he puts it into practice and looks at God's Word for himself. His emphasis on pure spiritual milk in verse 2 comes to fruition in verse 6 where he writes, 'It stands in Scripture:' and then he quotes from Isaiah 28:16; Psalm 118:22; and Isaiah 8:14.

God's promises in these verses use a stone as a metaphor for the coming Messiah. Peter has already alluded to the Messiah in this way back in verse 4 with 'a living stone rejected by men,' and then with the identical phrase 'chosen and precious', lifted from Isaiah 28. Therefore, Peter's point in verse 6 is two-fold.

First, Jesus *is* the chosen and precious Messiah of God as foretold by Isaiah 700 years earlier. He is the 'stone' who was (and is) rejected by most people. Peter directs his readers back to the Scriptures, quoting Psalm 118:22. People rejected the Messiah and that is one reason why he was killed. This is Peter's first point in verse 6.

Peter's second point, though, is that those who believe in Jesus will be saved. In other words, the result of the Messiah being rejected would be that he became the cornerstone upon which the whole building rests. Back in Matthew 21 where Jesus quotes from the same Psalm, he includes the next verse in the Psalm as well: 'This was the Lord's doing and it is marvellous in our eyes!' (Matthew 21:42). In other words, even the rejection of the Messiah (which resulted in his death) is part of God's marvellous plan. The fact that eternal salvation rests on this rejected Messiah is amazing. It does not depend on us, on the living stones being built into a spiritual house (v. 5). No—those living stones depend upon the cornerstone alone. Their salvation depends on Jesus alone. Those who believe in him will be saved.

Interestingly, Peter here gives more time to those who do *not* believe than to those who do. This is not because Peter is less interested in those who believe in Jesus. Rather, it is because he wants those who do *not* yet believe to come to 'a knowledge of the truth' (2 Timothy 3:7). Thus, he reiterates two points from chapter 1.

Firstly, people stumble over Jesus the Rock because they disobey the Word. In other words, he reiterates that to believe is to obey and to obey is to believe. Secondly, he reminds them that their disobedience was their destiny.

God chose Jesus and Jesus came willingly to live, to die, to rise and to ascend. Jesus had freewill and he chose to obey. God chose Jesus so that he would obey. The Spirit enabled Jesus to fulfil the plan despite his temptations and sufferings. Likewise, Christians are chosen by God to believe and to obey. We have freewill to choose to obey. God chose us so that we would obey. The Spirit enables us to fulfil the plan despite the temptations and sufferings we face.

Furthermore, the Spirit brings about the fulfilment of the plan in and through us *despite our sin*!

Fundamentally, Peter desires that his readers would respond in faith to Jesus, who is the Cornerstone. Rather than 'stumbling' over the stone, or being offended by his demands, he urges all those who do not yet believe to put their trust in Jesus. It is the only way to avoid shame and be given honour. Unless we submit to Jesus for our salvation, we stand ashamed and dishonoured and destined for disaster.

Peter is highlighting the binary nature of salvation. Either we *fall before* Jesus in submission and therefore our shame is removed and we have a glorious future before us, or we *fall over* Jesus and take offense and therefore our shame remains and our future is darkness and judgement. Every person alive will either fall before the Cornerstone or fall over the Cornerstone. Either Jesus is for us 'chosen and precious', or he is a 'stone of stumbling and a rock of offense'.

When it comes to our response to Jesus, we cannot simply add him as another brick to our life-build. Rather, we must tear everything down and begin building all over again with Jesus as our foundation upon which everything else depends. To change the metaphor, becoming a Christian is not simply adding another bead to the string of our lives. Rather, it is to change strings—now Jesus is the string upon which all other things depend.

The benefits are enormous, and Peter has alluded to them not just here, but also elsewhere in this section. Christians are never put to shame. They are honoured, chosen, royalty, priests, holy, God's people, and receivers of mercy. The requirement for these immeasurable benefits is that we believe in him, submit to him, entrust our lives to him. He becomes our king. We get off the throne and let him rule, because that is the only way to really live. It is the only way to taste that 'the Lord is good' (verse 3).

Have you tasted that the Lord is good? Either you disobey the Word, or you crave it so that you might grow up into salvation. Jesus is the Cornerstone and Peter's question is left hanging in the air. How are you going to fall? Like Luke Aikins jumping out of the aircraft, are you going to land on concrete, or in the only net there is? Will you fall before Jesus and live, or will you fall over Jesus and die? Either Jesus is your Cornerstone or he is your stumbling stone. I pray that you fall before him as Lord—the greatest and safest safety net there ever was and is.

Notes

1 Sproul, R.C., *1 – 2 Peter*, (Wheaton, Illinois: Crossway, 2011), p. 59
2 Piper, John, www.desiringgod.org/messages/long-for-the-pure-milk-of-the-word, January 30th, 1994

6 Suffering in submission

1 Peter 2:13–25

'Either you do as you are told, or I confiscate your phone until tomorrow!' This was me trying to exert some authority when one of our children was refusing to do as I asked. 'I'm not doing that!' This was me refusing to submit to authority at work when they asked all employees to do something I did not agree with. If I instruct my children to get ready because we are going out to eat pizza, they submit happily to my authority. If I instruct them to clean their bedrooms, submission is less whole-hearted!

In the first half of this chapter, Peter has explained that when it comes to the authority of Jesus, either we fall before him in submission and we are saved eternally, or we fall over him and are lost eternally. His Christian readers will have been comforted that submitting to Jesus as their final authority leads them to a glorious future, something Peter discussed back in chapter 1.

However, for the Christian, while submission to Jesus is a given, submission to human authorities is a knottier problem. In these verses, Peter provides a clear answer to the question of whether or not we are required to submit to human authorities. In the process, he anticipates and responds to the possible objections of his readers—objections which are all the more likely since they are facing increasing persecution at the hands of the Roman authorities. Peter couches his answer through four primary questions.

- How should Christians respond to those in authority (vv. 13–17)?
- What if the authority over us is evil and causes us suffering (vv. 18–20)?
- Why should we submit to suffering (vv. 21–23)?
- In what way is Jesus' suffering relevant (vv. 24–25)?

We begin, then, with the Christian response to authority.

How should Christians respond to those in authority (vv. 13–17)?

Notice how inclusive Peter is in his assertion in verse 13: 'Be subject to … *every* human institution.' This leaves no room for, 'Well, my boss does not understand my situation so I don't need to do as he says,' or, 'But if I do that, then an aspect of my ministry will suffer.' Peter does not give us those kind of options, but writes simply, 'Be subject to ('submit to' in NIV) … *every* human institution.'

This prompts the obvious question about what 'submit' actually means. Is 'submit to' the same as 'obey'? This is a similar question to the well-worn discussion about Ephesians 5, in which the same word is used to assert that wives are to 'submit to' their husbands. In both cases, it is important to recognise that the verb is a passive one. In other words, in talking to wives in Ephesians 5 and in talking to all Christians here in 1 Peter 2, the person being addressed is the one who is to submit themselves to the authorities. It is not for the husbands in Ephesians 5, or the authorities in 1 Peter 2, to make people submit to them. The word is not for them, it is for the people being addressed.

Submitting to authority is a decision and consequent action that is to be taken by the one submitting. For mature Christians, then, we know we are commanded to live in submission to authority. But we have no mandate from this text to try and force others to submit to our authority.

Peter provides the reason for submission here, too. We submit, 'for the Lord's sake'. We do not submit for our own convenience, our own sanctification or our own furtherance. Rather, we submit *for the Lord's sake*—we submit because of Jesus.

To put it another way, I do not submit to the authority of the government because I think they deserve it—whether or not they deserve it is irrelevant. I am to submit because I am a follower of Jesus. I do not submit to my boss at work because I think she deserves it—whether or not she deserves it is irrelevant. I am to submit because I am a follower of Jesus. A wife does not submit to her husband because he deserves it—whether or not he deserves it is irrelevant. She submits because she is a follower of Jesus.

This is a *good* thing, because it means that my response to those in authority is not based on whether or not I think someone deserves to be in authority. We submit for the Lord's sake. Submission is an action which Peter describes in verse 15 as 'doing good'. It is the 'will of God' (also verse 15) and so we submit because God wills that we submit. In doing this good, Peter argues, we may 'put to silence the ignorance of foolish people'.

Peter has not ignored the role of those in authority in these verses. He states that the role of the governors is 'to punish those who do evil and to praise those who do good' (1 Peter 2:14)—this is what governors are supposed to do. If you are an employer, or a parent, your primary role in exercising your authority is to punish evil and praise good. Both are necessary for good leadership.

However, Peter is focusing on Christians who live under authority of whatever kind, good or bad. This is why his words apply to us today as well. Whatever authority we live under, whether that be at home, at school, at work, or under our government, his focus is on how we respond to that authority.

Peter has already written: 'Keep your conduct among the Gentiles honourable, so that when they speak against you as evildoers, they may see your good deeds and glorify God on the day of visitation' (1 Peter 2:12). The aim in submitting to authority is not that I will receive the praise of those authorities (they may or may not supply that—that is their prerogative). Ultimately, the aim is that they will see our good deeds and *glorify* God, irrespective of their approach to leadership.

Peter's words in verse 16 are fascinating. He writes simply, 'Live as people who are free!' As far as Peter is concerned, submitting to those in authority is an act of freedom. We are not to say, 'I'm free, so I don't need to submit to authority'—such an attitude is 'a cover-up for evil' (verse 16). Rather, we are free *because* we are servants of God!

To put it another way, everyone serves something or someone. Perhaps, it is getting the nicest house or car, the latest gadgets, the best-paid job. Perhaps it is world travel or continued and varied experiences. Maybe we serve intellectual or academic progress. Maybe we serve others by living our lives seeking their approval or praise or applause. Maybe it is helping others or 'doing the right thing' or serving on a charitable trust board. Perhaps it is our family—seeking the best for them and driving for what we see as *their* success. But Peter is saying here that it is only when our driving force is to serve God that we are free. True freedom is to have our *raison-d'etre*, our focus in life, as serving God. Living any other way is not freedom—it is bondage.

As we come to verse 17, it is helpful to note that the whole verse is a miniature chiasm in the original. It is written in this way:

A. Honour everyone

    B. Love the brotherhood

    B. Fear God

A. Honour the emperor.

The first half is collective, while the second half concerns the leaders only. The outside concerns the world, while the inside concerns the people of God.

Honour everyone, Peter says—Christian or unbeliever, atheist or Muslim, enemy or friend. More particularly, though, over and above honouring everyone, we are to *love* the brotherhood. In particular, Christians should love Christians. Working from the other end, Peter's readers should honour the emperor. They should not undermine him or gossip about him or seek to usurp him. No—they should *honour* the emperor, recognizing his God-given earthly status and giving him due respect. More particularly, though, over and above that, they should fear God. Of all beings that exist, fear God—he is central. Peter is saying, 'Everyone, over whom is the emperor—honour him. Christians, over whom is God—fear him.'

So, the primary message in this first part is simple: be subject to, submit to, put yourself under the guidance and authority of, every human institution. 'Respect authority,' Peter is saying.

This is increasingly a highly counter-cultural message in our western world. To undermine authority, to stand against those over us, to push back against a parent or a boss or a government or a president, to disrespect them, to write amusing memes or witty putdowns against our leaders—all these are seen as good things. But they are not good things at all. They are bad things. Those in authority are only in authority because, ultimately, God put them there. If we claim to be servants of God, then we subject ourselves to those in authority over us.

Thus, Peter's first point here is that we should submit to the authorities over us, whether they be good leaders or bad leaders. This raises the obvious question: 'What if the one in authority is wrong, or causes us harm or suffering?' It is not a theoretical question of interest to the reader, though. It is a violently real question. These Christians are living under the authority of Rome. Increasingly they are facing persecution at the hands of (or at least as a result of) those in authority over them. So, the question is poignant: 'Do we submit to tyranny, or do we begin to mount some kind of resistance?'

What if the authority over us is evil and causes us suffering (vv. 18–20)?

Anticipating the question, Peter responds with a very clear instruction. He argues that we should subject ourselves not only to the good and gentle master, but also to the unjust master. 'The ones in authority over us are making us suffer. What should we do, Peter?' Peter responds: 'Subject yourselves to them, even though they are unjust.'

He does not leave it there, though. He provides them with a reason—a reason which he reiterates to drive the point home. 'This is a gracious thing ...', he writes in verse 19. In case we missed it, he writes again in verse 20: 'This is a gracious thing in the sight of God.' Unjust suffering is a gracious thing. What does he mean?

The word 'gracious' here translates the Greek root *charis*. Our problem with comprehension lies not in our failure to understand the word used, but rather in the fact that we imbue the word with all its soteriological connotations. In other words, we see the word 'grace' and we think of God's unmerited favour towards us in stooping down to our spiritually dead-in-sin bodies and rescuing us; making us alive in Christ; forgiving our sin and paying the price on our behalf by the death of Jesus; and now making us ready for eternity and preparing a place for us as we head towards eternal glory with Jesus. That is a lot to pack into a little Greek 5-letter-word! Sometimes in the New Testament, the word *is* imbued with all of that.

But here, Peter is using the word *charis* in its original, simple way, to mean 'favourable, pleasurable, that which brings joy'. We are to be subject to our unjust masters with all respect because this is pleasurable thing—a thing that brings joy.

It is tempting to wonder at this point whether or not Peter has finally lost his marbles. Being subject to unjust masters is definitely not a pleasurable or joyful thing. It is a painful and difficult thing which brings heartache and trouble. 'Wait,' Peter responds. Read carefully. 'If, when you do good and suffer for it you endure, this is a gracious thing in the sight of God!' (v. 20). It brings pleasure and joy not to you, but to God!

Now, this does not mean that God enjoys our suffering, like some kind of evil sociopath. God does not enjoy and find pleasure in the suffering itself. Rather, he finds pleasure in seeing his children endure despite (and in the midst of) their suffering. He has great joy in seeing us cling to him even in the furnace. When Satan approached God and asked to torment Job, he said, 'He only follows you and serves you because you've given him a great life' (Job 1:9–11). But God had great joy when Satan was demonstrated to be the father of lies. Job remained true to God despite his suffering.

So, Peter writes to these churches, 'Even under the emperor who persecutes you, continue to live God's way and endure—that brings great joy to God.' He delights to see his children live right whatever the consequences may be.

I had a student at school who often was amid trouble—causing it, being involved in it, getting himself into scrapes, and refusing to accept any responsibility. But sometime later, we noticed that when things happened around him, or when others were getting things a bit wrong, this student stayed out of trouble. My pleasure was in seeing a tutee who, formally, would be at least going along with it— if not instigating it—now refusing to be dragged in, sitting slightly apart, not getting involved. He was maturing fast and it brought me great pleasure. It was not a pleasurable thing for him, though. He no longer joined in with his friends. He had to stand out a bit. He had to stop being the one everyone enjoyed pushing the boundaries with. He felt a bit alone as he travelled against the tide. But it brought me great pleasure, not because I enjoyed his pain, but because I began to see someone who can get the small things right. He stood up under pressure and stood for what was right. He stood on his own two feet. The result was that, since he got the small things right, now I could begin to trust him with bigger things. I gave him greater responsibility. And when I saw him around, I praised and applauded and encouraged. Well done, faithful and committed student. I bragged about him to other staff. His resulting report was 'top-dollar'.

Why does God take pleasure in people enduring under suffering? Because it demonstrates they are maturing. They are getting the smaller things right, so now they can be given greater responsibility. They are standing on their own two feet. Their worship of God is their own, not dependent on what others decide to do. They are clearly God's children, and they experience his good pleasure. When they see him, he praises and applauds. He says, 'Well done, good and faithful servant.' His report of them is top-dollar, and he loves to applaud them.

When Stephen was being martyred at the end of one of the world's greatest sermons in Acts 7, remember what happens next. He sees heaven open and Jesus standing at the right hand of the Father to welcome him home, and his face is like that of an angel (Acts 7:56; 6:15). Whatever the world was saying about him and doing to him, God was welcoming him home. 'Well done, good and faithful servant.' He meets his greatest friend of all as he walks through the door of death into eternal glory.

Why should we submit to suffering? (vv. 21–23)

Peter has argued that we are to subject ourselves to those in authority, whether they are good or evil, whether we suffer unjustly or not. When we suffer and endure, this brings gladness to the heart of God—it is a gracious thing in his sight.

Peter anticipates further questions about *why* we should submit to suffering, so this is where he takes his discussion next in verse 21. He writes, 'For [that is, 'because'] to this you have been called, because Christ also suffered for you, leaving you an example, so that you might follow in his steps.' So, is it that we should suffer because we are meant to emulate Jesus, and Jesus suffered? Yes and no!

There is nothing good about suffering *per se*. It is not a holy thing to suffer. Peter is not upholding suffering as a positive thing in itself. After all, suffering is a result of the Fall back in Genesis 3, and there will be no suffering in eternity with Jesus. Suffering is a bad thing. We must read Peter carefully here. 'Christ also suffered for you, leaving you an example, so that you might follow in his steps. He committed no sin, neither was deceit found in his mouth. When he was reviled, he did not revile in return; when he suffered, he did not threaten, but continued entrusting himself to him who judges justly' (vv. 21–23).

The thing we are to emulate is not suffering itself, but rather that, increasingly, we should put sin behind us. We should not allow any deceit to come from our mouths. We should not revile when we are reviled, nor threaten when we suffer. Peter's point is that Jesus lived the perfect life, and it is the life of Jesus which we are to emulate. Living Jesus' way includes living right even when we suffer for it, just as Jesus did.

We cannot suffer for someone else as Christ did. We are not called to do that. But we can live in obedience to God, as Jesus did. That is our calling—to love Him and so to live his way day by day, whatever the consequences might be. In essence, Peter's call here is to the life of a disciple—growing in sanctification, growing to be more and more like Jesus.

In what way is Jesus' suffering relevant (vv. 24–25)?

It is hardly surprising that Peter finishes this whole discussion on submission to earthly masters with the relevance of the substitutionary death of Jesus on the cross.

To begin with, it is vital in the midst of suffering that we remember we serve a God who understands human suffering intimately. He is not distant, aloof and indifferent. No—Jesus himself suffered as he submitted to those in authority over him. He could have called on twelve legions of angels to rescue him (Matthew 26:53), but he did not. He could have come down from the cross, as he was challenged to do (Mark 15:30), yet he did not. Rather, Jesus himself suffered as a result of submitting to human authorities. He knows what it is like. He understands the pain from the inside. Peter is keen that his readers remember this.

Peter finishes this section with Jesus' suffering for a second reason, though. One of the key reasons that Jesus paid for our sin was that we would die to sin and live to righteousness. In other words, just as Jesus died because of our sin, so we should put sin to death and live because of Jesus.

We were running against God, like that student in my house at school. We were causing trouble, responding badly, instigating sin perhaps, encouraging others to live against God, reviling those who come against us, refusing to submit to those in authority, seeking to bring justice ourselves.

But now Jesus has paid for all of that. We have returned to the Shepherd and Overseer of our souls. We belong to him. He loves us, died for us, lives for us, leads us and encourages us. Note how Peter returns to the Old Testament yet again here, quoting from Isaiah 53.

Jesus' death fulfilled Isaiah's prophecy when the Lord laid on Jesus the iniquity of us all (Isaiah 53:5–6). Jesus was led like a lamb to the slaughter, but now he is the Good Shepherd who leads us, his sheep, to heavenly pastures. Our high calling is to submit to those in authority and so, somehow, to bring pleasure to our God, who loves us and who suffered to prove it.

7 Submitting to Christ

1 Peter 3:1–7

Chay Phillips was a highly accomplished climber. He had climbed all over the world and was one of the youngest Britons ever to conquer Everest. One spring, Chay helped lead a four-person climbing trip to the mountains with three friends, two of whom were less experienced than he was. Mark Tanton, one of those two, left the chalet early one morning with Chay for a dual climb before breakfast. Mark knew his own limits but he was utterly confident in the ability and competence of Chay. He knew the mountains were dangerous, especially in the spring, but with the energy and breeziness of youth, with their top-of-the-range equipment, and with one of the country's top climbers at his side, perhaps he felt that those dangers did not apply to him. Perhaps they both felt confident that conquering another mountain would be straightforward. Whatever the case, Chay and Mark never returned to the chalet that day. Their bodies were found the following day, and it seemed that, for some unknown reason, they had fallen 400 metres to their deaths.[1]

One of the tragedies of our human condition is that we often believe the rules do not apply to us. We know things are dangerous, but probably not for us—we think that we know what we are doing. We know we are supposed to do one thing, but we feel that doing something different would be just as good. Our prisons are full of people who, even just for a few moments, felt that the rules did not apply to them.

When we come to these first seven verses in 1 Peter 3, many readers sigh with relief as they gloss over the text. They respond, 'Well, it is all quite interesting and everything, Peter, but I'm single. Therefore, none of this husband/wife stuff applies to me.' Peter is explaining how wives and husbands should live. But for those who are too young (or feel they are too old) to marry, or for those whose journey has not included marriage, the temptation is strong to follow our natural human condition and say, 'This does not apply to me.'

Such an approach, however, is not right—it is dangerous, even. What Peter has to say applies directly to each of us, married or not. So, as we climb the heights of his argument, we must be alert to the dangers and keep our wits about us. It will take some time to reach the top, but once we arrive, we will have no doubt: these verses apply to every one of us.

Instructions to wives

Peter begins the section with the word, 'likewise', meaning 'in the same way.' In the previous chapter, Peter has asserted that servants are to be subject to their masters 'with all respect' (2:18). Now he writes that wives are to be subject to their husbands with all respect. This seems like a very controversial idea in our western world. With the emancipation of women, women's rights, and the feminist movement, the idea that a wife ought to be subject to her husband is almost anathema. The view is that in the 21st century, we have moved on from this primitive way of doing things.

But Peter does not agree. Thinking back to the servant in the previous chapter, we must remember firstly that the word 'be subject to' is almost a reflexive. It is a self-designated posture, not a posture to be imposed upon us. I am to subject myself to those in authority, not be subjected by them. Secondly, remember that the word 'be subject to' is a word that reflects freedom. As a servant, then, *because* I am free and live as a servant of God, so I can express my freedom by being subject to those in authority over me.

Likewise in chapter 3, firstly a wife can decide to be subject to her husband—he must not put his wife in subjection under him. Secondly, *because* she is free—*because* she lives as a servant of God—she can express her freedom by being subject to her husband.

For a wife married to a Christian husband, the husband should be seeking the best for his wife as he seeks to lead the family under God's authority. This is assumed of Christian husbands. The role of husbands is to love their wives 'as Christ loved the church and gave himself up for her' (Ephesians 5:25). In other words, the wife is to submit to the husband's oversight, and the husband is to give his life for his wife, if needs be. Wives are willing to submit; husbands are willing to die. That is Paul's emphasis.

Now, subjecting oneself to a husband who loves Jesus and is willing to die for you is one thing. It is quite another thing to subject oneself to a husband who is not a believer and therefore is not seeking to lead the family under God's authority. Perhaps in this case, the rules do not apply to the wife?

As with the servant in chapter 2, Peter disagrees. It is obvious in the way he writes: 'Wives, be subject to your own husbands, so that *even if some do not obey the word ...*' (3:1). In other words, be subject to your own husbands, even if they are not believers. Even if they do not follow God's law, and the Word of God is not paramount in their lives, nevertheless you are to be subject to him. We have noted before that we submit ourselves to those in authority whether or not they are worthy of our submission. Likewise, here, whether or not a wife is to be subject to her husband does not depend on whether the husband is worthy of that submission.

Now, to be clear, we explained last time that the word, 'be subject to' does not always mean 'obey'. Usually it does, but not always. If your husband demands that you do something contrary to God's written law, then, while you are to remain subject to your husband, you are also required to disobey! In such instances, you must respect him and submit to him, but not obey him. There are tragic situations of spousal abuse where respecting and submitting to a husband might include moving out and moving away. In these cases, wives are not to obey the ungodly demands and controlling behaviours of their spouses, simply because their obedience to God must always take precedence. In such situations, it can be the best thing for a husband to experience a break in the relationship as a route to possible repentance and faith (although sadly it does not always end that way).

Most of the time, though, submitting oneself to a husband and being subject to a husband involves staying in the relationship and living God's way. Peter explains why this is the case. He continues: 'So that even if some do not obey the word, they may be won without a word by the conduct of their wives.' The husband does not follow the Lord, but as he sees his wife seek to follow the Lord and love Jesus more and more, and as he sees the result of this reflected in beautiful submissive conduct (in which his wife is seeking to demonstrate love to him), so he is urged to consider Jesus for himself. Perhaps, one day, as a result of her prayer and conduct, he too will come to Jesus.

For any who are struggling with the pain of an unbelieving spouse, may I urge you to remember the apostle, Paul. He was running against Jesus, persecuting the church, and approving of the death of Stephen. But then God intervened. God met Paul on the road to Damascus, turned his life around, and made him a foundational pillar of the New Testament church. God is able to do amazing things—immeasurably more than all we ask or imagine (Ephesians 3:20). As you pray for your unbelieving spouse, remember that God is able. Keep praying. Even if your spouse has left you and there is great pain, still God is able. Your role is to continue to trust in Jesus who loves you and holds you.

They say that once you have dug a hole for yourself, it is worth throwing away the spade. But if we think Peter has already dug a hole for himself, now we notice that he keeps digging. As if his words so far are not controversial enough, he provides even more. In our day and age, heads will turn and tongues will wag. There will be disapproving looks. Read what he writes next—imagine having this read at a wedding!

Peter moves onto extremely dangerous ground, we might think. 'Do not let your adorning be external—the braiding of hair and the putting on of gold jewellery, or the clothing you wear ...' (3:3). Peter is a man—what right does he have to talk to women about how they should dress? And as I write this now, as a man, perhaps I should gloss over this bit at least—that would be much safer. 'Women should not braid their hair or put on gold jewellery.' Really, Peter? Are you saying that women should not look nice?

However, if we stop here and draw this conclusion, then we have not read properly. Indeed, we have not read to the end of his argument.

Firstly, Peter includes 'the clothing you wear'. Notice he does not say, 'wearing nice clothes'. He writes of wearing clothes *at all*. In other words, if we think Peter is saying that women should not braid their hair and that women should not wear gold jewellery, then logically he is also saying that women should not wear clothes! Each idea sits in the same category. So, since we can assume that Peter is not telling women to take their clothes off (!), then he is not telling them to take their jewellery off or to stop braiding their hair. He cannot be saying one and not the other.

More obviously, Peter is making a contrast. The point is not that braided hair, gold jewellery and clothing are a bad thing. The point is that the internal beauty of a gentle and quiet spirit is a better thing. Not only is it better, but it is also very precious in the sight of God.

In verse 5, Peter gets a little nostalgic. His train of thought appears to be a bit like this. 'In the 1st century, people think they know better don't they. Women have more freedom—freedom to stand up to, stand against, and even defy their husbands.' But, Peter argues, this is upside down thinking. Instead, it is because we are free that we can submit. Peter's thought continues, 'It is because Christian women are free—freed by the sacrificial blood of Jesus— that they are free to submit to their husbands. Modern women struggle to see the truth of this. But back then, back in the good old days, people understood. The holy women who hoped in God adorned themselves in this way: they submitted to their own husbands.' Peter could be one of our contemporaries, could he not?!

Notice that Peter takes his readers right back to Genesis. 'Sarah obeyed Abraham, calling him lord' (3:6; referencing Genesis 18:12–13). Now the feminists are slapping Peter in the face or sitting in an armchair wanting to slap me for being willing to write on such a text in the 21st Century. Peter uses that word, 'obey', a word which means to 'hyper-listen'. It means, 'to do as one is told'. Peter holds Sarah up as a model woman because she did as Abraham told her and she called him 'lord'.

In C.S. Lewis' *The Magician's Nephew*, when Queen Jadis tells Digory that his uncle must be a very great magician, Digory replies, 'Well...not exactly!' Polly responds, 'Not exactly? Why, it's absolute bosh from beginning to end!'[2] Likewise, here, Peter is saying that the best women bow and scrape to their husbands and do exactly as they are told, right? 'Well ... not exactly,' says Digory. 'Not exactly? Why, it's absolute bosh from beginning to end!' says Polly. And she would be right.

First of all, Abraham was about as far from an unbelieving husband as you can get. Abraham is not an example of someone who should be obeyed even though he did not obey God's word, rejected God, and was living against God. Quite the opposite. Abraham was someone who 'believed God and it was counted to him as righteousness' (Romans 4:3). He was someone with faith—someone with a more genuine faith than most others at the time (excepting Job, perhaps). If any man is worthy of respect, it is Abraham. Further, Peter is writing as a Jew whose history is traced back to this man—Abraham.

Notice, too, that Abraham's authority over Sarah did not mean that he always commanded her and she always obeyed. Yes,

Abraham led his family and retinue out of Haran and down to the Promised Land, and Sarah came along willingly. Yes, on Abraham's bad instruction, Sarah even agreed to pretend she was not married to him, so that Abraham would be safe. But, in Genesis 16, Sarah decided that Abraham should have a child through her servant Hagar, and she talked to Abraham about it. Abraham, rather than living in faith at the command of God, listened to the voice of Sarah (Genesis 16:2). Only after the event did Sarah realize that she had made a major mistake, and then she blamed Abraham for it. Partly, of course, she blamed him because she did not want to take responsibility for her lack of faith. But she also blamed him because he was the one in authority. It was because Abraham stood in authority over Sarah that their mutual sin was, at the end of the day, his fault! Authority is a two-edged sword.

When Sarah obeyed Abraham and called him, 'lord', this is not a blasphemous title. It is, rather, a word which translates the Hebrew for 'master'. In other words, she is asserting that Abraham is the one in charge—he is the one with overall authority. Sarah is commended not because she is bowing and scraping, but because she recognized the authority of her husband and happily lived under it (most of the time!). She did not always get it right, as we have seen. Indeed, she laughed in derision when told she would give birth to a son. Then she decided to try and make God's words come true by getting Abraham to have a child with her slave-girl. Sarah was not always right. But she is commended by Peter here as one who, in the main, submitted to her husband and lived under his authority. As we have noted, Abraham was a man under whose authority she should have been happy to live, because he lived under the authority of God himself.

Peter writes that all women are Sarah's children if they do likewise, living under the authority of a godly husband. In the good old days, this is how it was, Peter says. But now, women have moved away from this God-given design. Now their temptation is to do something different—to live differently.

I might add that husbands also have moved away from a fundamental desire to live as servants of Jesus. They have moved from being committed to their wives even to the point of death. Now, husbands seem more concerned about themselves and their own aggrandizement. A woman is not willing to submit herself to a husband and a husband is not submitting himself to God. The husband is not worthy of being submitted to, his wife does not submit, and there you have the seeds of marital disaster.

Peter finishes his survey of godly wives with two ways in which women can be like Sarah. Firstly, they can 'do good' (v. 6). That seems relatively self-explanatory—they are to live God's way in God's world. Secondly, they are instructed: 'Do not fear anything that is frightening.' This latter command seems to make little sense, and also seems a strange way to end the paragraph.

'Do not fear anything that is terrifying.' If it is terrifying, then I will fear it—is that not what *terrifying* means? And why does Peter put together in this way 'doing good' and 'not fearing scary things?' Perhaps Peter is thinking of the suffering endured due to an unjust master, discussed back in chapter 2. Such suffering may be a terrifying prospect. What if I seek to be subject to my husband and he lords it over me? The prospect of being taken for granted, put upon, bossed around, controlled ... these are frightening possibilities.

Nevertheless, Peter says simply to do good and not be frightened of anything in this world. God is sovereign over all things. Over everything else, the one we are to fear is *God*. Peter has already made this vital point (1 Peter 2:17), and now he reiterates it here. Do good, that is—fear God. Do not worry about things in this world—things that do not last—things that can only harm the body. Instead, fear God—the one who can throw both body and soul into hell, as Jesus puts it (Matthew 10:28). If we live in submission to God, then 'doing good' is what we will be about. Our life will involve bringing God's good Word and God's good work to a lost and dying world.

Instructions to husbands

Peter has spent six verses explaining how wives are to live. Now, he gives only one verse to speak to the husbands. This little fact might, in itself, hammer home our view that Peter is a misogynist. And when we actually read those verses, it gets even worse. 'Live with your wives in an understanding way, showing honour to the woman as the weaker vessel, since they are heirs with you of the grace of life, so that your prayers may not be hindered' (3:7).

This sounds very patronizing to women. Peter writes that women are weaker, so men should be understanding of their weakness. It is a small step to believing that men are better, but they should show understanding to the poor women. Now, if this is what Peter is saying, then I could understand why women might be getting a bit hot under the collar again. But this is a misunderstanding.

Peter follows his statement about women as the 'weaker vessel', with a note about an equality enjoyed by both men and women. Peter explains to the men that women are heirs '*with you of the grace of life*'. Men and women alike, if they are believers, are heirs of the grace of life. There is no hierarchy of current value or eternal outcome. Men and women equally are heirs of grace, made right in the sight of God by the death and resurrection of Jesus.

The inequality comes in the far less important physical realm. We live in a world where the physical is heralded as above everything. How you look, what you wear, what money you have, how many weights you pull, and so on—all these things reflect ways in which we are all different. Broadly speaking, too, men are taller and stronger than women. Not all men are taller than all women, of course, and not all men are stronger than all women, either. But, in the grand scheme of things, as a general rule, women are not as strong physically as men. This is why God has given men the role of protecting women and children. They are the stronger partner and so better able to defend and protect. We find this back in Ephesians 5, too. The wife should submit to the husband—that is her role. The husband is to love his wife even if it means dying for her—that is his role. Wives submit; husbands die.

As an aside, women may be the weaker vessel in terms of their physical capabilities, but you have only got to see a woman giving birth to know that their mental capacity for pain is mostly considerably stronger than that of men!

However, Peter's point here is that the husband is meant to protect his wife. He should stand in the gap and die, if needs be, to protect her. Wife—submit; husband—die; that is the deal. Live that way, and your relationship with God will be strong and your prayers will not be hindered.

Pointing to Jesus

If there is an equality in status, then, we return to the question posed earlier. We would be in good company if we were finding all these instructions about wives followed by a single verse about husbands a bit imbalanced, somewhat prejudiced—backward, even. Why does Peter write six verses for the wives and only one verse for the husbands? Even though we have worked through the text and tried to get to grips with it for wives and for husbands, it still seems a bit chauvinistic, does it not?

Going even further back, in what way is any of this stuff relevant to the many who are not married? Like the climbers in the alps, surely none of this applies to single people? As we noted at the beginning, though, such an attitude is not right. In fact, it is dangerous. This applies to us of all.

So why is this *not* chauvinistic, and why is this text for all Christians, male and female? It is for one very simple and wonderful reason. As we read through the New Testament, we discover that Jesus is the bridegroom and his church is the bride. All of us, if we are Christians, are the bride of Christ. This little fact makes sense of the whole text in a broader and deeper and more profound way.

Whether we are married or single, male or female, our role as the bride of Christ is simple. We are to submit to Jesus with a gentle and quiet spirit. We are not to push back or argue with what he calls us to do. We are not to be disobedient, but rather should subject ourselves to him. Because we are free, we can live under his authority. This is a very precious thing in the sight of God.

In the previous chapter we saw that submitting to one in authority, even if suffering results, is a gracious thing in the sight of God (2:20). It brings him joy to see his children remaining faithful whatever happens. Here in chapter 3, living under God's authority with a gentle and quiet spirit, is not only a gracious thing—it is also a very precious thing in the sight of God (3:4). God treasures that submissive attitude.

The role of the wife in these verses is the role of every Christian in their relationship with Jesus. An approach like this—gentle and quiet submission—is very precious in the sight of God. Why? Because God treasures it. To submit is a gracious thing in the sight of God—it brings him joy. To submit with a gentle and quiet spirit— this is a precious thing in the sight of God—he treasures it.

As Sarah obeyed Abraham, so we are to obey Jesus. What he says, we do. We call *him* Lord. We fear nothing else but God alone. In the light of this, we should have expected the majority of verses to be about the wives—instructions given for the bride of Christ. Instructions we need to follow.

The husband's instruction, though, is for Jesus himself. Now as we read verse 7 again, we discover that Jesus does not actually need the instruction because he has already done it all! He lives with us in an understanding way towards us. He understands our weakness and our failure to live his way. He recognizes we are weaker and need more help. As the bridegroom, he is even willing to have us as co-heirs. Paul writes this very thing, too: 'The Spirit himself bears witness with our spirit that we are children of God, and if children, then heirs—heirs of God and fellow heirs with Christ ...' (Romans 8:16–17).

The grace of life is ours because the bridegroom has already died on our behalf. He has died instead of us, protected us from the wrath of God against all our fallenness and brokenness and sin and rebellion. Now Jesus lives and reigns and we are called to submit to him, whether for the first time or for the thousandth time. He is our bridegroom and we are the bride.

Notes

1 I have used pseudonyms in relating this story.

2 Lewis, C.S., *The Magician's Nephew,* (Glasgow: Collins, 2001), p.82

8 Suffering and love

1 Peter 3:8–17

On Palm Sunday, 2017, two bombings and an ambush of a 'church bus full of men, women and children, [represented] an unspeakable evil towards [Christians] in Egypt ...' In the week following the attacks, 'Churches were filled with praying Christians ... Pain and agony are like seeds—growing up through the soil of our country to produce the fruit of the gospel. God is using these events—that Satan meant for destruction—as the greatest gospel platform in Egypt's history.'[1] So writes one of the contributors to Open Doors USA, a non-profit organization seeking to support persecuted Christians in over sixty countries.

Peter's original audience were no strangers to suffering either. In chapter 3, Peter continues with the suffering theme, and he focuses on three key motives which ought to underpin Christian behaviour. Before he gets there, though, he begins this next section by reminding his readers of something even more crucial—the need for them to love one another.

Verse 8 is the title, the headline, and the crux of all that follows. Peter begins the verse with the word, 'Finally ...', meaning perhaps, 'Above all else ...'. Then he structures the verse with a classic chiasm, to drive his point home. As God's people face persecution and pain, their need to love and support one another could never be greater. He arranges the chiasm roughly as follows:

A. Unity of mind.

  B. Sympathy

C. Brotherly love

B. A tender heart

A. Humility of mind

On the outside of this pattern, we find both unity of mind and humility of mind. In Philippians 2:2, Paul exhorts people to 'complete [his] joy by being of the same mind'. Peter's thoughts here in 1 Peter 3 are similar. Literally, he uses the more emphatic phrase, 'unity of mind'. If they are believers in Christ, then they should think the same way.

However, single-mindedness can easily morph into arrogance, so Peter uses the opposite side of the structure to highlight the importance of humility. In the opposite direction, humble-mindedness can easily mask a lack of conviction, so Peter begins the pattern by urging a collective single-mindedness. In a Christian community, Peter is explaining that a single-minded commitment to the truth must be coupled with a deep humility.

In the next section of the chiasm, Peter urges them to suffer alongside one another (this is what sympathy is truly about). Then he reiterates this need by using a deep, guttural Greek word meaning 'with strong bowels', which the ESV has translated, 'a tender heart'. In the West, we think of our deepest emotions as emanating from the heart, but in the ancient Near East, the deepest emotions were thought to come from somewhere rather lower down—the bowels. We would be 'sick to the heart', but they would be, 'sick to the bowels'; somewhat closer to the physical nausea that can accompany deep pain. Peter's point here is that alongside single-mindedness and humility should come a deep aching on behalf of one another.

Peter, thus, leads us through these ideas to the heart of community behaviour—placed in the centre of this chiasm—love. He uses a Greek word that describes a deep, filial, blood connection that goes beyond friendship and stays the course, even when people do not naturally get along. The central facet of Peter's exhortation to Christians is that we are to love one another. He is in total agreement with Paul's statement: 'Above all these, put on love' (Colossians 3:14). His key message of verse 8, then, is that, in the midst of suffering, it is vital for Christians to stand together in love.

Having made this point about the centrality of communal, filial love, Peter then explores three key motives in suffering. He begins with the right response to suffering, moves next to right reverence amid suffering, and then concludes with the readiness to reach out in suffering. All three aspects are underpinned by the love God's people are to display one to another. We will follow Peter's words as he works through each of these three motives.

The right response to suffering

It is almost natural for us to try to repay evil for evil. However, like Jesus' instruction to 'turn the other cheek' (Matthew 5:39), Peter implores his readers to respond to evil with blessing. In 2017, when those Egyptian Christians faced great pain, bereavement and injustice, the desire to seek vengeance could have been strong. Instead, though, they chose to love. In a similar manner, Peter argues that Christians should repay evil with blessing.

More than that, he writes that responding to evil with blessing is something to which Christians are 'called'. When Peter last explained about suffering injustice, he wrote: 'To this you have been *called* because Christ also suffered for you, leaving you an example, so that you might follow in his steps' (1 Peter 2:21). So here, the right response to evil and reviling is to bring blessing— something Christians are called to do, and for which there is great reward. We are called to follow Jesus in obedience, regardless of the suffering that such commitment might bring, and to bring blessing to any who persecute us. When we are treated badly, we should bless. It is utterly counterintuitive!

What does Peter mean by 'bless' (v. 9)? What is this 'blessing' we are to give? Peter does not use the more common word for blessing, but rather uses a word which means literally a 'good word'. This fits well with the context here. When we are reviled—when people speak ill of us—then we are to respond with good words. When people come against you with their words, Peter writes, respond with good words, uplifting words and positive words.

Most obviously, Peter is saying that our response to reviling is to give good words *to* the one reviling us. But perhaps also, Peter is urging us to give good words *about* the one reviling us. If so, this is even more challenging than the former—we are urged not only to speak well *to* the ones who come against us, but also to speak well *about* them.

This is the antithesis of gossip. Instead of speaking badly about our persecutors, we are to speak well about them. Why in the world would we do that? One reason we should respond to evil words with good words is because Peter writes it and therefore God commands it. It is, after all, exactly how Jesus responded to those who came against him. But Peter provides an even deeper reason. He writes, 'Do not repay evil for evil or reviling for reviling, but on the contrary, bless, *for* to this you were called!' Responding to words that push you down with words which lift them up is part of our Christian *calling.* Christians will be reviled—it is inevitable. Their response should be one of blessing.

But why are we called to answer evil words with good words? Peter answers this question in the same sentence: 'To this you were called, *that* you may obtain a blessing.' In other words, if people revile us, as they are bound to do, and we respond with good words, then the result will be blessing for us.

That is the economy of God. The result of responding to the world's rejection with blessing is that we obtain a blessing from God. And again, this 'blessing' we obtain from God is a blessing rooted in the idea of 'good words'.

It is fascinating that at this point in his discussion, Peter quotes from Psalm 34. David wrote this psalm as he reflected upon his experiences in Gath. He had been brought before the king of Gath (Abimelech) and, because formerly David had been an enemy of Gath, now his life was in danger. Thus, he resorted to feigning insanity, as a result of which King Abimelech released him and sent him away. In reflecting on this series of events, though, David writes that it was God who had rescued him. Thus, he praises God as the One who rescues. For David at least, God is the one who saves people from certain death. If our hearts cry to the Lord for salvation, then his face turns towards us and he rescues us. If, instead, we stop our ears to the Lord, then his face turns away from us and he condemns.

The 'good word' we receive from God, though, is not just a 'well done' sort of word. Rather, it is a salvific word—a word that says, 'You have sought rescue from me, so now I rescue you and adopt you and declare you to be righteous in my sight.' While it is true that no one who strives for what is good should be harmed, the reality in this broken world is quite different. Oftentimes people *do* suffer for righteousness' sake. When that happens, Peter declares that we 'will be blessed'.

Furthermore, the blessing to which David alludes in Psalm 34 is not limited to God's good word, 'well done,' nor even to God's salvific word, 'Welcome into my family.' Even more than this, David writes, 'The eyes of the Lord are on the righteous and his ears are open to their prayer' (v. 12). In other words, God sees us in our situation and listens to our prayers. Think of the wonder and glory of that for a moment. The Almighty God of heaven, the Creator and Sustainer of all things, the awesomely omniscient and the omnipotent God—*he* is attentive to our prayers. He listens and he acts.

Peter nails this point home by using the more usual word for *blessing*, when he writes, 'you will be blessed'(v. 14). If we bless those who revile us, then we receive a blessing. The blessing we receive is not only about God's 'good words' (which would be wonderful enough), but also concerns God's favour. He listens to us. James puts it this way: 'The prayer of a righteous person is powerful and effective' (James 5:16, NIV).

The right response to suffering is to repay evil for good. This means both that we respond to bad words with good words, and that we respond to bad behaviour with blessing. The result of living this way is to enjoy the blessing of God himself—his good words over us, and his attentiveness to our prayer.

The right reverence in suffering

Following the Palm Sunday bombings, those Christians could easily have responded with fear. But they did not fear the ones who place bombs or attack with guns and machetes. Instead, they feared the Lord who reigns. They revered God, not possible attackers.

As Peter approaches his next point, again he looks back to the Old Testament, this time to the prophet Isaiah: 'Do not fear what they fear, nor be in dread ...' (Isaiah 8:12). Isaiah's prophecy continues this thought with, 'But the LORD of hosts, him you shall honour as holy. Let him be your fear and let him be your dread' (v. 13). So, Isaiah argues that we should not fear those who can (and sometimes do) persecute us. Rather, we should fear God. Peter makes the same point: 'Honour Christ the Lord as holy' (1 Peter 3:15). Central to a right response to suffering is to have the right reverence in suffering. We are to live always in fear of the Lord.

Sadly, this doctrine is usually ignored by western Christianity, and sometimes it is even shunned. We have domesticated God and moved from thinking of Jesus as our Master to thinking of him as our mate. It is true that Jesus is the *friend of sinners*, but he is also the *fear of Israel*.

We might be tempted to think that the 'fear of the Lord' (Psalm 34:11), is intended as a motive for right living. We obey those we fear. If we fear our bosses, we obey them. If we fear our parents, we obey them. If we fear our government, we obey it. If we fear our leaders, we obey them. Thus, is it not true that if we fear God then we will obey God? We are to seek to live God's way in God's world, and if we truly fear God, then we will delve deeper into this obedience.

While there may be truth here, the Biblical idea is much deeper, and I am indebted to Bamberger for drawing it to my attention. In the Old Testament at least, the 'Fear and love of the Deity are not urged as motives for the good life, but are themselves the good life. They are means, not ends.'[2]

The essence of fear is not primarily 'terror at, or terror because'. It is not just that we fear God because he alone is able to throw body and soul into hell (although this is true). Neither is it that we fear God because we dread his displeasure at our sinfulness (although this, also, is true). Rather, *to fear God* is usually associated with worship. Nehemiah asserts that God's servants, 'delight to fear [his] name' (Nehemiah 1:11). Notice the word 'delight'!

The heart of 'fearing God' is not a terror or dread of some forthcoming divine thunderbolt that will hit us if we sin anymore. Rather, the 'fear of the Lord'—*reverence* for Him—concerns worship. The clearest example of this, perhaps, is when David writes, 'I will bow down toward your holy temple in the fear of you' (Psalm 5:7). Fear, reverence, and worship are three words which, biblically at least, can be nearly synonymous.

Isaiah's point was that God's people are to avoid the idolatry of those around them and to worship God only—they should fear God rather than idols. The same is true for us. In recent days, my wife and I have been noticing more and more the idol of self-determination in today's western world. We find it not only in the world at large, but also in the church. It creeps into the church's preached theology, too. 'We have free will!' is cried as a supposed refutation of God's divine election. But our freedom is limited and it is secondary. God is primary, and our idol of the self denies the sovereignty of God.

Peter is clear: we are to fear God and serve him only, because our Christian lives are not about us—they are about him. It is not about what I can do, or how I can be more holy, or how I can do amazing things for God. Rather, it is about God; what he has done for me; what he is doing in me; and where he leads me to go. It is about surrender to the God who is utterly sovereign. The God who should be our true 'fear'—the One alone whom we should worship. 'Self on the cross and Christ upon the throne,' as Timothy Dudley-Smith put it in his now famous hymn, 'Lord for the Years'.[3]

So, Peter writes, have no fear of the ones who cause you to suffer in this life. Rather, honour Christ the Lord as holy. Fear him. Worship him. Right reverence in suffering is the fear of the Lord.

The readiness to reach out

As mentioned in the introduction, our Christian Egyptian friends provide a challenging reminder that suffering can spread the gospel. Sometimes, suffering can destroy God's church. But at other times, Tertullian's words hold true—'The blood of martyrs is the seed of the church.'[4] The latter is certainly proving true in Egypt and the wider Middle East in our day.

Here in 1 Peter 3, Peter turns lastly to the way in which we express our worship of Jesus. He writes those famous words, loved by all apologists and evangelists: 'Always being prepared to make a defense to anyone who asks you for a reason for the hope that is in you' (v. 15).

In fact, as we shall see, from this verse right through to the end of 4:9, Peter is concerned about the way in which we make this defense to those who ask us for a reason for the hope that we have. How do we reach out in evangelism? How do we tell people the good news about Jesus? It is striking that Peter's encouragement to do so arises in the context of suffering.

Peter has just discussed the need for persecuted believers to live in fear of the Lord and not to fear people. From an outreach perspective, this is a great encouragement as we seek to speak out gospel truth to unbelievers around us. God remains sovereign and he is the one who takes his word to the nations. As we speak, we need not fear men—rather, we are to fear God and leave the outcome of our conversations in his all-powerful hands.

In these verses, Peter highlights the two primary aspects of evangelism: verbal and behavioural. He begins with the verbal in verse 15.

Peter writes that Christians should be 'prepared to make a defense to anyone who asks'. If you are a newer Christian or a Christian who has not spent time thinking about the reasons for your faith, Peter urges that you get prepared. This involves finding answers to common objections to our faith, such as the historicity of Jesus, the origins of humankind, the reliability of the Biblical documents and the issue of human suffering. If we do not yet have at least a rudimentary Biblical understanding, then we are not prepared in the way Peter urges us to be.

It should go without saying that our grasp of the Biblical perspective on those basic questions arises primarily from our ongoing growth in Biblical literacy—the extent to which we have indulged our craving for pure spiritual milk. We are not seeking to advance *clever theories* but rather to gain a hold of God's view of the world. More and more, we want to see things God's way and to be prepared to explain those things to the questioner. In short, we should all be able to answer the simple question, 'Why do you believe what you do?'

Peter is at pains to point out that it is not just about what we say, but also about how we say it. Whatever we say, we are to do so with gentleness and respect. We are not in an argument which we have to win. Rather, we are in a discussion and explanation of how we think God sees it—we are defending the Christian faith. It is a conversation in which we are at liberty to say what we know and admit what we do not yet know. It is a chance to display humility and empathy and love in the midst of those vitally important eternal questions.

Notice how he begins verse 16: 'having a good conscience ...'. I know that for me, when I am in the middle of these important discussions, my temptation is to assert a statistic as truth when, in fact, I cannot quite remember the details. When I do this, it means that my conscience is not clear anymore. But, since the central reason for these discussions (as for anything else) is to worship and bring glory to Jesus who is the truth (John 14:6), I fail at the first hurdle if I attempt to do so without honesty, openness and integrity.

On the other hand, if we do speak with integrity, then, when people revile us, they find themselves unable to revile our behaviour. Furthermore, if an argument begins to feel heated, over and above winning some theoretical point, we must love well. Then, when opponents attack us instead of attacking the argument (a common ruse when someone is unsure of their footing), we do not respond to reviling with reviling, but rather we bless. In turn, this puts their behaviour to shame and, more importantly, it means that God's words, our 'reasons' or 'arguments' for hoping in Christ, are left to stand for themselves without us getting in the way.

When we read verse 17, we might be tempted to think that Peter is simply repeating what he stated earlier in the letter—namely, that it is better to suffer for doing good than for doing evil (1 Peter 2:20). However, in fact Peter is writing specifically about the way in which we reach out to those around us. He is emphasizing the fundamental importance of the *way* in which we reach out, namely with gentleness, respect, and keeping a good conscience. As a result, when we are slandered, those who do the reviling find themselves put to shame. A godly perspective stands and the glory goes to God.

Notice Peter's dependence and convictions regarding the sovereignty of God. He writes, 'It is better to suffer for doing good, *if that should be God's will*, than for doing evil.' In other words, sometimes God's will is that we would suffer for doing good. Peter is not talking here about suffering from an illness, or because of a death in the family, or because of financial troubles. This is not a point about suffering in general. Rather, he is highlighting specific suffering—suffering because we are doing good and seeking to live God's way in a world hurtling in the opposite direction. We do not always suffer for doing good (and in this country at least, often we do not), but sometimes we do. And, even in the West, Christians may suffer through missing out on promotions or through ridicule from those around us because we love the name of Jesus.

Peter brings comfort because he writes that if we suffer because of our faith, then it is because God wills it. We do not suffer by accident, but because God wills that we suffer. Peter next provides the prime example of such God-willed suffering by pointing us to the suffering of Jesus.

Judas' betrayal of Jesus was a sinful act, and yet God willed it. The

Jewish authorities gave him an unjust trial, and yet God willed it. The Jews outrageously shouted, 'Crucify, crucify,' and yet God willed it. Pilate declared him innocent, but handed him over to be crucified anyway, and God willed it. The soldiers drove the nails through his wrists and ankles as they stabbed their Creator to the cross, and yet God willed it. When we suffer because of the will of God, we are in the very best company.

Furthermore, Peter wants to remind us that God always has excellent reasons for willing this suffering upon us, too. Without Jesus' betrayal, false trials, flogging and crucifixion—without his sacrificial death—salvation would be impossible for anyone. God's sovereign, omnipotent will was that Jesus should suffer, fulfilling all the Old Testament prophecies and thereby bringing salvation to all who are his. Jesus' suffering was hideous and horrific, but it resulted in his resurrection, ascension and crowning as King, forever over all, and was for the benefit of many.

Likewise, Peter is saying, when God wills that we suffer, sometimes that is for our own benefit, preparing us for heaven and making us more as we were designed to be—more like Jesus. Sometimes, too, our suffering is for the benefit of others. As we respond to suffering, so others are directed to see Jesus. Just as Jesus' suffering was to 'bring us to God' (verse 18), so our suffering can bring others to Jesus. Peter focuses once again upon the cross of Jesus because this is the heart of any discussion about the reasons for evangelism.

Conclusion

Peter has urged Christians to be united in love for one another as a key means for standing together under suffering, especially persecution. In the West at the moment, Christians have a duty to stand alongside our suffering brothers and sisters around the world—at least in prayer if not in other ways as well. Our love for one another should extend to all believers and is a real encouragement amid suffering.

However we suffer though, we should be prepared to give an answer and to suffer the consequences of those answers for two reasons. Firstly, Jesus was always prepared to give an answer, and our goal is to grow to be increasingly like him. Secondly, Jesus endured suffering—indeed went through death itself—to bring us salvation, so we should be prepared to do likewise for the sake of those who do not yet know him.

Somehow in the economy of God, suffering leads to joy. We are dead in the flesh, but alive in the spirit—eternally alive. Suffering should direct us and others to offer blessing to our persecutors, to live in reverence before God, and to reach out with the grace of the gospel of Jesus. After all, he is the only one who suffered, bled and died to bring life to many. We love him, we love one another, and so suffering should drive us onwards as we seek to love the world.

Notes

1 https://www.opendoorsusa.org/christian-persecution/stories/isis-attacks-egypt-spur-country-wide-evangelism/

2 Bamberger, Bernard J., 'Fear and Love of God in the Old Testament', in: *Hebrew Union College Annual, Vol. 6,* (Hebrew Union College Press, 1929), pp. 39–53

3 Dudley-Smith, Timothy, 'Lord for the Years', (Hope Publishing Company, 1969)

4 Tertullian, 2nd Century Church Father, https://www.quotestogether.com/quote/tertullian-11

9 Deep waters

1 Peter 3:18–4:11

Introduction

Following localized storms and persistent rain, the UK experienced unprecedented flooding on more than one occasion through 2019–2020. One evening, I was driving my family to visit our relatives—a drive which should have taken around 40 minutes but which, eventually, took over two hours. At one point, we drove down a road, over a hump-back bridge, and then came to a place where water was coming over the road. A truck some distance ahead of us was driving slowly through the floodwaters. Two or three cars were following tentatively. Others were backing away, not willing to risk it. In my younger days, I was more reckless and I would have pressed ahead. Possibly it would have been ok. But as the road disappeared beneath the water, and as the water got deeper, I could see the current racing across in front of the car and so I chickened out. I reversed a considerable distance before finding somewhere to turn around, and then we returned the way we had come. I was not prepared to venture into what looked like increasingly deeper and dangerous water.

I am aware, as we come to this next section in Peter's first letter, that we are approaching deep water. At the very least, the first few verses have generated countless discussions and questions, as theologians of all stripes have grappled to explain what is going on. Suffice to say, this is deep water indeed.

But as I study, I find myself refusing to chicken out. The water is deepening. The road is disappearing. The cross-current looks strong. But, somehow, I pray that all will be ok, and venturing forward will do more good than harm, and provide more help than hindrance. I hope I am not being reckless. Tentatively, then, I release the brakes and move us forward carefully through these deep waters. It could be a rocky ride.

Flood waters

To begin, I want to review a few ideas about verses 19 and 20. The questions tumble about us as we read. Did Jesus preach to spirits in the spirit-world? If so, does this give people who have died some kind of second chance to obey God? This does not seem to fit with the Bible's portrayal of salvation, but if Peter is referring to people who are alive, why does he use the word 'spirits'? Why does he describe them as 'in prison'? What does he mean when he refers to God's patience 'in the days of Noah'? Why does he bring Noah into the discussion at all? How does baptism (being immersed in water) correspond to Noah and his family who did not get wet at all? Over and above all that, how does baptism save people—surely salvation is by faith, not by baptism? There are so many questions here, and we will need to tread very carefully if we are to navigate this text successfully.

Some of these muddy waters can be cleared by recognizing that the context is one of evangelism. We have already discussed this in the previous chapter. Always be prepared to give an answer to the hope that you have, even if suffering results.

Since evangelism is the context, perhaps Peter is using Noah as an example of good evangelistic endeavour. Let me explain. In

Genesis 5, Noah was 500 years old when he had his three sons (Genesis 5:32). Following this, he was instructed to build the ark, and then we read that Noah was 600 years old when he entered the ark (Genesis 7:6). In other words, between God's instructions to Noah to build and the time he entered the ark, there could have been a period of nearly 100 years. In his second letter, Peter tells us that Noah was a herald [preacher] of righteousness (2 Peter 2:5). Thus, Noah preached to the peoples around him for many decades as he was building the ark. He did the two-fold job which God called him to do. Firstly, he built the ark, despite how crazy such an endeavour seemed to the world. Secondly, he preached the truth to those around him of their need to submit to God for salvation from the coming judgement.

God was very patient—Noah preached and built perhaps for nearly 100 years, warning the people of their need to repent and believe, or they would face coming judgement. In the end, though, Noah and his family followed the animals into the ark and God shut the door. Then the rain began to fall—God's judgement had come, and the results were devastating.

As we try to understand Peter's train of thought here, then, perhaps he is arguing that through the Holy Spirit (verse 18), Noah preached to the people of his day ('the spirits in prison'). They were not just spirits when Noah preached to them, of course—they were physical people with physical bodies. In the flood, however, their physical bodies died and, due to their unbelief, their spirits are now imprisoned as they await final judgement when Jesus returns to judge the living and the dead. In other words, they are spirits *now* (not physical anymore), and they are in prison *now* as they wait until the return of Jesus when final judgement occurs.[1]

Those people who heard the truth from God through Noah week by week, month by month, and year by year are utterly without excuse. They refused to respond to God, to turn from their self-determination and submit to God as sovereign, and the result was that the threatened judgement came upon them physically at the flood. In all of Scripture, the story of Noah is the greatest and broadest picture of the universal nature of the final judgement of God that we have. It is historical prophecy at its finest—real events, now in the past, foretelling even greater real events still in our future.

Noah and his family depended on God and were saved from those waters of judgement. They did not *bring themselves* safely through water, notice. Of course, they had to build the ark and do as they had been commanded. But Peter uses the passive voice to say that they 'were brought safely through' the flood (v. 20). They did not bring themselves through. Ultimately, their salvation was God's work and not their own.

I hope this has helped to navigate some of those 'deep waters'. Now Peter turns to more deep waters—this time, it is the waters of baptism.

Baptismal waters

First of all, notice in verse 21 that Peter *assumes* his Christian readers have been baptized. 'Baptism … now saves you …', he writes. No exceptions—all who are Christians have been baptized. This reflects what we see throughout the book of Acts, namely that repentance from sin, and trust in Jesus—becoming a Christian—is always intimately connected with baptism. At Pentecost, Peter himself (who wrote this letter) cried out, 'Repent and be baptized every one of you in the name of Jesus Christ for the forgiveness of your sins ...' (Acts 2:38). In other words, if you have repented (and thus received forgiveness), then baptism will automatically follow, proclaiming your forgiveness.

In fact, baptism is a *command* which all Christians are to obey. We are commanded to repent and we are commanded to be baptized, as a public sign of that repentance. If you are a Christian, the Bible says, then you will be baptized.

Secondly, also in v. 21, notice that Peter writes that baptism 'corresponds' to Noah and his family being brought safely through the flood. He explains that baptism is, 'not as a removal of dirt from the body ...'. It is not that the removal of dirt from your body in baptism removes the dirt from your soul. To put it another way, it is not an outward ritual which makes you right before God. If you are not already a Christian—if your life is not now submitted to Jesus—then getting baptized is not going to help you.

But, for the Christian, baptism signifies a spiritual washing that has already occurred. Baptism symbolizes dying to the old life, the washing away of sin, and then rising to new life, in which we are cleansed and renewed. To be clear, in baptism we are not dying to sin and rising to life or washing away the dirt of sin—those things have already occurred. Rather, baptism is the symbol of those things that have already happened. It indicates that a person has turned away from their sin, and trusted in Jesus for their salvation, living with Jesus as King from now onwards. To use another Biblical metaphor, baptism indicates that a person has been born again. They have moved from their old life to a new life, a life given by God.

When Peter writes, 'Baptism ... now saves you ...', he is not saying that the physical rite of baptism is what moves you out from under the wrath of God. He is not supporting any idea of 'baptismal regeneration', to use a theological term. Rather, because baptism follows justification so closely (in the New Testament at least!), he uses the word 'baptism' as shorthand for the whole process. When I am involved in a project and say, 'I need a hand with this,' I am really asking for a whole person to come and help, not just one of their hands.[2] Since baptism is a signifier of a person's justification—the loudhailer that makes a person's salvation known—Peter uses the word to describe the whole process of justification. Baptism appeals to God—'my conscience is clear' because it signifies repentance and faith.

So, baptism is an appeal to God through a good conscience, founded upon the saving work of Jesus Christ. Peter explains that baptism does not remove dirt from the spiritual person. Noah and his family did not get wet in the flood, and yet Peter uses the flood as a symbol of baptism. In a similar way, the people of Israel did not get wet as they passed through the Red Sea, and yet Paul used that event as a symbol of baptism in 1 Corinthians 10:1–2. So the heart of the baptism imagery is not water-washing—a ritual cleansing, as John's disciples may have thought (John 3:25). Instead, it signals an escape from God's judgement.

Noah and his family escaped from God's judgement in the waters of the flood. Moses and the people of Israel escaped from God's judgement in the waters of the Red Sea. Baptism signals an escape from God's judgement, an escape wrought not by any merit in the one baptized, but rather by the sovereign work of God in salvation.

Noah had a two-fold task. He had to preach and he had to build the ark—both were divine imperatives he was called to follow. But his salvation from the inevitable judgement of God came about only by God's divine intervention in rescuing him and his family. The people of Israel had to walk through the Red Sea—a divine imperative given through Moses which they were to follow. But their salvation from the judgement of God in the Red Sea, a judgement which befell the Egyptian army, came about only through a divine act of rescue, in which God held back the waters.

As evangelical believers, we are right to think of baptism as a symbol of dying to our old way of life and rising to a new life. We are right, too, to think of baptism as a symbol of being cleansed of our sin on the inside just as the water cleanses us on the outside. But baptism also is a symbol of being rescued from God's judgement—judgement which we deserve—a rescue brought about by the saving work of Jesus through his death, resurrection and ascension into glory.

As Peter puts it here, in our baptism lies an appeal to God—'My conscience is clear!' (1 Peter 3:21). Such an appeal is legitimate not because we have done nothing wrong—we are 'sinful from birth'(Psalm 51:5)—but because Jesus has done nothing wrong and his righteousness stands in place of our own. We know that this is Peter's line of thought, because the appeal to which he refers comes about, verse 21, 'through the resurrection of Jesus Christ', and his subsequent ascension to the place where he reigns as King over all.

My baptism says to God, 'I stand clean and cleared of all

wrongdoing. I stand free from the wrath of God which I deserve, because of the substitutionary death of Jesus—his death-defeating resurrection—and his power as the ascended and glorified King over all.' My baptism is a sign to my friends and family of my life, changed from rebellion against God to submission to God. It is, perhaps, the most powerful symbol of that *death-to-life* event, and it is a great witness to those who do not know Jesus. Underneath all of that, my baptism is an appeal to God the Father: 'My sin is paid for. I am free indeed. Because of Jesus, judgement can come upon me no longer.'

Worship

Having followed Peter's argument, we have examined the flood waters and the waters of baptism. Now, we reach chapter 4 where Peter explains that the result of the flood waters and waters of baptism should be one thing only: worship.

In verse 1, Peter writes, 'Since, therefore, Christ suffered in the flesh, arm yourselves with the same way of thinking …'. What was Jesus' thinking? He knew that suffering was part of his calling (remember 1 Peter 2v21). In fact, for Jesus, suffering was *the central part* of his calling. This is what God the Father wanted from him. And Jesus embraced it, knowing it was for the blessing of the nations, in dealing with the problem of sin. Thus, we arm ourselves with the same way of thinking, namely that suffering is part of our calling.

Jesus' suffering means that sin no longer has a hold over those who trust in him. Its debt is paid. Its power is broken. If we are

Christians, then while we *do* sin, we do not *have* to sin. Jesus is in control now, not our sinful natures. Sin is our master no longer.

Next, Peter argues that, while we suffer in the flesh (according to God's perfect sovereign will), we have 'ceased from sin' or we have 'finished with sin' (v. 1). Peter is not saying that we are already humanly perfect and sinless. After all, our sanctification is a lifelong process rather than a completed event now. His point, rather, is that we have ceased from sin's mastery. Sin is not our lord any longer— Jesus is our Lord. We have finished with the sin way-of-life and begun the Jesus way-of-life. We are heading to a better country where sin will be no more.

The result of this new life, this life in the Spirit, is that we no longer live for our human passions, but for the will of God. Sometimes God's will is that we suffer in the flesh (1 Peter 3:17). Christ suffered in the flesh according to the will of God, and we also live in the flesh for the will of God, even if the result is suffering.

Note Peter's approach to worldly living here. 'The time that is past suffices for doing what the Gentiles want to do, living in sensuality, passions, drunkenness, orgies, drinking parties, and lawless idolatry' (v. 3). I love that phrase, 'the time that is past suffices'! There is no place for someone to say, 'I just want to live life a bit more before I become a Christian and have to keep God's law. I just want one final fling before I get married and settle down. I'd love to just experience something of the world so I know what it's like.' Peter's response is an emphatic: 'No!' If he were Paul, this is where he would write, 'May it never be!' There has been enough sin already. In fact, any sin is too much sin. You gain nothing by indulging in the sin and mess of those who do not trust in Jesus.

There is plenty of immorality around, but for you—the time for that is past. Now you are finished with the sinful way of life. Now you live for the will of God.

When you do live God's way in this fallen world, people will malign you because you do not join in. Your view of the world is from a much higher plane and increasingly you see as God sees. But the world stops up its ears to avoid hearing the words of Almighty God, because for them, they want more time to do what God forbids.

Peter writes: 'the time that is past suffices' for all that. Everyone must give an account to God. God *is ready* to judge the living and the dead. Perhaps there is a hint in here not only that God will judge those who are currently alive and those who have died, but also that God will judge those who are spiritually alive (Christians) and those who are spiritually dead (those who are dead in their sin). There *is* a judgement for the household of God, not a judgement that could alter our eternal destiny, but a judgement of the way in which we have lived in light of our salvation. Further, of course, there is a judgement upon those not part of God's kingdom, those who face God's wrath and an eternity in hell.

In verse 6, Peter refers back to the preaching of Noah to make his point. 'For this is why the gospel was preached even to those who are dead,' (i.e., to those who are *now* dead, although they were not so when the gospel was preached to them). The reason for that preaching was to urge people to submit to God and live in the Spirit. Aside from Noah's family, however, no one in his day responded to the gospel. From that generation, only Noah and his family lived in the Spirit.

We make judgements about other people all the time. We judge them, 'in the flesh'. We might look at one of our peers and think: 'He's a nice guy—looking out for other people, not selfish, kind. I want to emulate him.' We might look down our noses at a homeless man—'I'm glad I'm not like him ...' We judge 'in the flesh' by what we see. But God does not judge according to the flesh—he does not judge us by our outward appearances (for which I am most thankful!). Instead, God looks at the heart (1 Samuel 16:7). He judges according to the Spirit, based on what is happening on the inside.

This is why the gospel needs to be preached to all people, even to those who are spiritually dead. They may be judged in the flesh by people who wish to emulate them, to learn from them, or even to revere them. More importantly, though, they will be judged according to the Spirit, and they are in desperate need of forgiveness and reconciliation to their Creator.

The flood waters were deep and spoke of the judgement of God. Rescue was possible only by God's hand. Only in responding positively to the preaching of Noah could those people be saved. Likewise, the waters of baptism do not wash away inner dirt. Rather, they speak of the judgement of God from which we have been saved if we have responded positively to the gospel preached to us. We repent of our sin and receive new life in Christ, an escape from the certain death that we would face outside of Jesus, as we stand before a God angry at our sin.

Likewise, here, Peter urges that we respond to the preaching we have heard—teaching from God's word—and live no longer in the flesh, but rather live for the will of God. That is what worship is about—bringing God the glory. This is the only real life that exists. Everything else is poor mimicry.

The first six verses of chapter 4 concern the negatives. Peter's argument is: 'If you are a believer in Jesus, then you will not …' and then he lists the things the world chases after and indulges in—sensuality, passions, drunkenness, orgies, drinking parties, lawless idolatry. A flood of debauchery (notice the reference back to Noah again). In the following five verses, though, Peter describes the positives.

Here, Peter argues, 'If you are a believer in Jesus, then you will …', and then he lists the things that the Christian chases after and indulges in—self-control, sobriety, praying, loving one-another earnestly, hospitality, stewarding the gifts we have, and so on. In other words, Peter is saying that now we are to be people of worship, as a result of which we will live God's way.

Peter's heading in verse 7 is, 'be self-controlled and sober-minded'. In other words, 'Get your body and your mind under control.' It is no surprise that Paul writes in Romans 12:2, 'Do not be conformed to this world, but be transformed *by the renewal of your mind.*' Of course we do need to get our bodies under control—Peter has already commented that if we are Christians, then we will no longer live for human passions. However, the way in which we get our bodies under control is to get our minds under control. Furthermore, the way we get our minds under control is not by some kind of eastern meditation or mindfulness or yoga or anything like that. Rather, our minds are renewed as we focus increasingly more upon the Lord Jesus himself. In other words, stop concerning yourself only with this world—'The end of all things is at hand' (4:7).

Jesus will return. Judgement is coming. Keep this eternal perspective and focus yourself on the Lord Jesus. As you do so, you will love him more and love the things of this world less.

Not only does Peter give the imperatives, though, he also provides a reason. 'Be self-controlled and sober-minded *for the sake of your prayers.*' This is not a new idea—he has already raised it in 1 Peter 3:7 when he was discussing the different roles of husbands and wives in the marriage relationship. Back there, he suggested that if we do not live God's way in marriage, then our prayers are hindered. So here, in 1 Peter 4:7, he broadens the idea and explains that if we do not live God's way in all of life—control of our body and control of our mind—then our prayers are hindered.

This chimes well with James' comment: 'The prayer of a righteous man is powerful and effective' (James 5:16, NIV). The more we live God's way, the more effective our prayers will be. Another way to look at this might be this: if we are Christians, then the penalty for our sin is fully paid-for by Jesus at his substitutionary death upon the cross, but our daily sin clouds our relationship with God—it gets between us. That is why we are called to repent every day—to live lives of repentance. As Luther put in the first of his 95 theses which he nailed to the door of the Castle Church in Wittenberg: 'When our Lord and Master Jesus Christ said "Repent" (Matthew 4:17), he willed the entire life of believers to be one of repentance.'[3]

If we have had a bath then, while we still need washing each day, it is only our hands and feet that need washing (John 13:10). The prime point of John chapter 13 is not service, but rather our daily need to repent. We walk around in a dirty world, a world full of sin, and we get ourselves dirty. We sin and thus we need daily forgiveness for our sin in order to keep us in a right relationship with God. For the Christian, a failure to repent regularly does not result in a loss of eternal salvation—if we believe, then we have (present tense) eternal life (John 3:16). That eternal life is, well, eternal—it goes on forever. If it could be lost, then it would not be eternal. If we are Christians, then our sin does not call into question our eternal destiny.

But our sin *does* result in a loss of communication with God. We no longer hear his voice as clearly and our requests to him are clouded by our sin. Regular repentance means good communication and our prayers are not hindered.

As Christians, then, we are to live God's way in the world in order to ensure our prayers are not hindered. Living God's way keeps that communication open. The prayer of a righteous man is powerful and effective, remember.

Thus, 'Be self-controlled and sober-minded,' is the headline. We are to be in control of our bodies and in control of our minds. If that is the headline, verse 8 is the heart. What is the most important way in which that self-control is expressed? Peter responds: 'Keep loving one another earnestly.' In so doing, he reminds us of verse 8 in the previous chapter.

The word he uses for 'love' here in chapter 4, though, is the Greek, '*agape*'. We know that as the apostles wrote the words of the New Testament, they looked at Jesus' understanding of love and thus imbued this Greek word, *agape*, with a much deeper meaning. According to Jesus, the law is summarized in two prime commands: 'Love God and love people' (Matthew 22:37–39). In other words, our Christian lives are summed up by that two-fold command to love.

Contrary to the view in popular culture, though, to 'love' in this way is not a feeling that happens to you. Rather, it is a decision of the will. It is a choice. We choose to love God (or not, if we are not Christians), and we choose to love others. It is a decision to focus on the well-being of people above yourself, without expecting anything in return. This kind of love expresses the heartbeat of God, and Jesus epitomized this approach to life. His command was as simple as it is revolutionary: 'love your enemies' (Matthew 5:44; Luke 6:27).

So, *agape* love is rooted in the Lord Jesus himself who expressed such love for us in giving his life 'while we were still sinners' (Romans 5:8). While we were living in rebellion against Jesus, while we were flogging him, shouting, 'crucify', and hammering in the nails, it was even and especially in that moment that Jesus loved us.

'Love covers over a multitude of sins,' Peter writes in verse 8, and this is true most clearly in the death of Jesus. Jesus did not hold our sin against us. He suffered the pain of rejection and rebellion from us—he swallowed that pain because his love covered over our sin. He suffered death itself because, gloriously and wonderfully, his love covered over a multitude of sins—all of our sins (past, present and future)—if we are Christians.

Peter's words here are phenomenal. He states that we are to love sacrificially from the heart *for the same reason that Jesus did*. We are to love earnestly *because* 'Love covers a multitude of sins.' Our love for our fellow believers ought to cover over, hide, veil, their sins even when to cover such sins is to endure their effects ourselves, to receive the injustices, to experience the pain of those sins. This reason which Peter gives for loving earnestly is hugely challenging.

He does not write, 'Be swift to forgive.' Neither does he write, 'Wait for God to sort out the issue.' Rather, he explains, 'Keep loving one another earnestly [from the heart] *since* love covers a multitude of sins.' They will be better off because you choose to love, despite the pain that entails. You will be better off because you are obeying the gospel of God. This is true worship—praise and honour and glory to Jesus in the midst of pain and betrayal.

Next, Peter unpacks some practical implications of this love. The negatives of verses 1 to 6 (what we are *not* to do) are counterbalanced with the positives of verses 7 to 11 (what we *are* to do). This sacrificial love to which he has alluded is demonstrated in some particular ways. He does not leave it as some theoretical idea—he illustrates with practical realities.

'Show hospitality to one another without grumbling' (v. 9). The word 'hospitality' which Peter uses is a word that, etymologically at the least, means 'love for strangers'. From what we can glean from the evidence, in the ancient Near East, hospitality was a social and societal necessity. The harsh, hot climate meant that any travellers required water, food and shelter as a matter of life and death. For most, refusing to provide this basic care was considered an insult. The general expectation was that a traveller would be welcomed as a friend and come under the protection of the household where he stayed.

The sharing of food together was a token of friendship, perhaps almost a covenantal commitment. As a result, eating with a person and then betraying them was seen as a despicable act (this is part of the horror of Judas' betrayal of Jesus—it followed immediately from the last supper). It seems, then, that the code of hospitality in the ancient Near East was both strong and widespread, and the author to the Hebrews reminded his readers of it: 'Do not neglect to show hospitality to strangers ...' (Hebrews 13:2).

It is in this context that Peter writes these words in chapter 4. The outworking of earnest love, one for another, would be showing hospitality to one another—eating together, providing basic needs, and so on. In other words, the love which Peter espouses in verse 8 is deeply practical. We are to recognize the needs of others and seek to meet them. Then he expands on this idea to include the mutual sharing of our gifts, whatever their nature. Gifts are given for service. We are to be 'good stewards of God's varied grace' (v. 10). If you have the gift of encouragement, then you are to use it in the church, serving God's people. If you have financial wealth, your role is to steward it well, sharing it with God's people and using it to serve them. If your gift is teaching or discipleship or leading or reconciliation ministry or whatever it may be, you are to use it in the service of God's people.

Peter finishes this entire section with the fundamental reason for life. He writes that we should live this way, 'in order that in everything God may be glorified through Jesus Christ' (4:11). The purpose of our lives is to glorify God through Jesus Christ. Life is about worship of Jesus. We do nothing for our own advancement, our own gratification, or our own promotion. Rather, we are to live in service of the King. For the Christian, our role is: to be a signpost that points to Jesus; to be a megaphone that shouts of Jesus; to be a tool in the hand of Jesus; to be a voice that brings praise to Jesus; all for the glory of God. It makes total sense that our rescue from the floodwaters of God's judgement, through the cleansing of his sacrificial blood on our behalf, should lead us to worship. As Peter writes: 'To him belong glory and dominion forever and ever. Amen.'

Notes

1 Peter's use of the word 'spirits' to refer to people is not unprecedented. The author to the Hebrews does the same thing in Hebrews 12v9.

2 Technically, this use of language is called synecdoche. It is when one part is used to refer to the whole thing.

3 Luther, Martin, *The 95 Theses*, 1517, https://www.luther.de/en/95thesen.html

10 A theology of suffering

1 Peter 4:12–19

In February 2020, a seven-year-old boy was knocked down and killed outside his home in Bristol. In March 2020, a friend of mine announced that he had just been diagnosed with prostate cancer. In April 2020, Covid-19 began to cause increasing alarm and pain across the world. There is no doubt that we are surrounded by suffering of many different types.

We noted earlier that when Peter urged, 'always [be] prepared to make a defense to anyone who asks you for a reason for the hope that is in you' (1 Peter 3:15), the context for that imperative was suffering. It is interesting, then, that suffering is a central question raised by unbelievers as a supposed attack on the Christian worldview. They ask, 'How can you believe in a loving God when there is so much suffering in the world?' as if Christians have not really thought it through. It is almost as if they are expecting the response, 'Oh yes—you're right. That's a great point. Oh dear—maybe the Christian faith is entirely wrong after all!'

Everyone faces the question of suffering close-up and personal, usually on numerous occasions through life. We do not have to live very long in this world not only to see, but also to experience personally, something of the suffering that pervades.

With the counter-cultural message of the cross, especially with regard to its implications for holiness in an increasingly, morally-confused and contradicted society, Christians are likely to experience ever more pressure to capitulate to the world's destructive and decaying values. In the light of this widening opportunity for persecution, we need a deeper theology of suffering. Helmut Thielicke was once asked what he thought was the greatest defect among American Christians. His response was simple: 'They have an inadequate view of suffering.'[1] The world flees suffering as a mouse flees a cat, but Christians are called to something very different. We are to embrace an approach to suffering which is rooted in the sovereignty and goodness of God.

In chapter 4 of his first letter, Peter summarises a godly approach to suffering. These few verses are crucial as we consider the problem of pain before a watching world. Peter makes two primary points. First, he considers the reaction to suffering, and then he examines the reasons for suffering. God is sovereign in this world—he has not lost control, dropped the ball, forgotten something or gone on holiday. Rather, he is in sovereign control over all things. He always has been and he always will be.

In the midst of suffering, it is helpful to remember that God has a strategy. There are reasons for all this pain. Covid-19 is not some cosmic accident in which God has to figure out an exit strategy. Rather, in some way the virus is part of God's overall plan, drawing people perhaps to recognise that they are not in control of anything in this world, and rather to begin to consider things of eternal value. God remains sovereign over all. As Sproul put it, 'If there is one maverick molecule in all the universe, then God is not sovereign. And if God is not sovereign, then he is not God.'[2] But there are no 'maverick molecules'. God reigns.

Peter takes us through these two points, which we will look at in turn.

The reaction to suffering (vv. 12-13)

Suffering is to be expected

Jesus commented that, 'You will be hated by all for my name's sake' (Matthew 10:22). Similarly, Peter writes here that we should not be surprised at the fiery trial when it comes upon us. It is to be expected. We should not throw up our hands and cry, 'Why is this happening to me?' Rather, James writes, 'Count it all joy, my brothers, when you meet trials of various kinds' (James 1:2). He does not say, '*if* you meet trials', but rather, '*when*'. Suffering is to be expected. As Jesus puts it elsewhere, 'In the world, you will have tribulation' (John 16:33).

As a side note, it is worth pointing out that suffering in the Bible is rarely divided into the two categories of 'normal suffering' and 'suffering for Jesus'. When Paul describes his suffering in 2 Corinthians 11:23–28, he speaks both of sufferings because of his faith (beatings, floggings, imprisonment) and also sufferings that are common to humankind (natural disasters, accidents, sickness). There is no distinction in Paul's description—it is just a simple list of various trials. Often when the Bible describes suffering, it is referring to all kinds of suffering—suffering that occurs for all kinds of reasons. This is why James explains that we suffer 'trials of various kinds' (James 1:2). Suffering is to be expected.

Suffering is to elicit joy

Peter reiterates that suffering leads to joy. This is very counter-intuitive and at loggerheads with the world's attitude which is to complain and run from suffering as much as possible. Peter says, 'Rejoice!' (v. 13). He is not alone in this idea, either. As we mentioned above, James writes: '*Count it all joy* ... when you meet trials of various kinds.' Notice James' expression, 'all joy'! Paul agrees when he writes: '... we rejoice in our sufferings' (Romans 5:3). Luke describes this in practical action. 'They left the presence of the council, rejoicing that they were counted worthy to suffer dishonour for the name' (Acts 5:41). Jesus himself, who 'For the *joy* that was set before him endured the cross ...' (Hebrews 12:2).

In 1 Corinthians, Paul writes to a church who are arguing about who is the better leader to follow: Paul, Apollos or someone else (1 Corinthians 1–4). Next, he highlights the church's riches, their strength and their worldly acclaim. He writes that they are highly privileged, and yet they argue and fight. They have forgotten that part of the gospel is a call to suffer. Paul wants to change their perspective, so he reminds them about his own situation: weak, dishonoured, hungry, thirsty, poorly dressed, buffeted and homeless, labouring, persecuted, slandered—the scum of the earth. They disagree about whether they follow Paul or Apollos or someone else. Paul responds by pointing out that they do not follow him or Apollos, whatever they may say to the contrary. If they truly followed him then, rather than worldly greatness, they would know heavenly greatness and the joy that comes through suffering. Paul knows that Christians are called to glory in Jesus alone, irrespective of the world, and to be joyful, irrespective of the suffering they endure. Perhaps Paul described them as 'infants in Christ' (1 Corinthians 3:1), because they had not suffered for Christ—instead, they were quarrelling about 'who was the greatest,' rather like some of Jesus' disciples did (Luke 22:24). Back in 1 Peter, we read, 'Rejoice insofar as you share in Christ's sufferings' (4:13). Our reaction to suffering ought to be rejoicing—we are to 'Rejoice in the Lord always' (Philippians 4:4).

The idea that joy follows from suffering is not obvious, so Peter now provides us with the primary reason. He writes: 'Rejoice insofar as you share in Christ's sufferings.' Paul has a similar idea: 'It has been granted to you that for the sake of Christ you should not only believe in him but also suffer for his sake' (Philippians 1:29). To put it another way, firstly, God granted them the gift of salvation, for which they rejoice. Secondly, God granted them the gift of suffering, for which also they should rejoice. This is not a new idea. Right back in the time of the patriarchs, Job proclaims with great clarity: 'The Lord gave, and the Lord has taken away; blessed be the name of the Lord' (Job 1:21). God gives good gifts to his children, but sometimes those gifts are hard ones. God himself declares, 'Who has made man's mouth? Who makes him mute, or deaf, or seeing, or blind? Is it not I, the Lord?' (Exodus 4:11). God takes credit not only for the things we enjoy, but also for the ailments of humankind. To repeat an earlier point: God is sovereignly in control. Different people are given different gifts— some easier (sight, hearing, etc.), others harder (blindness, deafness). All these things have been granted to us. Joy should flow amid suffering, because suffering is the gift of God!

The right reaction to suffering, then, is not to complain. It is not to ask, 'Why me?' It is not to run away. It is not to throw in the towel. It is not to think that God has abandoned us or forgotten us or lost control or dropped the ball. Rather, it is to rejoice. We are to react in this way because suffering is a gift.

Our natural response to this is to ask about the methodology behind God's sovereign work. What is His purpose, His grand design, in all the suffering that abounds? This moves us neatly to Peter's second point, namely his discussion about some of the reasons for suffering.

The reasons for suffering (vv. 14–18)

Suffering is to be expected and suffering should elicit joy—in some way, it is a gift from God. But what is it that we are to rejoice *about*? Peter anticipates this question.

Suffering proves genuine faith

To begin with, Peter writes, 'If you are insulted for the name of Christ, you are blessed, because the Spirit of glory and of God rests upon you' (v. 14). Through suffering, we know that God's Spirit rests upon us, which is certainly a cause for rejoicing. Your suffering demonstrates unequivocally that you belong to Jesus—that you have the Holy Spirit within you. You are more certain of your salvation when you have lived through suffering. This is a reiteration of Peter's point in 1:6–7—suffering proves that your faith is genuine. We said back then that this 'proving' works in two different directions.

Firstly, it proves *to you* that your faith is genuine. Suffering did not lead you to reject God, but rather deepened your love for him and your dependence upon him. You know you belong to Jesus because even amid suffering, Jesus kept hold of you. Your faith is not some imitation, shallow faith, but rather the conviction that clings simply to the cross of Jesus as your only hope. Suffering increases your assurance, and that is great blessing.

Secondly, suffering proves *to those around you* that your faith is genuine. In your suffering, those around you can see more clearly the genuineness of your faith. This is helpful to other Christians because seeing the depth of your faith challenges them to stand firm for Jesus (and also encourages them by proving that doing so is possible). It is also helpful to unbelievers. Indeed, perhaps an unbeliever *needs* to see you clinging to Jesus amid trial so that he or she can be challenged to consider Jesus for themselves. Undergoing suffering is an evangelistic tool in the hands of Almighty God, and again—that is a great blessing.

As a side note, suffering can be a blessing for the unbeliever more directly, too. I write amid the Covid-19 coronavirus outbreak, and one thing it has achieved is to make it starkly obvious that people are not in control of their own lives. It has broken through the barriers of self-reliance and self-dependence, because suddenly people are losing their jobs and worrying about losing their lives (or the lives of those close to them). This is a great blessing, because without a realization that 'I am not in control', there is no hope of submission to Jesus who *is* in control.

Suffering points people to God

For those who push back against the Christian gospel, suffering is often a primary objection. But as someone wisely pointed out, no one responds to personal suffering from the heart with: 'Since all of life is simply the random interplay of subatomic particles and chance, this suffering I am experiencing is meaningless and random.' No—even the most ardent atheist finds himself crying out, 'Why? Why me?' From their philosophical perspective, of course, such a question is misplaced—if everything is random then there is no 'why' or 'why not'. Suffering, however, has a great habit of undermining wrong personal, philosophical convictions. Again, it reminds us that we are not in control of our own lives, and it hints at a deeper reality beyond the physical world we inhabit. As C. S. Lewis put it so famously, 'Suffering is God's megaphone to rouse a deaf world.'[3]

Suffering encourages praise of God

It is striking that Peter describes the believers as 'Christians' in verse 16. It has been said that the word, 'Christian', was initially invented as an insult to those who followed a crucified man. In the New Testament, the word, 'Christian', is used only three times, and each could easily fit into this 'insult' category. Followers of Jesus were first called Christians in Antioch (Acts 11:26), and then King Agrippa II uses the word in consultation with Paul in Caesarea (Acts 26:28). Peter's use of the word here is in the same vein. Peter has stated that being insulted for the name of Christ brings blessing (1 Peter 4:14). Now, in verse 16, Peter writes 'If anyone suffers as a Christian,' (i.e., if anyone is ridiculed for the name of Jesus), they will 'not be ashamed'. Those early church believers took the insult, 'Christian', and wore the title as a badge of honour. They had the right human response to suffering for Christ, namely, to glorify God in the name of Christ.

Suffering, then, should result in praise of God. This was Job's response (Job 1:21). For Job, the blessing of God (the Lord gave) and also the sternness of God (the Lord has taken away), leads to, 'Blessed be the name of the Lord.' How different this is from the perspective of the wider world. There, even for the non-believer, the common response to that question of suffering is anger towards God (in whom the unbeliever does not believe!). But for the Christian, our response is very different—it is one of praise.

Suffering demonstrates God's love for us

Everything is under the hand of a Sovereign God who reigns as King over all and who loves his people. Even when we struggle amid suffering, the Omnipotent God has not lost control, or forgotten us, or failed to notice. Rather, our suffering has come for a reason and so our natural 'Why me?' question is absolutely right—for what reason has God brought this to me? What am I to learn here? How does this grow me to be more like my Saviour?

Suffering comes not because the Sovereign God has ceased to be sovereign, and neither does it come because God has 'allowed' it to happen and then tries to use it for some ultimate good. Rather, the master conductor of the whole cosmic orchestra has brought suffering about for specific reasons. In fact, the central reason for suffering, as far as I can understand it, is this: God loves us.

Because God is seeking for our best—because God is driving for a perfect eternity—God brings suffering into our lives. For the unbeliever, it is rather like the parent shouting to their child as they step into the road. They shout because they love the child and do not want them to come to harm. God shouts at an unbelieving rebellious world not because he hates them but because he loves them. It is a warning cry, an agonized shout that cost him his own life. It is a shout driven by love, that more people would recognize his Lordship and come in repentance and faith.

For the believer, God brings suffering into our lives to prove to us and to others that our faith is genuine, to teach us and train us in righteousness, and to grow our dependence on him. For some reason (often reasons beyond our comprehension at the moment), this suffering we are enduring is the best way. We are in desperate need of being made more like Jesus, and this suffering will help us to that end. Then, even if we do not know all the reasons, our response is to be one of worship. The Lord has given; the Lord has taken away; blessed be the name of the Lord. We should remember the answer to the first question in the *Westminster Shorter Catechism*: 'Man's chief end is to love God and enjoy him forever.'[4] All of life is about worship—direct worship of the Lord God who made us.

Suffering honours the gospel

For a person in the midst of suffering, Peter writes, 'Let him not be ashamed.' This is reminiscent of Paul's comments in Romans: 'I am not ashamed of the gospel, for it is the power of God for salvation to everyone who believes' (Romans 1:16). Whatever suffering comes to Christians, whether sickness, bereavement, ridicule, persecution or worse, we are not to be ashamed of the gospel. The gospel is the power of God for the salvation of everyone who believes. When Paul wrote Romans, perhaps he was remembering the persecution which he carried out against Christians earlier in his life. Perhaps he remembers standing in approval at the death of Stephen. Stephen spoke the word of God boldly, even as he was martyred. He was definitely *not* ashamed of the gospel, and the result of his lack of shame was a mighty witness to God. Soon afterwards, at God's instigation, the power of the gospel changed Paul's life entirely. The persecutor was saved through the power of the gospel and later became the persecuted. So, if we face persecution, we are not to be ashamed of the gospel—it is the power of God to change even those who persecute us. Rather, having been 'counted worthy to suffer dishonor for the name' of Jesus (Acts 5:41), we are to glorify God in the name of Jesus. Suffering honours the gospel.

Suffering is a privilege

Peter's overarching point is that, if you are insulted for trusting in Jesus, then you have God's blessing. You have the privilege of walking in the shoes of Jesus. You suffer, as he suffered. As God's Spirit rested on Jesus throughout his suffering, so God's Spirit rests on you in your suffering. You identify with Jesus in some small way, so that the suffering itself becomes a blessing from God.

Why do we suffer? For the unbeliever, it demonstrates that you are not in control. It urges you to consider the eternal rather than the temporal—to consider the love of God shouting to you to watch out and avoid the coming judgement. For the believer, suffering is about our discipline from God (1 Peter 4:17–18), our sanctification by God (1 Peter 1:7), having our sights raised to heaven (1 Peter 4:13), and our joy in the Lord Jesus (1 Peter 4:14). Perhaps also it is a preparation for us to be able to comfort others who suffer similar afflictions in the future. Suffering, however hard, is a privilege because through it we commune more deeply with Jesus himself.

In his remarkable book *The Heavenly Man* describing the life of a pastor in China towards the end of the last century, Paul Hattaway gives us a valuable insight into real suffering. Brother Yun commented, 'Christians who are in prison for the sake of the Lord are not the ones who are suffering. When people hear my testimony, they often say, "You must have had a terrible time when you were in prison." I respond, "What are you talking about? I was with Jesus and had overwhelming joy and peace in his intimate presence." The people who really suffer are those who never experience God's presence. The way to have God's presence is by walking through hardship and suffering—the way of the cross.'[5]

As a result of that attitude, he writes elsewhere, 'Don't pray for the persecution to stop! We shouldn't pray for a lighter load to carry, but a stronger back to endure! Then the world will see that God is with us, empowering us to live in a way that reflects his love and power. That is true freedom!'[6]

Suffering makes us more like Jesus

Moving forward in verse 17, Peter turns to the issue of judgement. 'It is time for judgement to begin at the household of God.' What an extraordinary statement! Is he saying to his readers that Jesus is about to return and final judgement is about to begin? If so, he was 2000 years wrong at the least. Is he warning them that judgement is coming and they had better make sure they are not found wanting and miss out on salvation? Again, judgement has not yet come, so his timing is very wrong. Furthermore, of course, their eternal salvation depends upon God and not on them. The Christians amongst them are *elect* exiles, after all (1 Peter 1:1). So, what does he mean?

The most obvious reading is that Peter is describing some events which are about to unfold, or which have already started to unfold. Therefore, the judgement to which he refers must be some kind of earthly, temporal judgement. Again, in the context it seems sensible to suggest that Peter is talking about increased suffering. This fits with the concluding verse in this section, too: 'Therefore let those who suffer according to God's will entrust their souls to a faithful Creator while doing good' (v. 19).

Peter is warning them that greater suffering is imminent. It is coming to Christians as part of God's 'judgement' of them. Peter is not referring to their eternal judgement—Christians have been rescued from the penalty of our sin already, at the cross of Jesus. Rather, he is referring to the disciplining hand of God as he brings suffering to his people, to bring them away from sin and closer to himself in the here and now. As they face suffering, they will be more sure of their own salvation. As they walk through suffering, those around them will be given more clearly the light of the gospel of Jesus. So, he asks the question, 'What will be the outcome for those who do not obey the gospel of God?' (v. 17). 'The righteous is scarcely saved' (v. 18)—only through the death and resurrection of Jesus is salvation possible. But, 'What will become of the ungodly and the sinner?' What happens to those who do not believe, those who live in rebellion against their Creator?

The hope, as always, is that amid the suffering that pervades, those who have not yet submitted to Jesus will see how his people respond to suffering and be drawn to the one who alone can save them eternally.

Conclusion

Overall, then, Peter has argued that suffering is good for us; it is good for the church; and it is good for evangelism. It is the means by which we are sanctified and it is the means by which unbelievers can be saved. It drives us into the arms of our faithful Creator to whom we entrust our souls as we seek to live his way in this world.

As Paul Hattaway noted, 'It is not great men who change the world, but weak men in the hands of a great God.'[7] In our weakness lies true strength, because when we are weak, we depend fully upon the Lord. God is sovereign over suffering and has a strategy in suffering. The ultimate goal is that we praise him. 'The Lord has given; the Lord has taken away. Blessed be the name of the Lord.'

Notes

1 Yancey, Philip, *Where is God when it Hurts?* (Zondervan, 1977), p.15

2 Sproul, R.C., quoted in: https://theologiainvia.wordpress.com/2016/06/28/no-maverick-molecules/

3 Lewis, C.S., *The Problem of Pain*, (New York: HarperCollins, 1940/1996), p. 91.

4 https://www.apuritansmind.com/westminster-standards/shorter-catechism/

5 Hattaway, Paul and Brother Yun, *The Heavenly Man*, (Hendrickson Publishers, 2009), pp.296–297.

6 Brother Yun, in: Yun, Yongze and Wang, *Back to Jerusalem*, (InterVarsity Press, 2012), p.58

7 Hattaway, Paul and Brother Yun, *The Heavenly Man*, p.14.

11 A pastoral conclusion

1 Peter 5

Once I worked for a domineering boss who was, without doubt, a 'control freak'. While doing very well in most areas, the business was struggling financially. As the new boss, he was required to make some difficult decisions to put the business on a much more secure footing for the future. To his credit, he had the courage to make those decisions and to stand by them. However, along the way he had neither empathy nor sympathy for anyone on the workforce, and even people who had worked for the business for many years were treated very poorly. As a result, perhaps 50% of front-line employees left in his first few years at the helm. Now, many years later, the business is far more financially secure. But the human cost at the time was huge, and he is remembered not for his good business decisions, but for his appalling lack of people skills.

Peter is well aware of the challenges many churches face from year to year. He is also aware that leading churches through those times of difficulty is a complicated task. As he concludes this letter to churches facing persecution, then, he has something to say to the church elders, something to say to the congregation, and then lastly some general comments. He begins with the elders—the 'shepherds' of God's people. For them, he provides some basic advice regarding how to lead in times of crisis and asserts that 'control freak' is an epithet that should never describe a church leader. Next, he turns to the church congregations (sheep) and provides some final instructions regarding how to live. Lastly, he makes some concluding remarks and sends his personal greetings. We will look at each in the order in which Peter writes.

Shepherds (v. 1–4)

In verse 1, Peter begins his exhortation to the elders on the basis of three things, arranging them in a typical Hebrew way. He puts the two secondary things on the outside (describing two ways in which Peter is like his readership). Then he 'fills the sandwich' with the primary thing at its centre (describing the one way in which he is unlike his readership). It is, in effect, a mini-chiasm.

On the outside of this chiasm, Peter identifies himself with them as a 'fellow-elder'. These leaders are elders of the church, and so is he. These leaders face church problems day by day, week in and week out, and so does he. He is reminding them that they are together 'in the same boat', and he empathizes with them. He knows what it is like to be on the front lines of gospel ministry in our broken world.

Secondly, he is like them because he is a 'partaker in the glory that is going to be revealed', just as they are. We might be tempted to think Peter is considering the glorious eternity with Jesus to which they are collectively headed, but the focus of Peter's thought here is probably Jesus himself—the one who *is* the glory that is going to be revealed. Jesus is returning in all his glory. The elders, and Peter with them, will share in the glory of the returning Christ. Remember Paul's words in Thessalonians: 'For the Lord himself will descend from heaven with a cry of command, with the voice of an archangel, and with the sound of the trumpet of God. And the dead in Christ will rise first. Then we who are alive, who are left, will be caught up together with them in the clouds to meet the Lord in the air, and so we will always be with the Lord' (1 Thessalonians 4:16–17). Peter and the elders will be 'partakers in the glory that is to be revealed', i.e., 'They will rise 'to meet [him] in the air'. They will share in this glorious future when they see Jesus face to face.

Thus, Peter encourages the leaders that they are as he is—'fellow elders', and he reminds them of the glorious Lord whom they serve. He is saying, 'We are simply bit-part players, far less important than the Lord Jesus who is the glory of God 'enfleshed' and who will be revealed in that final day.' It is a great encouragement. That is the outside of the chiasm pattern.

At the focus of this chiasm—at its centre—Peter is highlighting the way in which he is unlike them. He emphasizes their difference, and it is a difference of primary importance. Peter is an eyewitness of the most important thing of all: the sufferings of Christ. He has written this whole letter to help the church think rightly about the suffering they face—to help the church to live in joyful submission to Jesus, irrespective of the suffering they endure. The heart of their thinking about suffering must be to consider the suffering of Jesus.

Unlike the elders to whom he addresses these verses, though, Peter is an eyewitness. What he writes here is utterly dependable— it comes from one who knew Jesus personally as he walked the streets of Jerusalem and Galilee, who watched Jesus endure horrific physical suffering, who stood at the tomb when the angel announced Jesus' resurrection, and who watched as Jesus ascended into heaven. The atonement, the death of the Son of God and his subsequent resurrection—these are the core facts that underlie the Christian faith. It is hardly a surprise, then, that Peter puts Jesus' suffering at the heart of his exhortation to the leaders of the church. They can trust Peter's words because they are rooted in his personal testimony of the majesty of the Messiah.

Leadership in focus

In the light of all this, how should leaders lead in a crisis? What should they do when suffering comes upon the churches they lead? How should they direct God's people? Peter, using a well-worn metaphor to explain what to do, writes simply: 'Shepherd the flock' (v. 2).

Most likely, Peter has in mind his own commissioning on the beach after Jesus' resurrection (John 21:15–17). Back then, Jesus had instructed Peter three times to 'feed [or 'tend'] my sheep [or 'lambs'].' Thus, just as Peter was to 'shepherd the flock,' so he writes the same thing here. As he concludes this letter to the churches particularly close to his heart, he urges the elders in the same way: 'Shepherd the flock.' Then he provides them with some instructions on how to undertake that shepherding task.

He starts by reminding them that they are to exercise oversight *willingly*. They are not to oversee the flock just because they have to—just because it is their job description. Rather, they are to shepherd willingly, doing as God calls them to do eagerly (v. 2). Peter then exposes twin temptations in the midst of this description, temptations into which many leaders fall. These are the temptations to lead for shameful gain, or to lead in a domineering way.

It should come as no surprise that some leaders, even in the church, fall into the trap of shameful gain—'empire building' is a classic marker of this. People want to 'make a name for themselves,' as the people of Babel did in Genesis (11:4). Such leaders desire an ever-expanding influence, bigger and better facilities, etc., thus seeking to lead as the world leads. Some want more 'senior' ministry in order to deepen their own pockets, although this is uncommon in the UK due to the pitiful way in which churches often deal with remuneration. So many in ministry are paid far less than a living wage in the areas in which they minister, and faithful workers manage to survive, not because their churches pay them properly, but because they have spouses who work full-time, or because the benefits system supplements their wages. Worries about money dominate the thoughts of such workers, especially towards the end of each month, and this is a massive distraction from the ministry they are trying to do. Furthermore, of course, it does not speak of a church who values and looks after its staff. If senior doctors (who look after the physical well-being of humankind with temporary results) are paid well (and they should be), how much more should we pay well those who seek for eternal well-being? I digress.

Following his comments about 'shameful gain', Peter turns to the even more concerning problem of domineering leadership. Peter is clear: true leadership demonstrates right living through the example it sets. By contrast, domineering leadership tells people what to do. A good leader teaches people about gentleness and respect, both with words *and* by demonstrating gentleness and respect to those under their care. A good leader teaches people about giving, generosity and sacrifice in words *and* by example through their own giving, generosity and sacrifice. The key to good leadership, then, is word *and* deed: living as an example to the flock.

Why? Because leaders are only under-shepherds. They themselves live under the authority of another Shepherd—the chief Shepherd.

Like the leadership of my former boss, domineering leadership reflects a desire for control. It shackles people rather than freeing them. In the church, it hides sin and truth, rather than exposing them. It makes decisions 'behind closed doors'. It is a leadership running under secrecy rather than with openness. The result of such leadership is that for any under its influence, 'speaking out' is very difficult—something to be frowned upon. If questioned, such leaders suggest there must be some sin problem with the questioner, rather than doing some humble and much-needed soul-searching themselves. Such leadership binds people up rather than brings them freedom. It decides how others should live rather than living by example and praying for God's work to be done. It applauds its own orthodoxy and excludes any who see things differently. It fails to work with God's people for the gospel except within its own camp. It feigns humility when pride is rampant. It stands suspicious of anyone who comes from outside the 'inner circle'. It is insular and closed. This domineering leadership—this seeking to control others—is not just unbiblical, it is satanic at root. It desires to usurp God from his throne and take control. More, it causes great damage and pain to those who find themselves on the receiving end. Amazingly, God in his mercy and grace nevertheless uses such churches to bring people to salvation. But growing in discipleship in such environments is very unhealthy because its leadership is rotten.

Here, Peter urges leaders to shepherd the flock God's way. This means avoiding shameful gain and domineering leadership, and instead living as an example to the flock, honest about oneself and focused on the Lord Jesus. Leaders who are focused on Jesus receive the unfading crown of glory when he appears.

For many of his readers, the shepherding metaphor would have had two very obvious connotations: feeding and protecting. The author to the Hebrews writes, 'Remember your leaders, those who spoke to you the word of God. Consider the outcome of their way of life, and imitate their faith' (Hebrews 13:7). Notice how he emphasizes the twin peaks of right leadership—speaking the Word of God and living as an example.

Good leaders speak the Word of God—preaching and teaching God's Word is a church leader's primary task. In Acts 6, as the New Testament church began to grow, those leading the church responded to the practical problem of food distribution to certain widows. They said, 'It is not right that we should give up preaching the word of God to serve tables' (Acts 6:2). It was not that sorting out the practical needs of the church were not important—the apostles went on to appoint some people to fulfil that very task. However, the preaching of the Word of God was of *primary* importance for the leaders of the church. The Word of God is the food we need each day, nourishing us, growing us, moving us to love Jesus more. It helps guard against false teaching from both inside and outside the church, and it does so not by focusing on what is wrong with the false teaching, but rather by focusing on the truth and then preaching that truth 'in season and out of season' (2 Timothy 4:2). First and foremost, church leaders are to be engaged in word ministry—preaching and teaching. They should not be distracted from it by other things, however important those things may be.

Secondly, as we have already noted and as Peter says in verse 3, church leaders are to live out their faith—they are to lead by example. If we have good leaders, then we are to, 'Consider the outcome of their way of life and imitate their faith' (Hebrews 13:7). They undertake word ministry *and* they live a life of love for Jesus—trusting in him whatever the circumstances, even amid suffering, like the churches to whom Peter is writing.

Sheep (v. 5–11)

Following these important reminders about right leadership (how to shepherd well), Peter now turns to the flock. To begin with, Peter writes to 'those who are younger'. He does not mean biologically younger—remember Paul's words to Timothy: 'Let no one despise you for your youth …'(1 Timothy 4:12)—but spiritually younger. To those who are not elders—the general congregation.

The congregation, Peter writes, should submit to their elders—to those who do not domineer and those who are not in the role for 'shameful gain'. For those who preach the word tirelessly and live out their faith as an example to us, our role is to be subject to them. This submission Peter urges is not a submission leaders can impose—that would be domineering leadership which Peter has already denounced. Rather, this 'submission' is a submission voluntarily given by those 'who are younger'. Each of us can *decide* to submit—not because we must, but because we may (to pull a phrase out of context!). We emulate our leaders in as much as they emulate Jesus, as Paul urges elsewhere (1 Corinthians 11:1).

Peter now broadens his message to all in the church, elders and everyone else too. 'Clothe yourselves, *all* of you ...,' Peter writes as he begins this final section in v. 5b. In other words, here is something that applies to both the shepherds and the sheep, because all of us are under the Good Shepherd, and in that sense, we are all sheep. What should we all do? Peter urges: 'Clothe yourselves, all of you, with humility toward one another.'

The elders are to be clothed with humility, rejecting pride, rejecting shameful gain, rejecting a domineering approach. The elders are to humble themselves under the mighty hand of God. The congregation are to do the same (again, if the elders are living this way, then it serves as an example to the congregation). Peter is emphasizing the power of God (and consequently the weakness of humankind)—God's hand is mighty, not ours. This is as true for elders as it is for everyone else. God is mighty and we are not.

Then Peter does something which, at first, seems strange—he provides a surprising *reason* for humbling ourselves under God's mighty hand. He says that we should humble ourselves 'so that at the proper time [God] may exalt' us. Does this mean that the motivation for humbling ourselves is that God will exalt us? A sort of 'humble yourself and then God will make you great' idea? This has overtones of the prosperity gospel—'Give and God will make you rich; humble yourself and God will build you up.' Such a self-centred approach to life (and its consequent false humility) would be surprising on the lips of Peter. So how do we make sense of what he says?

Unsurprisingly, the answer is to read the second half of his sentence in verse 7! The humbling of ourselves, to which Peter is referring, involves casting our anxieties on him because he cares for us. To humble ourselves is to express dependence upon God. It is to throw ourselves at the feet of Jesus. It is to take those things which cause us greatest anxiety—the things which make us worry—and to submit all of them to Jesus. I am not to be anxious, but rather to cast my cares upon Jesus. We can be confident in such submission *because* Jesus cares for us.

In the midst of their current suffering, Peter knows not only that God is sovereign and has not lost control, but further that God has put everything in place—he is in charge of all the suffering, just as he is in charge of everything else. There is not one atom in the universe over which God does not declare, 'Mine,' to steal an idea from Abraham Kuyper.[1]

The exaltation to which Peter refers in verse 6 is not about God making us great in the world, either. Rather, it is about God lifting us from our worries and anxieties and concerns. We humble ourselves—we cannot solve this stuff on our own—we give it all to Jesus, because he cares for his children. When we humble ourselves in this way, God will lift us up. He will remind us of his care, of our standing as his child, of our eternal glorious hope. Even in the midst of suffering we can rejoice, not because we enjoy suffering, but because God uplifts us and fixes our sights on him and on his eternal glory which awaits.

This is not prosperity gospel; it is adversity gospel. This is survival in the midst of suffering because of the gospel. This is the true living gospel of hope which is rooted in the suffering of Jesus himself—the one who died but now is truly exalted.

Peter reminds his readers that this whole suffering experience is part of a spiritual battle. We are not to imagine that there is nothing going on 'behind the scenes'—that this is just a physical, earthly fight. Paul is adamant in Ephesians 6 that while we experience the struggle of the here and now through real people causing us real problems, in reality our battle is not 'against flesh and blood' (i.e., not against other people), 'but ... against the spiritual forces of evil in the heavenly places' (Ephesians 6:12). Certainly, it *looks* like we are in a battle against other people (and to Peter's audience suffering persecution under the authority of Emperor Caesar in Rome, it would have felt very earthly), but, in reality, the battle is even more serious.

It reminds me again of Job, whose battle looked like a very earth-bound battle: natural disasters, raiding enemies and personal sickness. But the reality was that behind the scenes a spiritual battle raged. Satan, his enemy, was seeking to devour him. The same is true in our circumstances, however 'human' the battle appears to be. The devil is seeking to devour us—that's what is really going on. So, like Paul's imperative to put on the whole armour of God, Peter likewise is clear—'resist' the devil! (v. 9). Stand firm in your faith. Christians throughout the world face suffering. You are not alone in the struggle and remember that Jesus suffered more than us all. So, stand firm.

To this end, Peter reminds us of our final hope and joy. He speaks of the 'God of all grace'. This includes grace to save us from our sin; grace to rescue us while we were still sinners; grace to impute the righteousness of Jesus to our account; grace to grow us into his likeness; grace to give us an eternal future; and grace to enable us to endure when we suffer. 'The God of all grace who *has* called you (past tense) to his eternal glory in Christ,' Peter writes (v. 10). Your eternity is secure because God has called you to it.

Notice the promise of God. Once we have suffered a little while (this could be a simple way of describing life in this world)—once we have suffered a bit—God will 'restore, confirm, strengthen and establish' us (v. 10). He is sovereign and he will do it—that is Peter's point. In the last analysis, your ability to keep going under suffering does not depend on you. It depends on him—the one who has dominion over all forever and ever. To him belongs all the glory!

Salutations (v. 12–14)

Peter completes his letter with some salutations, reminding us of some crucial truths as he does so. His personal messages here emphasize and underscore the need for God's people to stand together amid suffering. He begins by explaining that he has written this letter with the help of Silvanus (otherwise known as Silas). Very possibly, Peter dictated the words and Silas wrote them down.

In Acts 15, Paul was setting out on his second missionary journey (Acts 15:36–40). He had intended to take Barnabas with him, but Barnabas also wanted to take Mark—his cousin (Colossians 4:10), and Paul disagreed sharply. As a result, Paul took Silas and went travelling as planned, while Barnabas took Mark and they went by another route. To put it simply, Silas and Mark went in opposite directions. In Paul's letters, however, we discover that there has been reconciliation between Mark and Paul. Paul urges the Colossian church to welcome Mark (Colossians 4:10), and then, in 2 Timothy 4:11, we read, 'Get Mark and bring him with you, for he is very useful to me for ministry.'

Similarly, here in 1 Peter 5, we discover that Silas has helped Peter write this letter—Silas whom Peter describes as 'a faithful brother'. In the very next verse (v. 13), he describes Mark as 'my son'. He does not mean his biological son—rather, he means that Mark is his spiritual son. Perhaps Mark came to faith in Christ as a result of Peter's preaching, or perhaps Peter had been involved in Mark's growth into Christian maturity. Perhaps both. So, Silas, intimately involved in Peter's writing of this letter, writes of Mark as Peter's son in the faith. Reconciliation has definitely happened between Mark and Silas. Unity has prevailed despite their earlier breaking of fellowship. While there was disagreement and separation because of Mark's earlier behaviour—the details of which we do not know, other than that 'John [Mark] left them and returned to Jerusalem' (Acts 13:13)—now there was unity once more. For a church effective in gospel ministry, unity is vital. Peter encourages his readers to continue to 'stand firm' in the true grace of God (1 Peter 5:12), whatever their sufferings may be. Unity makes standing firm much easier—we stand together for the Kingdom.

Peter's phrase, 'She who is at Babylon ... sends you greetings,' probably refers to greetings sent from the church at Rome, with 'Babylon' used as a nickname for Rome. It is likely that Peter is writing from Rome, around AD 63, as persecution is beginning to break out against any who denied the divinity of the Caesar. Here, the Roman church adds its greetings to Peter's. Again, the church stands together—the Roman church alongside all the churches to whom Peter is writing. He reminds the people of God to continue with their warm fellowship one with another—'Greet one another with the kiss of love' (v. 14), he writes. This 'kiss' was a common greeting, perhaps similar to the French way of greeting today. They are united, and they stand on the truth, looking to Jesus, the author and finisher of their faith.

Finally, as an elder over the church, Peter pronounces a benediction of peace to all who belong to Jesus—to all who are part of the true church of God. Even in suffering, there is peace for those who know and are known by Jesus, the Prince of Peace. Suffering leads to glory. That is God's clear message throughout the writing of 1 Peter—suffering comes now, but glory will follow. So, even when we suffer for whatever reason, we can be joyful in hope and patient in affliction (Romans 12:12), because the God of all glory is leading us home. To him be all glory!

Notes

1 *Sphere Sovereignty* (p. 488) cited in: Bratt, James D., ed: Abraham Kuyper, *A Centennial Reader*, (Grand Rapids, MI: Eerdmans, 1998).

2 Peter
SUFFERING AND CERTAINTY

12 Salvation belongs to our God

2 Peter 1:1-11

There was a restaurant in Croydon where you could order a heart-stoppingly enormous burger. The aptly named 'Beast' is a 7lb steak burger, topped with half a pound of cheese, seven rashers of streaky smoked bacon, a whole lettuce and seven whole tomatoes. Even more than that, it is served with a pound of skinny fries and a full-size milkshake containing two scoops of ice-cream. If you could eat the lot within an hour, it was free, but otherwise it would set you back £60. Apparently, hundreds of people have tried to conquer the 'Beast', but none have succeeded. So, if you are stuck for dinner one night and do not live too far from London, you could try and find it for a free meal, plus (probably) a free ride to the hospital afterwards.

As we come to study 2 Peter 1:1–11, it is rather like sitting down before the 'Beast'. There is so much meat here, and so many side dishes—too much to digest. We will not manage it all. Some things we will have to skirt over. Some things we will not be able to dig into. Unlike the 'Beast', though, this spiritual meal is extremely healthy—a meal that will keep you going for days and is very good for you. It truly satisfies the soul.

In one way, these first 11 verses outline the whole Christian life. They cover the past, the present and the future. Peter begins with justification, in which a person is forgiven and put right before God at the moment of their conversion—a past event for all Christians. Next, Peter moves to sanctification, in which a person becoming increasingly more like the person God designed them to be—a present ongoing event for all Christians. Then Peter finishes with glorification, in which a person is finally perfected and enters eternity with Jesus after judgement—a future event for all Christians. Justification, sanctification, glorification.

While Peter will go on in the letter to spend considerable time discussing true prophecy and false prophecy, to remind us about Christology, and, to expand on what happens at the end of time, he grounds it all with the great truths of these first 11 verses. His focus is upon a person coming to faith, growing in faith and being completed in faith—the three aspects of salvation which we will work through in this chapter.

Before that, though, we need to take a look at Peter's salutation in verse 1. What do we learn about Peter from the way he introduces himself?

Salutation

Peter begins by describing himself as 'a servant and apostle of Jesus Christ'. The words, 'servant', and, 'apostle', urge the recipients of the letter to take note of what Peter is going to write.

As a *servant* of Jesus, Peter is saying that he comes in the name of the King. He is part of the royal household. His occupation is obedience. His focus is upon Jesus. His ultimate goal is to serve Jesus. In other words, as one commentator has put it, Peter has grasped the sometimes-bewildering truth that 'to serve God is to reign'.[1] What a life lesson with which to begin a letter! To serve God is to reign.

Secondly, though, Peter reminds them that he is an *apostle* of the

King. That means he is sent by the King. Despite various convoluted arguments to the contrary (arguments which have arisen only in the last hundred years or so), it seems obvious that this letter was written by Peter who was part of the twelve. This is the Peter, the former fisherman who walked with Jesus, even on the water of the sea. This is the Peter who saw Jesus at his Transfiguration; who denied Jesus three times on the night of his arrest; who was restored by Jesus on the beach; who preached at Pentecost and 3000 people became Christians; and the one who wrote 1 Peter to encourage Christians facing suffering. This is the Peter who soon would himself die a martyr's death. It is this Peter who wrote this letter probably within a year or two of AD 63.

While it is possible that Peter has the churches of 1 Peter 1:1 in mind, in this second letter he does not specify a particular group, so his writing probably is to a broader readership. He writes, 'To those who have obtained a faith of equal standing as ours.' He is writing, thus, to all Christians. This means that those of us who are followers of Jesus today are directly included. If you trust in Jesus for your salvation, then Peter is writing to you. If you are not a Christian at the moment, then Peter's writing gives insight into what being a Christian means, so there are many things for you here as well.

Now, then, we return to Peter's focus on the past, the present and future.

Justification (1:1–4)

As Peter begins this letter, he writes that salvation—trusting in Jesus—is something given by God. Justification is by grace alone through faith alone. 'To those who have obtained a faith of equal standing with ours by the righteousness of our God and Saviour Jesus Christ,' he writes in v. 1. While the original is an active verb, the word, 'obtained', here is rightly translated in this gloriously passive way—to those who *have obtained*. Christians have obtained salvation not by their own righteousness, but 'by the righteousness of … Jesus Christ', as Peter puts it. Verses 3 and 4 hold a similar idea. 'His divine power *has granted to us* all things …' and 'by which he *has granted* to us …'. In other words, Christians are people who have faith in Jesus, not because they have figured it out, or because they are more morally upright than others, or they have read all the evidence, or because they have studied the Bible. Rather, they are Christians because they *have obtained* a faith. And this faith is obtained through the righteousness of our God and Saviour Jesus Christ.

To put it another way, a Christian has faith in Jesus because Jesus gave them faith. It is a gift, to be received with heartfelt thanks. It is not given because we deserve it in some way. It is not given because of our own righteousness, or our own morality, or our own upstanding life, or our own intelligence, or our own money, or our own achievements. None of those qualify us for faith. Rather, Christians receive faith *through* (because of) the righteousness of their God and Saviour Jesus Christ.

Jesus is perfect in every way from all eternity past to all eternity future. He lived a perfect life on earth. He died a substitutionary death. He rose victoriously from the grave. He ascended triumphantly into heaven. He reigns supreme over all things. In all of this, his obedience was perfect—it was an obedience to death, even death on a cross. His obedience paid the price for your sin and for mine, and the result of it is that he gives faith to Christians. We deserve a forfeit rather than faith. We deserve justice instead of joy. We deserve punishment instead of pleasure. We deserve condemnation instead of comfort. We have rebelled against Almighty God, after all.

But the punishment we deserve, the forfeit we deserve, the justice we deserve, and the condemnation we deserve, are all taken by Jesus upon himself in our place. Perfect justice is meted out on Jesus, not on us. It is only because of his perfect righteousness that we can have faith. The faith we have is a faith given *by* God, a faith *in* God, and a faith *for* God.

Peter, then, begins his second letter with justification by grace alone through faith alone, because of the righteousness of Jesus. But how could Jesus achieve perfection and so stand as our substitute before the wrath of God? This is the question to which Peter turns right here in verse 1. Jesus could do all this for us for *one* reason and one reason only.

When we read the prologue to John in John 1, we find an unequivocal assertion that Jesus, the Word, *is* God. At the end of John's Gospel we find the disciple, Thomas, falling on his knees in worship before the resurrected Jesus saying, 'My Lord and my God' (John 20:28). When we study Colossians, we read, 'In him [Christ] the whole fullness of deity dwells bodily' (Colossians 2:9; compare with Colossians 1:19). Here, in 2 Peter 1, we have again that clarion call of the New Testament: Jesus is Saviour and Jesus is God. Peter is abundantly clear in this verse, where he writes, 'our God and Saviour Jesus Christ'. The Greek behind this translation is unequivocal. Jesus is identified both as Saviour and as God.

There was great controversy about this assertion, especially back in the 4th century. Arius taught that Jesus was made by God and is *not* God.[2] But the Council of Nicaea of AD 325 asserted that Jesus is of one essence with the Father—of the same being and co-eternal.[3] The Nicene Creed did likewise.[4] The council of Chalcedon in AD 451 again affirmed the full deity of Christ.[5] These councils affirmed it, not because they figured it out or speculated, but because the Bible is clear on the matter. Theologians did not invent the idea that Jesus is God. While the word, 'Trinity', does not appear in the Bible, it is the clear teaching of the Word of God, and 2 Peter 1:1 provides one clear example.

We may wonder why Peter chooses to focus here upon Jesus' divinity. R.C. Sproul clarifies for us: 'The One who saves us is our God, and our God is our Saviour, which means, by way of application, that if God has saved you, you are saved indeed.'[6] If you are a Christian, then your faith is a faith *given to you by God*—a faith *received*. Christians are saved because Jesus saved us. It is his work. Justification is by grace alone.

How does Peter describe this received faith? He writes that it is a 'faith *as precious as ours*' (NIV). More literally, he says that it is a faith 'equally honoured', or 'of *equal standing*'—as ours. Peter is saying not only that our received faith is precious, but also that it is *the same faith* as his own. Peter had great faith, say the Roman Catholics. Peter replies, 'All Christians have great faith—their faith is equally precious and of equal standing as mine.' So why is this faith so great? It is unimaginably great because it does not originate with Peter, but rather it originates with God. The faith we have is *given to us*, not engineered by us. It is from God. If God has saved you, then you are saved indeed. Justification is by grace alone.

Having just noted the divinity of Jesus, it seems to me that Peter now broadens our view by reminding us of the Trinity: 'Grace and peace be multiplied to you in the knowledge of God [that's the Father] and of Jesus our Lord [that's the Son]. His divine power [that's the Holy Spirit] has granted to us all things that pertain to life and godliness ...' If I am right, then he describes the Holy Spirit as the 'Divine Power'. In some circles, it is not uncommon to lose sight of the Holy Spirit and to hold to a sort of Di-unity rather than Tri-unity. But the Holy Spirit is the One who has made our hearts *strangely warm*. He is the One who has breathed new life into our dead souls. He is the One who grows us into Christ more and more. He is the One who has given us everything we need for life (that is the principle) and godliness (that is the manifestation—the result). As the third person of the Trinity, the Holy Spirit is co-equal and co-eternal with the Father and the Son, so it is vital we do not distort the object of our trust by forgetting him.

Notice that Peter focuses on knowledge in these two verses. He desires grace and peace in abundance '*in* the *knowledge* of God and Jesus and the Holy Spirit' (v. 2). We have life and godliness 'through the *knowledge* of him who called us by his own glory and excellence (v. 3). Peter is urging us to grow in knowledge. It is knowing God better that results in grace and peace in abundance in the life of the believer. The more we know him, the more we think his thoughts after him, the higher our perspective on life and the more we can live in grace and peace. We gain life because the divine power—the Holy Spirit—has given us life. We grow in godliness because the

Holy Spirit gives us all we need for that, too. And we grow more like him as we learn more of him.

They say that the longer a couple are married, the more they become alike. My wife and I often find ourselves thinking the same things or saying the same things. The more we know one another, the more like one another we become. In similar fashion, Peter is arguing, the more we know God, the more we grow to be like him.

Notice the order in which Peter writes here—'[he] has granted to us all things that pertain to life and godliness ...'. It is not that godliness leads to life, but rather completely the other way around. Life comes first, and that leads us to godliness. You cannot be godly without being God's. He gives us life, and this leads to our godliness.

God's promises to us are precious and huge and magnificent and overwhelming and wonderful and utterly undeserved. The Holy Spirit has given us *all things* that pertain to life and godliness, so that his words to us are secure and certain promises, upon which we may rely.

Peter finishes this first section by reminding us in verse 4 that justification is a gift—'He *has given us* his very great and precious promises, so that through them you may participate in the divine nature' (NIV). The ESV puts it like this: 'He has granted to us his precious and very great promises, so that through them you may become partakers of the divine nature ...' The result of this justification, the result of coming to trust in Jesus for ourselves, is that we may partake of the divine nature.

It is important to understand what Peter means by this. Is he making an argument that when we trust in Jesus, we become divine—we come to be little gods ourselves? No, of course not. That would run counter to the whole tenor of Scripture. We are made in God's image, which means we were imbued with God's *communicable attributes* (such as the capacity to love, to experience joy, to reason). But God's *incommunicable attributes* (such as omniscience, omnipresence, omnipotence, and sovereignty) remain God's attributes—they can never be ours. So, as we grow in our knowledge of God, we become more like God, not in terms of his *essence* but in terms of his *holiness*. The role of the Divine Power (v. 3) is to make us more like Christ and so enable us to partake in the divine nature.

To put it another way, participating in the divine nature is about growing more and more like Jesus. In fact, this is called sanctification, and it anticipates what is about to come in the next few verses. So, Peter has made it abundantly clear that Christians are saved, forgiven, restored, declared innocent, freed, and regenerated, because of the objective work of Christ alone. If you have faith, then you have it because God produced it in you. Justification is by grace alone.

And if you *are* saved, if you *are* a Christian, then your justification has happened and now you are living in sanctification territory, to which Peter now turns.

Sanctification (vv. 5–9)

Notice how verse 5 begins. 'For this very reason ...' When Peter writes, 'make every effort to supplement your faith with virtue ...', he is arguing that we should seek to live God's way *because* God has saved us. We are heading for eternity with Jesus, and nothing we ever do can change that. We have complete eternal security, and because of this—because Jesus has saved us—then we make every effort to grow in sanctification. Good works follow salvation—the point Peter has already hinted at in verse 3 when syntactically he put life before godliness, reflecting the temporal order of events. Life first, godliness follows.

There is a great picture of this truth in the Old Testament. Consider the following order of events. The Israelites were rescued from slavery in Egypt through the sacrifice of the 'Passover lamb' (just as we are rescued from slavery to sin through Jesus, our Passover lamb). Next, they moved through the Red Sea (which Paul uses as a picture of baptism in 1 Corinthians 10:1–5). Finally, they receive the law through Moses on Mount Sinai. In other words, the nation was saved first, then baptized, and then they were given the law—*This then is how you should live.* In short, then, justification comes first and sanctification follows.

Likewise, here, Peter is attesting to the fact that good works *follow* salvation (you can never *earn* salvation). The word used in verse 5 is really 'furnish your faith with,' rather than 'add to your faith', as the NIV has it. Allow me to illustrate.

Shortly before we were married, Emma and I purchased a house. It took 6 short weeks from our first visit to our receipt of the keys (an extremely rapid turnaround for a house purchase!). But when we got the keys and went in, we realized something. We had the house, but we had nothing to put in it. We had the house, but we had no furniture. Notice—furniture *should* fill the house. The bedrooms should contain beds. The kitchen cupboards should contain crockery and things. The lounge should have things to sit on. There would be something wrong if the house did not get furnished, even if the furnishing process takes some time. But none of the furniture helps towards getting the house.

Imagine we had decided to furnish the house before we had a house. That would not make sense, would it? We would not go into a furniture store (or, more likely for us, a freecycle website!) and collect sofas and tables and lamps and crockery and so on, if we had nowhere to put them. They would be of no benefit or use to us. And they would not help us to buy the house, either. In fact, using our money in that way would have made purchasing a house a bit more difficult. The furniture does not help us to get a house. Rather, the house must come first and the furniture comes later.

The same holds true for salvation. Good works and trying to keep God's laws are good things, but they will not help you get saved. In fact, they might make salvation more difficult. You may begin to think that you might be good enough for God to accept you, but you would be wrong—you can never be good enough for God. Salvation comes only as we throw ourselves at God's feet, pleading for mercy and asking for forgiveness through the death and resurrection of Jesus. Salvation is a free gift, remember, given by God to those who recognize their desperate need. Then, once we are saved, we are called to become more like Jesus—to furnish ourselves with good works. The furniture comes in now that the house has been purchased for us.

The word, 'supplement', which Peter uses in verse 5, means 'furnish'. He is saying that now that you have faith (given to you by God), you must furnish your faith with these things. Put these things in the house of faith—things that will help you to live well.

In a house, it would be hard to decide upon the order in which your furniture should come. Do you get a cooker and then later on a bed and then a sofa later still? Or do you get a bed first and then a fridge? Whatever the case, there are some essential items you need to work on getting for the house from the very beginning. Likewise, here, I am convinced that Peter is not supplying us with a sequential list—first faith, then goodness, then knowledge, as if we cannot move to the next one before we have the previous one. Rather, Peter is providing a list of furnishings. We have the faith house, so now we are to furnish the house with goodness and knowledge and self-control and the rest. We are to make every effort to grow in these things, Peter is saying, because true Christians do not stop growing in Christlikeness.

What can be said about these seven qualities which Peter mentions? We will explore each one briefly.

Firstly, the word, 'goodness', concerns *moral excellence*. The root of the word is used forty-two times in the New Testament, and almost everywhere else it is translated 'excellence' or, 'things that are pleasing'. Peter's point is that our faith should be furnished with moral excellence. He uses exactly the same word in verse 3 to describe Jesus—'who called us by his own glory and *goodness*' (NIV). As Christ is morally excellent—pleasing to God—so should be anyone who is indwelt by the Holy Spirit. Justification always leads to a growth in morality.

Secondly, the word, 'knowledge', concerns relational knowledge of Jesus, a relational knowledge to which Peter has already referred. In verse 2, he writes that it is through the *knowledge* of Jesus that grace and peace are ours in abundance. In verse 3, he explains that it is through the *knowledge* of Jesus that the Holy Spirit imparts life and godliness. Justification always leads to a growth in knowledge.

Thirdly, 'self-control' refers specifically to fleshly desires and is the final aspect of the fruit of the Spirit in Galatians 5:23. The irony is that before we become Christians, we try to control our lives and ourselves in our own power, and we find that we are unable to do it. But when we relinquish control and submit to Jesus as our King, then we find that we have the power to exercise the self-control we could never achieve on our own. Justification always leads to a growth in self-control.

Fourthly, 'steadfastness' is about endurance—keeping-on-keeping-on-ness. In the New Testament, steadfastness is often tied to suffering. 'The testing of your faith produces steadfastness' (James 1:3). 'You have heard of the steadfastness of Job' (James 5:11). 'Suffering produces endurance' (Romans 5:3). This chimes well with the message of Peter's first letter, in which he urges Christians to keep going through suffering. Furthermore, it reminds us of the steadfastness and endurance of Jesus in his own suffering, to which Peter has already alluded in v. 1. Justification always leads to a growth in steadfastness/endurance through suffering.

Fifthly, 'godliness' concerns becoming like Jesus. Peter told us that his divine power (the Holy Spirit) 'has granted to us all things that pertain to life and *godliness*' (v. 3). Increasingly, Christians are changed into the image of Christ. Note that the power to become more like Jesus comes from the Holy Spirit. It is not that we can somehow drum up enough of our own strength to make it happen; rather the strength comes from God. Leaning on God brings strength for godliness. Justification always leads to a growth in godliness.

Sixthly, 'brotherly affection', or 'brotherly kindness', refers to inter-familial love, i.e., love for our fellow-Christians. It refers not to those outside the church of God, but to those within it. We are to love especially those who are inside the church. As Jesus put it: 'By this all people will know that you are my disciples, if you have love for one another' (John 13:35). Justification always leads to a growth in brotherly affection.

Seventhly and finally, Peter links this brotherly kindness with 'love', as Paul does in Romans: 'Love one another with brotherly affection' (Romans 12:10). This love, of course, refers to all people, not just to those within the church. Justification always leads to a growth in love for others.

The original text of verse 8 does not include the word, 'if'—Peter is saying that these qualities *are* yours (yours to be had), and they achieve something in you. They keep you from being ineffective and unproductive in *your knowledge of our Lord Jesus Christ*. In other words, if you grow in these things then you will know Jesus better, and secondly, if you know Jesus better then you will grow more in these things!

We know that justification is by grace alone through faith alone. Peter has been very clear about this in his first letter, as well as in this one. But what about sanctification—what about becoming more and more like Jesus. Is Peter telling us that once we are saved, then we are in the business of trying harder and harder to stay saved? The root of the word, 'ineffective', is 'lazy' or 'idle' or 'useless.' It is about not bothering. And Peter goes right on to say, 'Whoever lacks these qualities is so nearsighted that he is blind, having forgotten that he was cleansed from his former sins.' Is Peter arguing that 'Salvation is by grace alone through faith alone, not by works. But once you come to faith, then it's all about works. You must try hard and dig hard and study hard and do all you can to get rid of sin in your life. Otherwise, you might lose your salvation. In fact, you might fall further and further from God past the point of no return.' In verses 10 and 11, Peter writes, 'Be all the more diligent to confirm your calling and election, for if you practise these qualities, you will never fall. For in this way there will be richly provided for you an entrance into the eternal kingdom of our Lord and Saviour Jesus Christ.' The implication, then, is that if you do these things, then you will get into the eternal kingdom, but if you do not do these things, then you will fall and you will not get into the eternal kingdom. Right? If there is no sanctification then there is no glorification.

But such a position would completely undermine the point with which Peter began. We spent some time in verses 1–4, and especially verse 1, where Peter is writing to Christians who 'have obtained' a faith as precious as ours, whose divine power (v. 3) *has granted to us* everything we need for life and godliness. Here, Peter was clear that God has done the work and so we have complete security. Anyone who has repented of their sin, and submitted to Jesus as King from now on, is eternally secure—saved by the grace of God and raised from spiritual death to spiritual life. We have complete security.

So, what does Peter mean here? I think it helps to consider what he does not say. He does not write: 'If anyone does not have these qualities, he is short-sighted and blind, and has *lost* his salvation.' Rather, he declares that he has *forgotten* his salvation, which is a very different thing. A number of theologians have made the helpful point that justification—becoming a Christian, if you like—is a monergistic event. In other words, it is all of God. It is all his work and his way. It is his freely-given life. On the other hand, sanctification—becoming more and more like Jesus—is synergistic. God works in us as we work in Him.

Paul makes this point in Philippians 2, where he writes, 'Work out your salvation with fear and trembling *for* it is God who works in you to will and to act in order to fulfil his good purpose' (Philippians 2:12b–13). We work because God is working. We have no hope of success on our own, no hope of irradicating sinful behaviour if we try in our own strength. We are powerless. But if we work 'by the strength that God supplies' (1 Peter 4:ll), then putting sin behind us is increasingly possible.

Here, Peter is arguing from both directions regarding the qualities of goodness, knowledge, self-control and the others. His point is that as we grow in our knowledge of the Lord Jesus, so these qualities will grow, and as we grow in these qualities, so our knowledge of the Lord Jesus will grow.

This notion that the knowledge of God leads to our own growth in righteousness is the point Peter makes back in verses 2–3. God called us by his own goodness to make us good. If we do not grow in these qualities, then we are forgetting what Jesus has achieved in dying for us. We are *forgetting* it. But we are not *losing* it!

This becomes abundantly clear again as we look more closely at the final two verses in this section—verses which consider glorification.

Glorification (vv. 10-11)

Peter writes in the way he does in vv. 10-11 because he recognizes that there can be security without assurance. Making sure of (or 'confirming' as the ESV puts it) our calling and election is not about whether our faith and consequent eternal life *exist*, but rather it is about the *evidence* of them. It is helpful, I think, to consider the object of that 'confirming'. To whom should I 'confirm'? Since God needs no confirmation of his calling and election of us (he knows all things, after all), the 'confirming', must refer to confirmation either to others or to myself. How do I *know* I am one of God's children? One clear way is to consider whether or not these qualities Peter has highlighted are growing in me. How do I know if someone trusts in Jesus? The qualities growing in their life should indicate it. 'By their fruit you will recognize them' (Matthew 7:16), Jesus said.

So, Peter is not writing about security. For the Christian, future life with Jesus for all eternity is already totally secure. Nothing you can do can extract you from the omnipotent grasp of the eternal God—Jesus is clear on this point (John 10:27-29). So, these verses are not about security. Rather, they are about assurance.

Peter does not write, 'Be all the more eager [or 'make every effort'] to make something new happen.' Rather, he writes 'Be all the more diligent to confirm your calling and election,'—to bring assurance of something that is already true. How do I have assurance in my heart that I am heading for heaven? The clearest way is to look back over your life since you first professed faith in Jesus and ask the question: 'Does it look like I've been growing? Am I different? Are things changing? Have I persevered under trial? Is my house of faith slowly being furnished with goodness and knowledge and self-control? Do I love others more? Is my knowledge of God growing? Is my love for God growing?' If the answer to any of those questions is 'Yes, undoubtedly,' then that gives us assurance.

As John Piper once noted, a person's spiritual genuineness (whether or not they are a Christian) is judged not by how close they are to heaven, but by how hard they are swimming.[7] These qualities are not our wages to earn our way to heaven. No—they are evidence of our salvation. The question is not, 'Will this sheep escape from the hand of Jesus?' but rather, 'Is this person a sheep?' The 'fall' in verse 10 is not a fall from salvation; a fall into eternal separation from God; a fall into hell. Not at all. Rather, the fall of v. 10 is a fall into sin—a moral fall. The point is that a moral fall is never brought about by goodness, knowledge, self-control, perseverance/ steadfastness, godliness, brotherly affection and love. These seven characteristics buttress us against a moral fall.

The more we grow in these things, what happens? Peter concludes: 'There will be richly provided for you an entrance into the eternal kingdom of our Lord and Saviour Jesus Christ' (v. 11). Again, to be clear, Peter is *not* saying that if we do not evidence these seven things well enough, then we will lose our salvation. Absolutely not. Rather, he is saying that if we are truly saved, then there will be increasing evidence of these things.

An illustration here may help. After a long period embattled at sea, a ship finally makes it into the harbour, limping a little because of battle scars. The crew are tired because they have fought hard and struggled through the war. Now a huge crowd is gathered on the beach. The BBQs are alight. Perhaps there is even a Beast Burger or two on the grills. The tables are laden. A loving family awaits. As the crew arrive, they receive a rich welcome. They may be bruised and battered. They may be war-torn and weary. But a rich welcome awaits.

Contrast this with the vessel that goes off to war but comes back within days. The battle was too hard. The crew are mostly untouched by the troubles of war. This vessel also comes safely into harbour. But there is no rich welcome – just the safety of the sandy beach.

If you practise these things, Peter is saying, if you strive to know Jesus better and to love him more, and so grow in holiness as Peter has just described, then you do not just have a place in the eternal kingdom of our Lord and Saviour Jesus Christ, but you have also a rich welcome. If you do not practise them, sure you will still enter the eternal kingdom, but there will be no rich welcome for you. Perhaps like the bad leaders Paul refers to in Corinthians, 'he himself will be saved, but only as through fire' (1 Corinthians 3:15).

Thus, Peter is saying that if you are a Christian, then it is God who has made you so. It is all his work, raising you to spiritual life, giving you forgiveness, freedom from guilt, eternal life, the righteousness of Jesus, and everything else. Now, you work with him to grow into his likeness. It is not, 'Salvation is not by works, but once you are saved, you jolly well better work or you might be lost again.' No, salvation is not by works. Once you are saved (v,3), his divine power, the Holy Spirit, *has given us* (past tense)—*has given us* everything we need not only for life (that is the being-saved part) but also for godliness (that is the becoming-like-Jesus part).

Yes, we must work hard, but not on our own, and not for the purpose of remaining secure. We do not fight alone. The Holy Spirit of God—God's *Divine Power* (the power which raised Jesus from the dead)—now works in us and with us. We work in conjunction with God himself. The key is growing in the knowledge of Jesus— something Peter has mentioned four or five times in these eleven verses.

Conclusion

So, whoever you are, your only hope of an escape from the punishment you are due and the separation from God, which you deserve, and your only hope of freedom from guilt and the blessing of eternity with Jesus, is to turn from your sin and turn towards God—to submit to Jesus as King. Only then will you be justified. And then, you will have eternal security.

Once you are a Christian, Peter urges, grow in these seven qualities, with the help of God Himself, not because these qualities save you, but because they give you increasing evidence that you are saved. This is the road to assurance.

Most importantly, there is a huge encouragement and spurring on which Peter gives us here. If we strive to grow in these things, seeking to love Jesus more and more and so to become increasingly like him, then we have not only the joy of an eternal Kingdom ahead, but also a rich welcome into that eternal Kingdom. We have the prospect of those glorious words we so desire to hear: 'Well done, good and faithful servant.'

Notes

1 https://livingbulwark.net/serve-is-reign-with-christ/
2 According to the teaching of Arius, the Son was a "created god", created by, and lesser in essence than, the Father, and the one who reveals the ineffable God. Gervase N. Charmley in: https://banneroftruth.org/uk/

resources/articles/2016/arianism/

3 According to Wikipedia, all but 2 of the '250-318' voters came against Arius. And one of those two was Arius himself. https://en.wikipedia.org/wiki/First_Council_of_Nicaea

4 The relevant portion in English reads: 'We believe in one Lord, Jesus Christ, the only Son of God, eternally begotten of the Father, God from God, Light from Light, true God from true God, begotten, not made, of one being with the Father.' http://anglicansonline.org/basics/nicene.html

5 Bindley, T. Herbert, ed., *The Oecumenical Documents of the Faith*. (London: Methuen, 1899), quoted by Wikipedia in their article on the Chalcedonian Definition: https://en.wikipedia.org/wiki/Chalcedonian_Definition#CITEREFBindley1899

6 Sproul, R.C., *1–2 Peter*, p.208.

7 Piper, John, https://www.desiringgod.org/messages/confirm-your-election

13 Bible bedrock

2 Peter 1:12-21

I am known for having a poor memory. When they were younger, sometimes one of my children would give me something for safekeeping, such as a favourite toy. Later, they would ask, 'Dad, where did you put my toy?' Sadly, it was not uncommon that not only would I not remember where I put it, but also, I would not even remember that they had given it to me. Moving house was a time of joyful discovery when we found all those things I had put away for safekeeping!

In my job as a teacher, when exams were approaching, I might introduce a revision lesson on equations by saying, 'Now just pretend that you do not remember how to solve trigonometric equations. For some of you, pretending will not be too difficult!' I say it that way because I know that I am not the only one with a bad memory.

Memory is a problem with more important things, too, and Christians have notoriously bad memories. We attend church happily on a Sunday and sing about the wonder of salvation and the glory of Jesus, but when it comes to Monday morning when we have some particularly difficult or tedious task to perform, we forget all those fundamental things for which we were praising God just a few hours ago. That is one good reason for being in church every seven days. We get out of kilter during the week and we forget the truths we know. Thus, we need to come back into line and remember our salvation. As Luther is wrongly attributed as saying, 'We need to hear the gospel every day because we forget it every day.'

Peter picks up on our need for repeated reminders here in chapter 1. He expresses our need to remember our salvation, and then emphasizes the reliability of those things of which he reminds us. To put it another way, firstly Peter makes repeated reminders about salvation (vv. 12–15) and secondly, he proclaims reliable revelation of salvation (vv. 16–21).

Repeated reminders of salvation (vv. 12–15)

As we noted in the previous chapter, up to this point Peter has expressed that salvation is monergistic. In other words, justification is God's work—it is by grace alone through faith alone. Peter then moved on to explain that sanctification is synergistic—we work as God works in us. After covering those two core truths, what might we expect Peter to write next? Perhaps something like, 'We've discussed justification and sanctification, so now I'm going to tell you some deeper things, some more secret things of God ...'. But he does not do that at all. Rather, he writes, 'Now that you understand salvation, I am going to remind you of your salvation.' For Peter, his role—his mission—is to remind us of salvation. Peter writes that he will '*always ... remind* you of these qualities'. His focus is on reminding them of the fundamental truths he has just outlined. He uses the same *memory* word three times in four verses to emphasize his point: 'I intend always to remind you ...' (verse 12); 'I think it right ... to stir you up by way of reminder ...' (verse 13); 'I will make every effort so that after my departure you may be able at any time to recall ...' (verse 15).

Peter writes that he will 'always … remind you of these qualities, though you know them and are established in the truth that you have'. Notice, too, that he refers to the truth not just as something they *know*, but also as something they *have*.

As Peter moves into verse 13 and beyond, it becomes clear that he is anticipating his forthcoming death. The year is probably around AD 63, and most likely he is now in Rome and awaiting his execution at the hands of the Roman authorities. As death awaits him, what is his passion? To remind Christians over and over and over again of the salvation they have in Christ.

You may be aware that as the people of Israel moved around in the wilderness in the Old Testament, the tabernacle (a large, specially designed tent) was known as the dwelling place of God. The tabernacle moved with them because God was in their midst. You may remember, too, that when Moses came out of the tent, his face shone with the glory of God because he had met with the Lord in the tent. Here in 2 Peter 1:13, Peter writes literally, 'As long as I live in this tabernacle …'. He describes his body as a tabernacle because, as a Christian, God lives within him. He is indwelt by the Holy Spirit.

The same is true for all Christians. Paul puts it just as clearly: 'Do you not know that your bodies are temples of the Holy Spirit, who is in you?' (1 Corinthians 6:19). Every Christian is Spirit-filled. You cannot be a Christian without having the Holy Spirit live within you. It is the Holy Spirit who brings us to life and comes to live inside us. You do not become a Christian by accepting Jesus into your heart— Jesus lives and reigns in heaven. Rather, you become a Christian by turning to Jesus and turning away from your sin, asking for his forgiveness and submitting to him as your Lord and King. At the point when you do this, it is God the Holy Spirit who comes and lives within you. Peter earlier described the Holy Spirit as the *Divine power* (verse 3), and this One who is God's power now lives within you if you are a Christian.

Peter emphasizes the fact that it is the Holy Spirit who lives in him because he wants to be clear that he is not talking about his own work, but rather the work of the Spirit. He will always remind them of their salvation as long as he is in this body—as long as the Holy Spirit is living in him. The Spirit is the driving force, reminding Christians of their salvation in Christ. He desires to stir them up, to arouse them, and to wake them from sleep. If you are a Christian, then Jesus has *saved* you and the Holy Spirit works *in* you. Do not forget these glorious truths as you go through life. As Jerry Bridges was fond of saying, 'Preach the gospel to yourself every day.'[1] Furthermore, just as Peter wanted to 'always ... remind you of these qualities', so also, we should always remind one another of these things.

Could it be the case that the role of the Christian is to remind ourselves and others of the gospel of Jesus Christ? Could it be that everything else is secondary, or in support of that one aim? Why do we endure suffering? To display the gospel of Jesus. Why do we give of our finances? To further the gospel of Jesus. Why do we come together to sing and pray and read the Bible? To applaud and demonstrate and glory in the gospel of Jesus. The gospel displays in vivid technicolour the justice of God, the love of God, the holiness of God, the grace of God, the transcendence of God, the immanence of God, and the depth of riches of the wisdom of the knowledge of God. The gospel drives us to praise. The gospel impels us to cry, 'All to Jesus I surrender. All to him I freely give.' (Judson W. Van de Venter, 1855–1939).

Overall, then, Peter makes repeated reminders of the gospel in verses 12 to 15. Next, though, he considers the reliability of that gospel revelation.

Reliable revelation of salvation (vv. 16–21)

God's audible voice (vv. 16–18)

Peter begins with audible revelation. As he writes in verse 16: 'We did not follow cleverly devised myths when we made known to you the power and coming of our Lord Jesus Christ, but we were eyewitnesses of his majesty. For when he received honour and glory from God the Father and the voice was borne to him by the Majestic Glory, "This is my beloved Son, with whom I am well pleased," we ourselves heard this very voice borne from heaven, for we were with him on the holy mountain.'

Peter is referring back to the Transfiguration and reminding his readers that he was an eyewitness of Jesus' majesty. Note that Peter does not consider here Jesus' amazing miracles—walking on water, feeding the 5000, calming the storm, healing the sick, or even raising the dead. He does not consider Jesus' own death and all the glory of God that his death displayed. He does not even refer to Jesus' resurrection, and his meeting with the resurrected Jesus in the upper room or by the lake. He even bypasses the coming of the Holy Spirit at Pentecost and the resulting 3000 people who came to faith. Instead, he points us to the mount of transfiguration.

Peter has made known the power and coming of Jesus not because of cleverly invented stories, but because he was an eyewitness of

Jesus' majesty. Being an eyewitness is a consequence of an event beyond your control. When there is a road-traffic accident, often the police appeal for eyewitnesses—people who happened to see the events unfold—events over which they had no control. Here, Peter is discussing not an event he controlled, but rather an event he witnessed. It was a truly remarkable event, in which Jesus was transfigured and God spoke from heaven in an audible voice, probably through the agency of the Holy Spirit.

It is helpful at this point to consider the question: 'What was the purpose of the Transfiguration?' It seems to me that if we know the purpose of the Transfiguration, that should help us to understand why Peter chose this event above all the others as the one that proves the power and coming of the Lord Jesus Christ.

The way Matthew records the Transfiguration in Matthew 17 is instructive. There, Jesus (along with Peter, James and John) goes up a mountain (probably mount Tabor) in order to pray. Jesus was 'transfigured'—he became radiant in appearance. Then Moses and Elijah—key Old Testament believers—met with him and talked with him. Finally, God's voice came down from heaven: 'This is my beloved Son; with whom I am well pleased.' What was the purpose of these events? I think there are two reasons, one narrow and the other broad.

The narrow reason is that the Transfiguration was for the benefit of Peter, James and John. In Matthew 16:16, Peter has just confessed Jesus to be the Christ of God. Jesus responds by talking about his pending death and resurrection. Then they go up a mountain to pray and there the three disciples hear God the Father reiterating Peter's confession: Jesus is God's beloved Son. In other words, God is audibly affirming Peter's confession. The Transfiguration endorsed Peter's affirmation of Jesus as Messiah. Jesus *is* the Christ, the Son of the living God.

The broader reason is that it pictures what happens to us as believers. Let me explain. Consider for a moment Jesus' glory *now*, as he has ascended and is seated in the heavenlies. Revelation chapters 1, 4 and 5 give some insight on this. The Lamb is seated on the throne; blazing with light; with a sash of gold; with eyes like burning fire; with feet glowing like bronze in a furnace; and with four living creatures and the twenty-four elders bowing down day and night and forever crying, 'Holy, holy, holy, is the Lord God Almighty' (Revelation 4:8).

In other words, whatever Peter, James and John saw at the Transfiguration, it was not the Divine Jesus in his final glorified state. Certainly, it pointed *towards* that, but it was not that. They saw not a glorified divine Jesus, but rather a glorified human Jesus. This glorified human Jesus was conversing with other glorified human beings (who had gone to be with the Lord centuries earlier)— Moses and Elijah. In other words, the Transfiguration is a picture of what happens to us if we belong to Jesus. As David Mathis once put it, it is 'the story of *our* glory'.[2]

Yes, the Transfiguration affirms the divinity of Jesus, and it does display the Trinity more clearly. But beyond that, the Transfiguration displays our own future. In it we see the glorified humanity which awaits all Christians—a glorified humanity in which we are able to converse with other Christians who have gone before us, just as Jesus conversed with two giants of the Old Testament era.

So, back in 2 Peter chapter 1, why does Peter refer to the

Transfiguration at this point? Again, I think there are two main reasons—a narrow reason and a broad reason.

The narrow reason is that Peter knows his own death is approaching. He does not have long to go—'I know that the putting off of my body will be soon,' he writes of his own body in verse 14. But he remembers the Transfiguration, and he is comforted and encouraged. It shows him where he is heading.

The broader reason, though, is that it urges his readers to take his words and the words of the gospel seriously. These are not cleverly devised myths. This is not make-believe or delusion. No—Peter is an eyewitness. He is an eyewitness of Jesus' life and teaching and miracle-working, and he is also an eyewitness of his majesty. He has seen the Lord in glorified humanity. Beyond that, he has seen Jesus discoursing with two men who stand as representatives for all of the Old Testament Scriptures. Moses represents the Law and Elijah represents the Prophets. So why is the Transfiguration recorded in the Gospels? Because it reminds us that the whole of the Old Testament points towards Jesus. Peter uses the Transfiguration as his reference point not just because *he* is an eyewitness of the majesty of Jesus, but because the whole of the Old Testament stands witness as well. Moreover, it is God in heaven who endorses and proclaims the Lordship of Jesus. Notice verse 17. Peter does not write: 'He received *our* honour and glory when we saw him on the holy mountain,' or even, 'He received the honour and glory of Moses and Elijah when he met with them on the holy mountain.' No—he writes, 'He received honour and glory *from God the Father* and the voice was borne to him by the Majestic Glory, saying, "This is my beloved Son."'

There is one other confirmation that this is Peter's point, too. Peter describes the mountain as a 'holy' mountain ('sacred' in the NIV). Perhaps the mountain is holy not because there was something special about the mountain but because of the one who was transfigured upon it. Throughout Jesus' life on earth, he had a 'holy-making' effect, to invent a word. In the Old Testament, people were urged not to touch things that were unclean, because it would make them unclean. But when Jesus touches a leper, the result is not that Jesus becomes unclean but rather that the leper becomes clean. When a woman who has been bleeding for 12 years touches Jesus, he does not become unclean but rather she becomes clean—she is finally and fully healed. Jesus' touch results in holiness—clean-ness—rightness. So perhaps this mountain is holy not because there is something special about the mountain, but rather because there is something special about the one transfigured upon it.

It is the same for us, too. How do we become holy? Only by the touch of Jesus. You cannot make yourself holy. You cannot drive yourself to perfection. More likely, you will drive yourself to distraction. What you need and what I need, every day and always, is the touch of the Holy One of God—*he* makes us holy. Peter has already made this point in 1:3—the Holy Spirit (divine power) 'has granted to us all things that pertain to life and ...' what? 'Godliness'. Holiness. *God* does it. We strive, yes, but *he* works within us to will and to act according to his good purpose.

Think back to Mount Sinai where the Law was originally given. Despite describing the mountain as covered in darkness and fire and smoke and earthquake as God descended upon it, Mount Sinai is never described as a 'holy mountain', in all of the Bible. Never. In fact, the phrase, 'holy mountain', or ,'holy hill', does not appear in the Old Testament until we reach the book of Psalms, where it appears regularly and then again sporadically throughout the prophets. In virtually all of those texts, 'holy mountain' is used to describe *Zion*. The word, 'Zion', sometimes refers to Jerusalem, the city of David. More often, though, it is used to describe the place where God lives, and thus the place where we will one day live, if we belong to Jesus.

Why is this important? Because when it comes to the New Testament, the phrase, 'holy mountain', appears only once, right here in 2 Peter 1:18. The cross, the resurrection and the ascension all concern what Christ does on our behalf. He brings us our salvation past—*justification*, and our salvation present—*sanctification*. At the Transfiguration, what do we find? Our salvation future—*glorification*. The Transfiguration gives us insight into what our final glorified state will be like. It points to the eternal Zion where God reigns, and where we will reign *with* him in resurrected and glorified bodies.

As Jesus stands, as a glorified man, his Father thunders from heaven: 'This is my beloved Son.' It seems that Peter is saying, 'Out of all that has happened, the thing that finally gives me the impetus to get up and live God's way is the cross, the resurrection, the ascension of Jesus, of course but, at heart, it is the Transfiguration.' Why? 'Because here I saw what it will be like for me one day if I belong to Jesus.' And in some way, this is where we are heading if we belong to Jesus, our own *transfiguration* if you like. Then, finally, we will be perfectly in the image of God; physically perfect; morally perfect; relationally perfect; gloriously exactly as God designed us to be. Jesus' *transfiguration* demonstrates *our* glorification. That was sight and sound enough to spur Peter into action, that he, too, might hear those words, 'This is my adopted Son, with whom I am well pleased.' Or, to put it another way, 'Well done, good and faithful servant' (Matthew 25:21). This is reliable revelation because it is God's audible voice.

God's written voice (vv. 19–21)

Next, Peter writes, 'We have the word of the prophets ...' (or, more literally, 'the prophetic word'). In other words, not only does Peter tell his readers about God's audible voice, he also reminds them of God's written voice. Notice the way he expresses it: 'the prophetic word *more fully confirmed* ...'. Peter is not suggesting that the prophecies of the Old Testament were not certain before Jesus' transfiguration and that now they are more certain. Far from it. As far as God is concerned, once he has declared something then it is more certain than you are of the ability of the chair upon which you sit to hold you up. If God says something, then it is, by definition, certain. Nothing could make it more certain.

We met a similar problem back in chapter 1, where Peter wrote, 'Be all the more diligent to *confirm* your calling and election' (2 Peter 1:10), or 'make your calling and election *sure*' (KJV). This 'confirm' or 'sure' is the same word as the one Peter uses in v. 19. In 1:10, Peter was not saying that we can make our calling and election more certain than it is. No. If you are a Christian, then your calling and election are already certain. You have total security. However, working under the authority of God the Holy Spirit who lives within us, as we 'furnish our house' with the qualities listed in verses 5 to 7, so we gain increasing assurance of our eternal salvation.

In essence, I think this is the difference between objective fact and personal conviction. I teach Pythagoras' theorem to my students. His theorem regarding right angled triangles is true irrespective of the personal convictions or beliefs of the students. If one of them does not understand it, or even chooses not to believe it, that would not stop it from being true. Conversely, as they come to accept it for themselves, this does not make it more certain than it was before. But, the more students use the theorem, the more certain they become of its truth.

If you are a Christian, then your calling and election are certain. It is a 'done deal' because of the death and resurrection of Jesus. However, if we live the way God intends, then *we* gain increasing assurance of its truth. When Peter urges us to make every effort to ensure our calling and election are sure, he is simply asserting that the more we live as God calls us to live, the more sure we will be of the truth. If we fail to live God's way, our calling and election are certain, definitive and objective truths, but we will lack assurance ourselves, like my students doubting Pythagoras' theorem.

So, it is here in verse 19, where Peter argues that the prophetic word is made more certain. The prophetic word is already certain. Whether or not you are a Christian, the words of the Bible are certain. Trouble in this world is certain. The fact of God as the Triune Creator and Sustainer of all things, including you, is certain. Jesus' return in power and glory to judge the living and the dead is certain. Judgement for those in rebellion against Jesus is certain. Life for those in submission to Jesus is certain. The complete renewal of our broken world is certain. Eternal punishment for those who have not submitted to the Lord is certain. Eternal joy without problem or pain for the Christian is certain. The prophetic words are already certain.

But now, Peter is saying, the prophetic word is 'made more fully confirmed' for Peter and his companions because they have seen its fulfilment in Jesus himself. Peter and his companions are much more certain of the truth than before. They knew the Old Testament prophecies about the coming Messiah. Peter has already confessed to Jesus, 'You are the Christ [the Messiah], the Son of the living God' (Matthew 16:16). At the time of the Transfiguration, many of those Old Testament prophecies had already been fulfilled. By the time Peter is writing this second letter, many more have been fulfilled, not least because Jesus has suffered, died, risen, and ascended. But it was at the transfiguration that God affirmed Peter's own declaration about Jesus, and thus Peter is more certain of the truth of the prophetic word than he was before.

During Jesus' earthly ministry, Peter moved from understanding truth about Jesus to incomprehension about Jesus' mission. He vacillated between walking on the water to sinking beneath the waves. Now, though, Peter is convinced. He is sure. Thus, he writes, 'You will do well to pay attention, as to a lamp shining in a dark place, until the day dawns and the morning star rises in your hearts' (2 Peter 1:19).

You would be forgiven for thinking Peter has lost his fire in his old age. This seems far from the thunder of Acts 2: 'Repent and be baptized every one of you...'. It seems much softer to write, 'You will do well to pay attention.' But, of course, that is not really what is happening. In Acts 2, Peter was crying out to a crowd full of people who were not Christians—people who had not yet submitted to Jesus as Lord. The message, 'Repent and be baptized every one of you,' remains unchanged, even for you today if you are not trusting in Jesus. 'Repent and be baptized! Turn to Jesus—he is your only hope.' That fiery message in which alone hope is found, thunders on down through history.

But here in 2 Peter, Peter is writing to Christians, and he knows that Christians easily forget—the very point he was making earlier in this chapter: 'I intend *always* ... *remind you* of these qualities, though you know them ...' (2 Peter 1:12). Constant reminders are required. Thus, he writes, 'You will do well to pay attention.' The prophetic message (the Bible) is easily forgotten. It fades in our minds, and so our thinking gets darker and we have less clarity—we walk around as people in a fog. For many Christians, they rarely even *read* God's word for themselves, so the fog is thick and choking.

What are we to do, Christian? We are to pay attention to the prophetic message. It is a light shining in a dark place. According to Peter, if we pay attention, day by day by day, then the day will dawn and the morning star will rise in our hearts.

What does this mean? Jesus asserts, 'I am the root and the descendant of David, the bright morning star' (Revelation 22:16). Peter is explaining that Jesus, by the Holy Spirit, will rise in your hearts. The more you read, the more you will see him. The light will shine. He is urging his readers—Christians particularly—to pay attention to the Old Testament and, by extension, to the whole Bible. He realizes that some Christians still feel like they walk in a dark place, perhaps for a short while, or perhaps for years. His response is to say: 'Keep paying attention to God's Word. Each day, every single day, pay attention to it. Then, at some point, the day will dawn and you will know Jesus' light in your heart, either for the first time, or once again.' The Word of God, the Bible, is like a lamp shining in a dark place (Psalm 119:105). As Christians, we have submitted to Jesus and asked for his forgiveness. But many of us still struggle. We struggle with the circumstances of life in which we find ourselves. We struggle with difficult relationships in our homes, in our workplaces, in church, at the office, in the classroom, and at the school gate. We struggle with sin. Peter urges that the only way forward is to pay attention to God's Prophetic Word. God's Word is confirmed because of Jesus' life, death and resurrection. It is confirmed because of the voice of God from heaven pronouncing Jesus as God's beloved Son. 'Pay attention,' Peter insists.

The final two sentences of chapter 1 focus on the reality of what theologians call the *verbal plenary inspiration of Scripture*. Let me explain.

Firstly, some people believe that some parts of the Bible are true—inspired by God—while others are not. Peter's words here put paid to that idea: '*No* prophecy of Scripture comes from someone's own interpretation' (v. 20).

Secondly, some think that God gave the writers of Scripture the ideas, and then they wrote what they thought; or they think that God only inspired the writers when they were writing about specifically religious topics, not history or poetry or genealogy or whatever. But, when Paul writes on the subject, he writes not '*Some* Scripture is breathed out by God ...', but rather, '*All* Scripture is breathed out by God ...' (2 Timothy 3:16).

Thirdly, some think that God (sort of) dictated letter by letter and word by word and the apostles and prophets simply 'held the pen'. But you only have to read the Bible to see the personalities and emotions of the writers shining through—this was not automatic or robotic writing. Rather, the human author wrote using their own style, their own language, their own idiosyncrasies, and somehow, underneath it all, God the Holy Spirit made sure every single letter and word was exactly what he wanted.

Fourthly, some people think 'verbal inspiration' means that our English Bibles are letter by letter, word by word, directly from the mouth of God. But they are not. They are translations of God's Word into a language we can understand.

Fifthly, some people think it means that the Hebrew and Greek texts we have are directly from the mouth of God. But does not quite mean that either. The fact is that we do not have any of the original documents that were written. We only have copies of them. In fact, we have hundreds and hundreds of different copies from different geographical locations and from a wide variety of time periods. Our current Greek text is modern scholars' current 'best guess' at what the original documents say. Now that sounds pretty uncertain, does it not? The words 'best guess' make it sound like we cannot be sure about the Bible at all.

Nothing could be further from the truth. If you were to open the Greek text and read one verse at random, you would be extremely unlikely to pick a verse about which there is much doubt. We do not have the time to explore in detail now, but the crucial point is that 99.9% of what we find in an up-to-date Greek text is exactly what was originally written. In fact, if you happen to pick a verse where there is any uncertainty at all, the uncertainty will probably be one of three things:

- Which way did the writer spell this word? We know what the word is, but which way did he spell it?
- We know what the sentence says, but we are not sure whether the writer used this word or that word at a particular point. Whichever one it was does not alter the meaning of the sentence.
- Is this word or phrase in the original or not? This sounds more serious than it is. Imagine someone was scribing 2 Peter 1:17. The temptation would be to write, 'This is my beloved Son; with him I am well pleased. Listen to him.' Why? Because in the gospel accounts, when the voice comes from heaven, this is what God says. But you will notice that the, 'listen to him', is missing from 2 Peter 1:17. The vast majority of the manuscript copies do not have, 'listen to him', in 2 Peter 1:17, even though we expect it. A very few, and not very reliable ones at that, include the phrase here in 2 Peter. The consensus of the scholars is that a few scribes added it in, not because they wanted to add to God's Word, but because they thought the text they were copying had missed it out when copying the words of Peter. They tried to correct a previous mistake, but since it was not a mistake, they, in fact, introduced a mistake. We realize this when we put all the manuscript evidence together and discover, 'Oh—Peter did not include it.' (We do not have the time here to consider *why* Peter did not include it—that is one for your ongoing study this coming week!)

Overall, then, we can have complete confidence in the original text of the New Testament. The same applies to the Old Testament, too, of course, although that was written in Hebrew.

Going back to our original question, what *does* 'plenary verbal inspiration' mean? *Plenary* means, 'all parts of Scripture and all subject-matter of Scripture'; *verbal* means, 'every last word'; and *inspiration* means, 'breathed out by God'. It refers to the original manuscripts, of course. All of the Scriptures, every single word, were breathed out by God. Our English Bibles are translations. They are the result of a group of eminent scholars seeking to be faithful to the original languages, doing their level best to bring the Word of God into our own heart language. We can refer to our Bibles as God's inerrant word—we need not be squeamish about saying that, even though, technically, it is the original texts about which we argue for 'Plenary, verbal, inspiration.'

Finally, it has been helpfully pointed out that a correct view of God will lead us to a correct view of His Word. Because God is all-powerful, all-knowing, and completely perfect, his Word will, by its very nature, have the same characteristics. The same verses that establish the inspiration of the Scriptures also establish that it is both inerrant and authoritative. Why? Because God is inerrant and authoritative.

And this point is the one Peter made back in verse 17. That is why he pointed us to the Mount of Transfiguration. It is not just that Peter and his associates are telling us the truth about Jesus. In fact, it is not even that Moses and Elijah (the entire Old Testament) are telling us the truth about Jesus. Rather, the voice came from heaven, borne by the Holy Spirit from the mouth of the Father, 'This is my beloved Son, with whom I am well pleased.' Peter is saying that *God* is the one who endorses the message. Thus, you will do well to pay attention to it. Do not miss the message. Stay focused on the text of Scripture. It is God speaking.

Conclusion

So, if, like me, you have a poor memory, then take note of Peter's point here. Christians need repeated reminders about our salvation, and we can have assurance of that salvation because the revelation of it is utterly reliable. I may forget where I put my child's special treasure, but God treasures his children, he has given them salvation, and he will never forget.

Therefore, if you have never started, begin reading through God's Word, the Bible. If you are reading through the Bible—keep on reading. If you got stuck somewhere and gave up, go back there and pick it up. Keep on keeping on with your study of God's Word. It is a light shining in a dark place, but the day will dawn and Jesus himself will bring light to your heart. The Holy Spirit in you will bring you into truth and light and life. The purpose is to drive us ever deeper into the gospel—always being reminded of all Jesus has done for us and raising our sights to him—our gloriously risen, enthroned and exalted Lord.

Notes

1 Jerry Bridges, *The Discipline of Grace: God's Role and Our Role in the Pursuit of Holiness*, (Colorado Springs: NavPress, 2006).

2 Mathis, David, https://www.desiringgod.org/articles/the-story-of-our-glory

14 Charlatans in the church

Peter 2:1–22

In various hospitals in Australia, Dr Shyam Acharya treated people with migraines, viruses, influenza, chicken pox, fevers, measles, mumps, blood disorders, personality disorders, cancer, Alzheimer's, asthma, back pain, gout, gallstones, and on and on and on. We might imagine all the good he did and the problems he diagnosed and put right. But we would be wrong, because it was discovered recently that he was a charlatan—a fake. He had worked as a hospital doctor for eleven years, but he had stolen his name and qualifications from a doctor in India. He was a pseudo-doctor. Dr. Shyam Acharya was completely unqualified.

The apostle Peter has spent some time at the end of chapter 1 discussing the reliability of revelation through God's audible and God's written voice. As he moves through chapter 2, Peter turns from the reliability of true revelation to a revelation which is really no revelation at all, to borrow phraseology from the apostle Paul in Galatians. Peter runs an exposé on charlatans in the church.

He discusses these pseudo-Christians in four stages. Firstly, he warns of the church's imminent danger (vv. 1–3). Secondly, he affirms God's inevitable justice (vv. 4–9). Thirdly, he describes their inventory of corruption (vv. 10–19). Finally, he explains their impulse for rebellion (vv. 20–22). We will study each one in turn.

The church's imminent danger (vv. 1–3)

Peter has spent the whole of the first chapter on true believers and teaching the truth. Now in chapter 2, Peter writes to his readers not only about Old Testament false prophets, or *pseudo-prophets*, but also about New Testament *pseudo-teachers* among the Christians there. The reality of false prophets in times past (in the Old Testament) is reflected in Peter's certainty about false teachers in the future (the New Testament and beyond). Wherever the true gospel is presented, a false gospel will never be far away. There are charlatans in the church, an imminent danger to which Peter devotes all of chapter 2.

Never be the person who says, 'I'm not really into doctrine stuff—that's for the theologians. I'm into Jesus.' Peter has said that where the true gospel is taught, so a false gospel will be present. Thus, if you are not into doctrine, then you may well be into false teaching. Peter is writing to urge true Christians to be vigilant. Right doctrine—right teaching—is essential, he is saying, and he calls Christians to recognize error and to deal with it.

This call to root out false doctrine is a deeply serious one. Those who teach false doctrine, and those who yield to it, are in danger of the condemnation of God himself, Peter writes. Hold fast to the truth! Those who do not are pseudo-Christians—charlatans in the church. They are false teachers heading for destruction.

The temptation at this point is for each of us to start thinking that our own church has good teaching and plenty of mature Christians who will root out error, so we need not be concerned. But Peter does not let us get away with such arrogance. Notice how clear he is in verse 1: 'Just as *there will be* false teachers *among* you.' If any church teaches the true gospel, then be certain of this: there are pseudo-believers or pseudo-teachers there as well, whittling away at the edges of truth. This is true of the whole church of God from the time of Peter to the present day. It is true in your church, too. If we preach the truth, then the fake will not be far away. Probably it is in the building, always trying to edge us away from the heart of the gospel. It pays lip-service to the exclusivity of Jesus and his Word, but underneath it is always looking for 'Jesus *plus* something'.

Peter comes against it like a hammer against a nail. He has already reminded us that through the Holy Spirit, Jesus provides everything for life and godliness (2 Peter 1:3). Jesus provides *everything*. No more is needed for salvation; no more is needed for life; no more is needed for godliness; no more is needed to remove guilt; no more is needed to forgive sin; no more is needed to overcome sin; no more is needed to be restored; no more is needed to be accepted; and no more is needed to be certain of a glorious inheritance. This second chapter is a hard but necessary warning. Watch out, Peter commands—there are charlatans in your midst.

Notice, also, how Peter describes the work of these 'pseudo' or 'false' teachers in these opening verses.

Firstly, he explains that they 'secretly bring in ...'. The word for 'secretly bring in' usually means simply to 'introduce', rather than about something being secret. However, it is unlikely that false teachers in the church would get anywhere if their false teaching were not secret in some way. The things of the devil are often secret and hidden (that is what 'occult' means, after all). Things in the church that are secret or hidden (such as decisions that are made behind closed doors or 'on the quiet') are a neon warning-sign. Such things reek of the satanic, not the saintly. The things of God tend to be open and honest and up-front and available for scrutiny. Things done in the open reflect the heart of God.

Secondly, Peter writes that these pseudo-Christians secretly bring in 'destructive heresies'. This word 'heresies' is to do with divisions, factions, a *sect*, i.e., a group of people who hold certain things as non-negotiable beliefs for genuine salvation, even though Biblically, some of those things are not necessary for salvation. In order to emphasize the depth of the problem, Peter deliberately uses a tautology to describe it: 'destructive heresies'. If it is a heresy, then it will be destructive, so he need not have used the word, 'destructive', but he does so to emphasize the danger that lurks beneath the shadows. He uses exactly the same word in the middle of verse 1 as he does at the end of the verse to describe the destiny of such pseudo-teachers—'destruction'. That is how bad heresy is. Not only is it divisive and causes confusion and problems in the church, but, even more seriously, it urges people towards destruction rather than towards repentance and faith in Jesus.

In Peter's day, false teachers taught a number of false doctrines. They taught salvation by works. They taught about a need to go beyond the cross, to move on from the cross and resurrection of Jesus to deeper things of God. They taught that Gentiles needed to live by Jewish customs—something Peter himself had been guilty of suggesting. What sort of things do false teachers push today? Common things include Christianity as 'therapy' ('Become a Christian because it'll make you feel better'), or Christianity as 'cure' ('Jesus will be your friend if you ask him,' or 'Jesus will sort out your problems'). All of these are a far cry from Peter's Pentecost sermon: 'Repent and be baptized every one of you ... for the forgiveness of your sins' (Acts 2:38). In many places in the world, a 'Prosperity gospel' is taught ('give to God and he will give back to you 100-fold,' or 'God wants you to be healthy and wealthy and wise'). More subtly, and therefore perhaps more dangerously, some churches push at the edges of the inerrancy and supremacy of Scripture, or they emphasize certain moral behaviours or expected social behaviours or certain secondary doctrines, rather than emphasizing Jesus. The impression is given that Christians must dress a certain way (especially on a Sunday), or be in a particular social or financial bracket, or do church a particular way, or believe particular non-central doctrines, otherwise they are not really proper Christians. There are so many subtle errors to fight against, but fight is what we must do.

Thirdly, Peter writes that these pseudo-Christians were even 'denying the Master who bought them'. Of course, the question that springs to mind here is, 'Were these pseudo-teachers ever Christians?' The text says that the Master *bought* them. So, are we to believe that they were saved but now they have fallen away somehow? We will deal with this vital question a little later, but for now, note that they *deny* the Master. They turn their backs upon— they refuse to bow the knee to—the Master who bought them, who paid the price for them, who gave his life for them. They refuse to submit to him.

Finally, as well as describing these false teachers and false believers, Peter now summarizes the results of their teaching. He gives three outcomes from unchecked false teaching.

Firstly, he writes that *many* (that's a worrying word, isn't it?) will follow their depraved conduct (2 Peter 2:2). There is no safety in numbers—*many* will go astray, Peter writes. Do not follow them.

Secondly, the way of truth will be brought into disrepute (2:2). We see this every time a pastor falls, every time there is a scandal in the church—in such cases the way of truth is brought into disrepute and the world laughs in derision.

Thirdly, Peter writes that they will exploit you with fabricated stories—'false words' in the original (2 Peter 2:3). Teachers are meant to bring the true Words of God to God's people, but these pseudo-teachers bring false words and use them to exploit God's people. Pseudo-teachers use manipulation. They explain things in particular ways to try to get people to behave in particular ways. They avoid explaining things in other ways in order to avoid uncomfortable questions. Instead of freedom, they use carefully crafted false words which then exploit God's people. True teachers must fight to avoid all this, to live by truth, to cling to the truth and to preach only the truth. God's people must strive to discern the truth and Peter has already explained how to do this in the previous chapter. Reliable revelation comes from God in the Bible—you would do well to pay attention to it. That is the only way to be certain of discerning truth from error.

God's inevitable justice (vv. 4–9)

Having exposed the church's imminent danger, Peter now spends the next few verses describing the inevitability of God's perfect justice. In fact, verses 4 to 9 form one sentence in the original. In these verses, Peter explains the reality of judgement on those who reject Jesus and of salvation for those who embrace him. His prime aim is to demonstrate that the God of justice is fully in command.

It is worth noting that Peter writes a threefold chronological list describing God's justice. He begins with the judgement meted out on the angels who sinned and were committed to chains of darkness to be held for judgement. This concerns the fall of Satan and his angels in Genesis 3. Next, he describes the judgement meted out on the ancient world through the flood, but the sparing of Noah and his immediate family because of their submission to God (Genesis 6–9). Finally, he outlines the judgement of Sodom and Gomorrah (as an example of what would happen to the ungodly) and the rescue of Lot because of his submission to God (Genesis 19).

Each incident begins: 'if God did this …', and so we are expecting a 'then'. Peter answers that question in verse 9. If this is how God dealt with the wicked and the righteous in the past then be assured that the Lord knows how to rescue the godly from trials and to keep the unrighteous under punishment until the day of judgement.

It would be easy to get the wrong impression here. Peter is not speaking of salvation by works. He is not saying, 'If you live right, then God will save you. If you are wicked, then God will condemn you.' If he were saying that, he would be undermining most of what he said in chapter 1. Instead, Peter is using the words, 'righteous' and 'unrighteous', to distinguish between those who have received a faith as precious as ours (Christians), and those who have not (those who continue to live in rebellion against Jesus).

We may wonder why he uses these terms, 'righteous' and 'unrighteous', rather than the more obvious, 'Christians' and 'non-Christians'. Partly this is because the title, 'Christian', was not yet widely known as Peter writes (and, furthermore, that the term was considered a derogatory one). More importantly, though, Peter uses 'righteous' and 'unrighteous' because the way we live reflects the one for whom we live. He made this very point back in chapter 1:9. If you are truly saved, then your life will increasingly demonstrate it. You will display the qualities of 1:5–7 more and more in your life—you will display 'righteousness' or 'godliness', as he put it back in verse 3. So, Peter uses 'righteous' because the one submitted to Jesus should be characterized by a growing righteousness. To misquote Jesus, 'Out of the abundance of the heart, the life speaks.'[1] 'Righteous' and 'unrighteous' are a very natural shorthand to distinguish between Christians and non-Christians. God will rescue the righteous (Christians), and judge the unrighteous (non-Christians), just as he did in the three instances in Genesis which Peter has mentioned.

Another important question to ask is this: 'Why did Peter choose these three events, when there are so many others he could have chosen?' Our first thought might be that Peter simply picked the first ones in human history. But we know this is not true. At the very least, he ignores God's judgement against Adam and Eve back in Genesis 3, God's judgement against Cain for killing Abel in Genesis 4, and God's judgement against the people seeking to build the tower at Babel in Genesis 11. So, he does not select these events from Genesis because they are the first ones—they are not.

Why, then, does he choose the fall of angels, the flood and Sodom and Gomorrah? I think it is because collectively they cover all possibilities for created sentient life. If angelic beings are unrighteous, God will judge them (the fall of Satan and his demons).

If a world full of people is unrighteous, except for just a very few, then God will judge the whole world but save those few (Noah and the flood). If cities are unrighteous, God will judge those cities (Sodom and Gomorrah), but God will save the righteous, even if there are very few of them (Lot and his two daughters).

In other words, regardless of the numbers involved—many or few—and regardless of the status and power of those involved— angels, princes or paupers—God will rescue the righteous and he will judge the unrighteous. He is the perfect judge and he will do right. You can count on it. However many, however few, however powerful, however weak, whoever you are reading this now, if you are submitted to Jesus, then God will rescue you. If you are not submitted to Jesus, then God will judge you. There is no doubt.

Peter has not chosen trifling examples to demonstrate that the God of justice is fully in command, either. No, Peter writes of the Devil and fallen angels. He speaks of two cities full of people standing against God. He speaks of virtually the whole world standing against God. There are three groups standing against the God of heaven, but even taken together—all of humanity and all of the fallen angels—they are no match for the judgement of Almighty God.

As long as you refuse to make a decision; as long as you refuse to submit to Jesus; as long as you fail finally to admit your sinfulness and need of a Saviour; as long as you do not nail your colours to the mast and say, 'Yes—now I belong to Jesus,' then you continue to stand against God. And if you continue to stand against God, then do not be arrogant enough to think that God's judgement will not come upon you. Make no mistake, Peter says, God the judge is fully in command and he will judge those who do not submit.

Gloriously, though, Peter does not write about judgement alone. In the midst of a judgement upon the whole world, he reminds us of Noah and his family. In the midst of a judgement coming on two cities, he reminds us of Lot, Abraham's nephew. As Noah and Lot were submitted to God, God rescued them. If you are interested in rescue from the hands of God the judge, then you need look no further than here. Submit to God, and your rescue is certain—inevitable. Cry, 'Yes, Jesus—I am yours,' and you will be saved. Call out, 'I turn from my sin and turn towards you,' and you will be saved. God, who is a just judge, will bring his justice (his impartiality and its consequences are inevitable) and he will save those who trust in him.

Moving forward, Peter presents us next with a catalogue of problems concerning these pseudo-teachers and pseudo-Christians.

Their inventory of corruption (vv. 10–19)

In chapter 1, Peter describes what is true—the true teacher and the true believer. Now in chapter 2, he describes what is false—the false teacher and the false believer. He exposes ten contrasting differences which help us to recognize the false teacher, because the best way to discern whether or not something is false is to compare it with the genuine.

- First of all, true believers and pseudo-believers have different masters. A true believer trusts in Jesus and has Jesus as his master, 'Lord and Saviour' (1:11), whereas a false believer denies Jesus (2:1).

- Secondly, true believers and pseudo-believers have a different mindset. A true believer humbly accepts salvation as a gift (1:3), whereas a false believer is arrogant (2:10), perhaps believing that he deserves salvation in some way.

- Thirdly, true believers and pseudo-believers have a different muse. A true believer has Jesus at the centre (1:3,11), because Jesus gives us 'all things that pertain to life and godliness'—it is all about him. A false believer, on the other hand, introduces destructive heresies and even denies Jesus (2:1).

- Fourthly, true believers and pseudo-believers have a different message. A true believer speaks truth and not cleverly invented stories (1:16), whereas a false believer exploits with stories they made up (2:1).

- Fifthly, true believers and pseudo-believers have a different mode of existence. A true believer is free from corruption (1:4), whereas a false believer is enslaved to corruption (2:19).

- Sixthly, true believers and pseudo-believers have a different measuring line. A true believer appeals to Scripture (1:19), whereas a false believer appeals to human lustful desires— what people want to hear (2:18).

- Seventhly, true believers and pseudo-believers have a different manner. True prophecy is carried along by the Holy Spirit (1:21), whereas false prophets speak words they themselves have made up (2:1).

- Eighthly, true believers and pseudo-believers have a different morality. A true believer pursues virtue, knowledge, self-control, steadfastness, godliness, brotherly affection and love

(1:5–7). A false believer is characterized by arrogance (2:10), slander, greed and never stops sinning (2:14).

- Ninthly, true believers and pseudo-believers have a different marking. A true believer is effective and productive (1:8), whereas a false believer is a spring without water, promising much but giving nothing (2:17).

- Lastly, true believers and pseudo-believers have a different morrow (future). A true believer receives a rich welcome into the eternal Kingdom of our Lord and Saviour Jesus Christ (1:11), whereas a false believer experiences swift destruction and their condemnation has long been hanging over them (2:1, 3).

In sum, then, the false believer in the church has a different master, a different mindset, a different muse, a different message, a different mode of existence, a different measuring line, a different manner, a different morality, a different marking, and a different morrow. He is utterly opposed to the true things of God, so the church needs to be protected from such pseudo-believers and pseudo-teachers.

There are some who come into the church and will do the church more harm than good. They do not believe in the inerrancy of Scripture. They do not believe in the exclusivity of Jesus. They do not speak of Christ and him crucified. They push at the edges of truth with poisonous lies. Peter describes them as 'natural brute beasts who are made to be taken and destroyed' (2 Peter 2:12, KJV). Peter's description is strong, and it gets even stronger as we read on. Pseudo-believers blaspheme about things they do not understand. Most people sin more at night when it is dark, but these people live in sin in broad daylight (2 Peter 2:13). They are 'blots and blemishes', the very words Peter will use again in chapter 3 to say to believers, 'Be diligent to be found by him without spot or blemish ...' (2 Peter 3:14). More, 'They have eyes full of adultery' (2:14). The men cannot see a woman without wanting sexual relations with her. The women seek to seduce. They entice those who are weak. They are experts in greed. Peter's language gets stronger still, and he calls them, 'Accursed children!' (2:14), who will be devoted to destruction.

It is noteworthy that Peter uses the story of Balaam here to describe their sinfulness (Numbers 22–24). Balaam was a 'prophet for hire', who agreed to do something wrong for financial gain. When he found himself unable to do that wrong (he was unable to curse Israel—God's message was one entirely of blessing), he missed out on that financial gain. Balaam thus dreamed up another way for the Moabites to bring the Israelites into sin, telling the Moabite women to seduce the Israelite men. The results were Israel stepping into idol worship and sexual sin. The final outcome of Balaam's efforts as a pseudo-believer was God's judgement, and the death of 24000 Israelites. A pseudo-teacher or pseudo-believer can have profoundly negative effects among God's people.

Peter tells his readers that pseudo-believers are following the way of Balaam—they are 'for hire' and dream up ways to cause God's people to stumble (v. 15). They are 'wells without water' (v. 17), who promise much but give nothing. They make foolish boasts and, like Balaam, they entice by the lusts of the flesh. They promise freedom but are themselves enslaved.

Suffice to say, Peter's words are an inventory of corruption. The obvious question now is this: 'Why would people behave in this manner?'

Their impulse for rebellion (vv. 20–22)

What is the root cause of the problem? 'If, after they have escaped the defilements of the world through the knowledge of our Lord and Saviour Jesus Christ, they are again entangled in them and overcome, the last state has become worse for them than the first' (2 Peter 2:20). Is Peter saying that such people were once saved but have now lost their salvation, and that is why they are behaving in such dreadful ways? I mean, look back to verse 1: 'The Master who *bought* them ...'. This refers to the redemption price that Jesus paid at the cross, does it not? Peter goes on to write, 'It would have been better for them never to have known the way of righteousness than after knowing it to turn back from the holy commandment delivered to them' (2:21). So, the reason for their rebellion is that they have fallen away from faith in Jesus, right?

Wrong. Peter most certainly is *not* arguing that people can become Christians and then fall away and lose their salvation. This is not his point, because this is not his doctrine. In fact, his warnings here in 2 Peter are similar to those found in the book of Hebrews (Hebrews 6:4 onwards being the most well-known). But in each of these cases, to conclude that a person can lose their salvation is, I think, a careless reading of the texts.

Consider Peter's long sentence from verses 4 to 9 and think about the words he uses. 'If God did not spare angels when they sinned but cast them into hell ...' (2 Peter 2:4). Clearly Peter is not referring to Christians here. 'If he did not spare the ancient world but preserved

Noah ... when he brought a flood upon the world of the ungodly' (2:5). Again, Peter is not speaking about the destruction of believers. We find the same thing in verse 6: 'If by turning the cities of Sodom and Gomorrah to ashes he condemned them to extinction, making them an example of what is going to happen to the ungodly...'. Verse 9 completes the idea: 'Then the Lord knows how to rescue the godly from trials and to keep the unrighteous under punishment until the day of judgement ...'. In other words, all these instances of God's judgement refer not to Christian believers, but rather to those who have not submitted to God.

And then remember how he describes the destiny of such people: 'These, like irrational animals, creatures of instinct, born to be caught and destroyed ... will also be destroyed in their destruction ...' (2:12). 'For them the gloom of utter darkness *has been reserved*' (2:17). Finally, 'They themselves are slaves of corruption' (v. 19). These are not Christians—far from it.

So, the question, then, is this: 'To whom is Peter speaking in these verses at the end of chapter 2?' Clearly, he is not speaking of those who have never heard the gospel of Jesus. He is not discussing those 'outside these walls' if you like, who do not know that repentance— turning to God—is required for salvation. He is not describing those who do not know that unless we bow the knee to Jesus then we will remain in our sinful, broken, rebellious state and, one day, be cut off from God and one another eternally. Rather, he is speaking about those who *do* know. He is speaking of those who are well aware of the gospel, who know they are sinful and rebellious people who need repentance and faith and who know that they need to bow the knee to Jesus. He is speaking to those who know that Jesus died to pay the price for their sins. Jesus paid the price for them, he purchased them, he *bought* them as he puts it here in 2:1. They know all that. But, nevertheless, they are not Christians. Instead of responding to the truth of Jesus in faith, these people refuse to turn. They continue to rebel. Indeed, they bring in false teaching, trying to entice others away from Jesus as well.

The passages in Hebrews are similar. They are not passages directed at Christians who might be in danger of losing their salvation—no, such an interpretation does violence to the clear teaching of the rest of the Bible. They are passages directed at those within the church—those in the 'covenant family' if you will—who hear the truth regularly and repeatedly and clearly but yet refuse to bow the knee.

Perhaps they have been helped by the covenant community to steer clear of some of the defilements of the world because Jesus' way has been demonstrated not just to be commanded by God (which does not affect them) but also to be better for us as human beings (which *has* affected them). Then, slowly, over time, they fall in with those defilements of the world. Perhaps it happens as they grow up physically and struggle through the teenage years. Perhaps it happens later, once they have left home and become independent and got a good job or whatever it may be. And despite all the warnings and encouragements to the contrary, finally they give in and get entangled. Why? Not because they are Christians who are losing their salvation, but rather because they were never Christians in the first place. These are the people about whom Peter writes.

So why do these pseudo-teachers and pseudo-Christians behave in the ways Peter has described? The answer is simple and is found in verse 22. It is because they are like vomiting dogs and wallowing pigs, returning to their filth. They remain unchanged. They have never submitted to Jesus. They are not Christians. The impulse for their actions is sin from an unregenerate heart.

Now we need to be careful here—clearly there are genuine Christians who get entangled in the defilements of the world. Sadly, the list of morally fallen pastors and ministers grows numbingly longer week by week as scandal after scandal hits the church of God. Do such people lose their salvation? Perhaps less obviously or dramatically, all of us as Christians fall every day as we fail to live for the glory of God alone. Do we lose our salvation? No. There is a whole raft of reasons, but two will suffice for now.

Firstly, if heading for heaven depends on my 'getting it right' then Paul has it back to front, and salvation *is* by works alone and not by grace so that people can boast in their achievements, which would be prideful boasting and thus would annul their salvation! This is clearly backwards-thinking. Salvation depends on God's work not your work or mine. If he has saved you to eternal life, then eternal life awaits you and you cannot lose that inheritance, because the Holy Spirit lives in you. The Holy Spirit is a guarantee of your inheritance—a guarantee! (Ephesians 1:14).

Secondly, 1 Corinthians 3 seems to me to be important in those instances where supposed Christian leaders seem to fall into grave error and sin or fall away from God. In the final judgement, Paul tells us, such people, if they were genuinely saved, will still be saved, but only as one escaping through the flames. Their work among God's people will be burned up—worse than useless. Judgement will be a horrible experience for them as they face the justice of a holy God, but nonetheless they will be saved eternally.

So, if a pseudo-believer and a true believer can look similar, how do we spot a true believer and a true teacher? Even closer to home, how do I know whether or not I am a true believer?

One sure sign of the true believer is a private and public attitude of repentance. Look at King David whose moral fall was meteoric when he committed adultery with Bathsheba and then had her husband killed in battle to cover up his sin. Surely, he was like a dog returning to its vomit? Surely, he was a sow returning to wallowing in the mud? No, he was not. How do we know? Because of Psalm 51:10–14, where David cries out to God: 'Create in me a clean heart, O God, and renew a right spirit within me. Cast me not away from your presence and take not your Holy Spirit from me. Restore to me the joy of your salvation and uphold me with a willing spirit .... Deliver me from bloodguiltiness, O God ...' and so on. You cannot read it and not recognize genuine repentance. The clearest mark of a true believer and a true teacher is genuine repentance. Prayer like David's prayer. 'Cleanse me and I will be clean.' This is *the* mark of true Christians.

In chapter 1, Peter has described already the route to genuine assurance. The qualities of 1:5–7 are growing in us. We can be certain because we are being changed, bit by bit. The change is slow—painfully slow in my case—but slowly we are changing to be more like Jesus. The direction of our life overall is clear—it is towards Jesus. This is how we spot true believers and genuine teachers.

Here in chapter 2, Peter is not arguing that Christians can lose their salvation. Instead, he is arguing that these 'teachers' and 'believers' are, in fact, not Christians at all. They are *pseudo*-teachers and *pseudo*-Christians—charlatans in the church.

Conclusion

Peter, then, is deeply concerned about charlatans in the church—pseudo-teachers and pseudo-believers—who are leading others astray. He has explained the church's imminent danger, God's inevitable justice, their inventory of corruption, and their impulse for rebellion. Pseudo-believers are a major problem to which Peter has addressed a third of his letter.

So, if you are not a Christian yet, then please, I urge you, do not miss the dire warning Peter gives: 'If, after they have escaped the defilements of the world through the knowledge of our Lord and Saviour Jesus Christ, they are again entangled in them and overcome, the last state has become worse for them than the first. For it would have been better for them never to have known the way of righteousness, than after knowing it to turn back from the holy commandment delivered to them' (2 Peter 2:20–21).

If you sit in church, week in and week out, but never bow the knee to Jesus; if you continue to live without Jesus at the helm of your life, without him as your captain, without him as your saviour, redeemer, deliverer, justifier, friend, then you are in a worse state than someone who has never heard the gospel. You are more responsible for your sin than they are. The truth has been explained and expounded to you over and over again. When you meet Jesus at your death, or when he returns if that be sooner, you will have nothing to say. Your mouth will be stopped. The horror of your condition will finally hit you with full force, but it will be too late.

When Job said, 'It would have been better had I never been born' (Job 3), he was wrong, because he belonged to God. He was a believer. But if *you* reach that final day without submitting to Jesus, then it would be true for you—it would be better for you if you had never been born. That is why Paul, the great evangelist, cried, '*Now* is the day of salvation' (2 Corinthians 6:2). Or, to quote Joshua, 'Choose *this day* whom you will serve' (Joshua 24:15). *This day.* Come to him and find living water for your soul—forgiveness, reconciliation, freedom, joy and life. Do not be like the dog returning to its vomit. Stop being a pseudo-Christian or a pseudo-believer. Perhaps at church, people think you belong to Jesus. But perhaps you have another secret life—the real you, who rejects Jesus and exists only for yourself and the things of this short life. You are a charlatan. And if that is you, my friend, it is not worth it. Deny the Master no longer. Come before Him in sorrow at your sin and trust Him. If you do, your future is secure and certain, and heaven awaits.

Notes

1 Matthew 12:34 actually reads: 'Out of the abundance of the heart the mouth speaks', but it is a similar idea.

15 Passion and purpose

2 Peter 3:1–9

Perhaps the greatest and also the most common philosophical question is 'What is the meaning of life?' In other words, is there more to life than wake, eat, work, socialize, sleep, and maybe parties at weekends, round and round and round, week after week, month after month, year after year? Is there anything more? Is there any meaning or purpose to it all?

Of course, these questions are not new. People have posed them for millennia. The *Westminster Shorter Catechism*, written back in 1647, begins with the question, 'What is man's chief end?'[1] In other words, 'What is the purpose of life?' Does life have any meaning?

Peter tackles this very question in the third chapter of his second letter. In the first few verses, Peter expresses his own passion and purpose in life, and then he writes about God's passion and purpose. Why does he do that? He does it because if the Creator and Sustainer of all things has a passion and purpose for you and for me, then there is no doubt that life *does* have a purpose.

Peter structures this next part of his letter in a four-way pattern (reminiscent of a chiasm) as follows:

1. Peter's passion (v. 1a)
2. Peter's purpose (vv. 1–2)
3. God's purpose (vv. 3–7)
4. God's passion (vv. 8–9)

We will work through each in turn.

Peter's passion (v. 1a)

To begin, then, what is it that Peter is passionate about? Back in chapter 1, he explained that coming to spiritual life—being born again—is by grace alone through faith alone in Christ alone. In other words, salvation (or 'justification') is 'monergistic'—it comes about by the work of God alone.

Next, Peter argued that Christians becoming more like Jesus, growing to be less sinful, is by the work of God within us as we strive to grow more like Jesus. To put it another way, sanctification is 'synergistic'—a partnership—God's work in us as we work together with Him.

Peter spent the remainder of chapter 1 pointing to the Old Testament and to the Word of God through the apostles. He reminded his readers repeatedly of the certainty of God's Word. Peter is passionate about Jesus and he is passionate about the means by which we may know him better—the Bible.

Then in chapter 2, Peter describes the presence and the eroding effect of pseudo-teachers and pseudo-believers in the church. Peter took us through 22 very hard verses in this chapter. They were hard not because they are difficult to understand, but because their message is difficult to accept—they are hard to swallow. But he brought us these words because he is passionate about upholding the truth of God's Word.

When we arrive at the beginning of chapter 3, then, what does Peter write next? We have discovered that he is passionate about God and passionate about God's Word. So, we may wonder whether his passion extends further. And we see directly that it does.

He writes: 'Dear friends ...', or more literally: 'Now this, beloved.'

In other words, 'I have written many hard words to you, so I'm reminding you of my heart in all this.' Peter wants to remind them of his passion—not just passion for Jesus and for the Bible, but also passion for them. He is affirming, 'You are my dear friends, the ones whom I care about deeply. I write not for your harm but for your good.' While Peter uses the term, 'beloved' for the first time here in 3:1, he uses it on a further three occasions in this final chapter. Yes, he is passionate about Jesus and passionate about the Bible, but he is also passionate about his readers—he loves them deeply.

This reminds us of the way Paul writes: 'I do not write these things to make you ashamed, but to admonish you as my beloved children ...' (1 Corinthians 4:14). In a similar manner, in the midst of the hard words which Peter has been compelled to write, he re-affirms his love for them.

If we are passionate about Jesus and passionate about the truth, then sometimes we need to speak (or write, in Peter's case) to someone with words that may be hard for them to accept or to hear. If so, Peter models how to do it. If such words need to be said, they should be said not only from a heart of passion for Jesus and passion for the Bible, but also a heart of passion for the person to whom we communicate. Hard words should be designed to gather up the other person in love and urge them nearer to Jesus. They are words we may speak only if we hold deep love for the other person. The Biblical principle is clear: if we do not love, then we must not speak such words. When Jesus provides a summary of the law, he quotes, 'Love the Lord your God with all your heart and with all your soul and with all your mind and with all your strength.' In other words, hold a passion for God and for his Word. But Jesus did not stop there.

He also quoted, 'Love your neighbour as yourself' (Mark 12:30–31). This latter is a passion for one another.

Peter models passion in three directions, then: God, his Word, and one another. For that reason, Peter expresses his passion here in chapter 3—'Now this, beloved ...'. He loves these Christians and wants them to stay on track. That is his passion.

Next, Peter explains his purpose.

Peter's purpose (vv. 1–2)

His readers would be sure to wonder why Peter writes as he does, so he tells them. 'I am stirring up your sincere mind by way of reminder, that you should remember the predictions of the holy prophets and the commandment of the Lord and Saviour through your apostles' (2 Peter 3:1).

In chapter 1, Peter finishes describing justification by faith alone and sanctification by God's work in us as we strive to love him more. Then he moves to emphasize the need for them to remember. 'I will always *remind* you of these things' (2 Peter 1:12); 'I think it is right to refresh your *memory*' (2 Peter 1:13); and 'You will always be able to *remember* these things' (2 Peter 1:15). In other words, he provides a three-fold encouragement for them to remember.

Now, in chapter 3, he returns to this important need to refresh our memories. 'I have written ... as reminders to stimulate you to wholesome thinking. I want you to recall ...' (NIV). More literally, this reads, 'In both of them, I am *stirring up your sincere mind* by way of *reminder*, that you should *remember* ...' (ESV), To reiterate, Peter provides a second three-fold encouragement for them to remember.

What does he want them to remember? It is no different from

what he wrote back in chapter 1. They are to remember justification by faith alone and sanctification as we grow into Christ, and they are to remember that we need continually to immerse ourselves in the truth through God's Word.

What does Peter want his readers to do? He wants them to recall the words of the prophets (that is the Old Testament), and to recall the words of Jesus given through the apostles (2 Peter 3:2).[2] Peter has already written about how certain we can be of the Scriptures (that was the second half of chapter 1). Now, once again, he is reminding his readers to pay attention to God's Word. This is his purpose.

Notice how closely it is linked with his passion. He is passionate about God, God's Word, and his fellow believers. Therefore, his purpose is to direct his fellow believers back to God through God's Word, that they may be passionate about Him.

Did you notice how he describes the Old Testament: 'words spoken in the past by the holy prophets' (2 Peter 3:2, NIV). The ESV has it this way: 'the predictions of the holy prophets'. It is instructive that while the Old Testament is full of history, poetry, apocalypse, genealogy, and law, Peter describes all of it as 'prophecy'. Why does he do that?

Luke 24 provides a clue. There, Jesus is speaking with two disciples on the road to Emmaus the morning following his resurrection. 'Beginning with Moses and all the prophets, he [Jesus] interpreted to them in all the Scriptures the things concerning himself' (Luke 24:27). In other words, whatever else may be happening in the Old Testament writings, all of it is about Jesus, all of it points to Jesus, and all of it is fulfilled by Jesus. In Genesis 1 and 2, Jesus (the 'Word' of God), created all things. In Genesis 3, Adam and Eve are clothed by God in the Garden, pointing towards Christians being clothed by God with the righteousness of Jesus. In Genesis 4, the righteous Abel was killed by the unrighteous Cain as a picture of the death of the righteous Son of God on the cross, rather than the unrighteous 'son of Adam' who deserves to die. Jesus is to be found in all of the Scriptures because it is all about him. Thus, whatever else it may be, the Old Testament is prophecy about Jesus—words spoken in the past not just about the future generally, but about Jesus specifically. This is why Peter describes the whole of the Old Testament as 'prophecy'.

If the Old Testament is prophecy about Jesus, how does Peter view the apostolic writings (or the New Testament as we know it now)? Again, Peter describes it with one word: 'The *command*ment of the Lord and Saviour ...' (2 Peter 3:2). This word 'command' is singular, not plural. He does not write that the Old Testament is prophecies and the New Testament is commands. Rather, he explains that the Old Testament is prophecies plural, but the New Testament is 'command', singular. Again, the apostolic writings include history, genealogy, poetry, prophecy, and, later, apocalypse, but to sum them up, Peter describes them as one command. Why does he do that?

The New Testament is clear that Jesus, though he had never done anything wrong, fulfilled the Old Testament prophecies by dying on the cross and then being raised to life. As sinners we recognize this perfect fulfilment. As people who have done so much wrong, we realize that we deserve God's judgement and condemnation. As a result, our cry is, 'What shall we do?'

When Peter preached to the crowds in Jerusalem at Pentecost, he explained to them that Jesus, the sinless, died and they, the sinful, deserve God's judgement and condemnation. The crowd responded with the same cry as our own: 'Brothers, what shall we do?' (Acts 2:37).

Peter's response in Acts 2 is a single command: 'Repent.' It means to turn around—to turn away from the old rebellious life and turn towards the One who created you, loves you and died to save you. It means to seek his forgiveness and life through submitting to him. Repent. There is but one command to be obeyed: 'Repent.' Everything else follows from obedience to that one command.

The Old Testament is all about Jesus, pointing towards his substitutionary death, his resurrection, his glory and our eternal hope in him. The New Testament is, in essence, a single command from God. It is a command we find explicitly on the lips of the apostle Peter in Acts 2, and again through Peter's words here in 2 Peter 3: 'Repent.'

If you have not yet submitted to Jesus, then, as you hear of your own fallenness and guilt in the eyes of Almighty God, and as you hear of your desperate need for forgiveness and of the possibility of freedom from that guilt, your obligation is to obey a single command: 'Repent.' If you do, then your relationship with God is restored and an eternal and joyful future is assured.

What is Peter's purpose as he writes this letter? He desires for his readers to come to the cross and to keep returning to the cross; to keep reminding themselves of what Jesus has achieved for them; to keep submitting to the Lord Jesus who died for them; to keep striving to love Jesus more and live his way more closely; and to keep reading God's word as the stimulus to staying close to Jesus.

Peter is passionate about God, about God's Word, and about God's people. His purpose is to point people back to God through his Word. What if every Christian had Peter's passion and purpose? What if I did? What if you did?

We might think, 'Well, that's all very well, but that's just Peter's purpose. Mine might be different.' So, Peter turns next to consider God's purpose.

God's purpose (vv. 3–7)

Peter makes the point that we should pay attention to God's Word not just because there are pseudo-teachers and pseudo-Christians in the church, but more specifically because of what those pseudo-teachers are saying. 'Scoffers will come in the last days with scoffing, following their own sinful desires. They will say, "Where is the promise of his coming?"' (2 Peter 3:3–4). In other words, these pseudo-teachers are arguing that life goes on as it always has. People are marrying and giving in marriage. People are being born, growing, working, marrying, making money, having families, retiring and life simply goes on and on. They argue that the warnings of the Bible can be ignored. 'Nothing has come of Jesus' threat to come back,' they scoff. So, they follow their own sensual desires.

But if we do not pay attention to God's Word (2 Peter 1:19), then we will begin to capitulate to the ways of the world. Like a hot coal taken from the fire, slowly we will grow cold and become ineffectual in shedding the warmth and light of the gospel to others. If we ignore God's Word through the prophets and the apostles, then we will give in to the world. If you have never submitted to Jesus and given your life to him then you are already a scoffer who is 'following ... [your] own evil desires'.

There is a direct link between scoffing and following your own evil desires. According to Peter, those who scoff will live as they please. They think of themselves as king of their own lives. What they want is what they do. They live for themselves, ultimately. Sure, they may help other people or look out for their neighbours or have compassion on others. But in the end, they put themselves first. Remember the condemnatory words from the book of Judges in the Old Testament: 'Everyone did what was right in his own eyes' (Judges 21:25). They live the way they think they should. There is no submitting to a higher authority here, and no desire to come under the command of Almighty God.

Such people may live right, provided they are not too inconvenienced. They may live right, provided they are not required to sacrifice too much. Perhaps they live right because it makes them feel better about themselves, or because other people will then think better of them. Sometimes people seek to live right because they think that doing so will somehow make up for their own failings and misdeeds and brokenness. But the reality is that none of these are 'living right' at all.

This should stand in stark contrast with believers. For someone who has submitted to Jesus, Jesus is King. Our priority is not to follow our own fleshly desires, but to follow in the footsteps and rule of our King.

The scoffers will say 'Where is the promise of his "coming"? For ever since the fathers fell asleep, all things are continuing as they were from the beginning of creation' (2 Peter 3:4). Have you ever thought this? Have you listened to preachers always giving these warnings about God's holiness and Jesus coming back to judge? And perhaps you think: 'But nothing ever happens. The world goes on as it always has.' Well, that is the argument of the scoffers in Peter's day, and many take the same view in our day as well.

Peter attacks this position with punishingly direct logic. He points his readers to Noah and the flood. Some people think that Peter deciding to talk about the flood is strange, but often this is because they do not understand the purpose of the flood. Just prior to the flood, we read: 'The Lord saw that the wickedness of man was great in the earth, and that every intention of the thoughts of his heart was only evil continually' (Genesis 6:5). As a result, many people think that the purpose of the flood was to get rid of all the sin and start all over again. In other words, the flood is a sort of large wash to clear away the evil and make way for a new world.

But this is a demonstrably false idea. Immediately after the flood, 'I will never again curse the ground because of man, for the intention of man's heart is evil from his youth' (Genesis 8:21). The whole world has been washed clean. All the people steeped in sin have died, and now only Noah and his family remain. But, as God describes Noah and his family, he says, 'The intention of man's heart is evil from his youth.' With regards to the problem of sin, the flood achieved nothing. If God's idea was to wash everything clean and start again so that sin would be no more, then He failed.

But God did not fail, because that was never the point of the flood. To begin with, the flood demonstrates the seriousness of sin. It shows us how seriously God takes rebellion against himself. The flood is not a children's story so that kids can colour in fun pictures of giraffes and hippos. The flood is a real-life movie, certificate 18. It is a horror movie through which the truth about God and the need for repentance is clearly preached by Noah, perhaps for a period as long as a hundred years, with zero positive response from anyone. Eventually, the ark was complete and time had run out. Noah and his immediate family enter the ark. And then God rains down his judgement upon the world for over a month until all humankind outside the ark have perished. That is how seriously God takes sin and rebellion and a refusal to repent.

On a deeper level, though, the reason for the flood is painted in bold letters here by Peter. 'The world that then existed was deluged with water and perished. But by the same word, the heavens and earth that now exist are stored up for fire, being kept until the day of judgement and destruction of the ungodly' (2 Peter 3:6–7). To put it another way, Peter is saying that the prime purpose of the flood, in all its terror and horror, is to provide us with a picture of the coming judgement of God upon the world. It is the clearest picture of final judgement that we have in all of history.

We can miss the force of what is happening at the flood in Genesis. We know that Genesis 1–3 is all about the beginning of the cosmos, the creation of humankind and the fall of humankind. In other words, human history does not really get underway until chapter 4, where Cain and Abel are born, Cain kills Abel, Seth is born and the families begin to grow. And then we are pretty much at chapter 6.

We are tempted to think that probably there are not that many people around—not much has happened. But this is a very distorted view because it ignores chapter 5. That chapter is a genealogy—we are good at forgetting those! But Genesis 5 is of deep significance, for many reasons. One reason is that it tells us something about the time span. The period from the birth of Seth—Adam and Eve's third son—to the time of the flood is not short; it is something over 1500 years. That is about the same as the time from the New Testament church to the time of the Reformation.

By the time of the days of Noah, there were thousands of people around. What were they doing? They were being born, growing, working, marrying, making money, having families, etc. In the middle of it all, Noah was preaching of the pending judgement of God, but the people scoffed. They ignored the ongoing warnings of Noah. They said, 'Where is this judgement you're telling us about? Nothing has changed. Everything goes on as it always has.' They scoffed.

Back in 2 Peter, do you notice Peter's devastating logic? He brackets the creation of the world and the flood. The scoffers 'deliberately overlook this fact, that the heavens existed long ago, and the earth was formed out of water and through water by the Word of God' (2 Peter 3:5; see Genesis 1). 'By means of these, the world that then existed was deluged with water and perished' (3:6; see Genesis 6 to 8).

When Peter writes, 'in the last days' (3:3), he is referring to his own time and ours. What happens then? 'Scoffers will come ... with scoffing, following their own sinful desires.' They will be saying, 'Where is this coming? Where is this coming judgement you keep talking about? Everything goes on as it always has!' The scoffers in Peter's day and in our day make an identical argument to that given by those in the days of Noah. And what happened to those in the days of Noah? God's judgement fell suddenly and devastatingly, and the scoffers perished in a matter days.

Peter's argument is that people in his day are saying exactly what people were saying prior to the flood. They have heard the words of the prophets and words of the apostles, and so they think that the idea, that Jesus is returning and judgement is coming, is clearly rubbish. So, Peter shouts from the rooftops: 'Remember the Flood!'

The same holds true in our day, too. People are living in rebellion against God. People ignore all the warnings of God's people. 'Nothing has changed for hundreds, no thousands of years,' the scoffers say, 'so why should I be worried about a so-called "coming"? Why should I concern myself about warnings of pending judgement? Nothing has happened until now. Maybe I'll worry about it when I'm really old. Maybe I won't. But don't try and make me do what you want with your made-up stories and scaremongering. I'll decide how to live my life thank you very much.'

Peter breaks into such dangerous thinking with a clarion call: 'Remember the Flood.' 'Watch out!' Judgement is coming—there is no doubt about that. Just like before the flood, so it is now.

This time, however, it will not be a watery grave. This time it will be a fiery inferno. The burning judgement of God will fall, terrifyingly, upon all those who have not bowed the knee to Jesus. Justice will be done. This is God's purpose. His inescapable, conclusive and burning holiness ensures that judgement is coming. Have no doubt and do not be a scoffer. Instead, tremble and recognize the purpose of Almighty God.

This leads us finally to God's passion in judgement.

God's passion (vv. 8 – 9)

Peter writes now: 'Do not overlook this one fact, that with the Lord one day is as a thousand years, and a thousand years as one day' (v. 8). Do not forget that the way the world really works can be understood only from the perspective of our divine Creator and Sustainer. God is not bound by time in the way we are. To us, a thousand years seems forever. Jesus has promised to return and judge, but it has not happened for centuries, so why should we worry—it looks like it is never going to happen at all.

But, as we look at what leads up to verse 8, we see that while you may think God is taking a long time to fulfil his promise to return and bring judgement, it is not a long time as far as God is concerned. He has a much broader and wider view of history than we do. He stands outside the bounds of time looking in, and the fact that we have not seen this judgemental act for a long time does not mean he has forgotten it, or he has rescheduled, or he has changed his plans, or the plans are in fact just made up to try and coerce humankind to live a particular way.

Looking forward from verse 8, we see that it also says that this is to do with God's patience. The reason his judgement has not yet come is simple: he is being patient. He is waiting for you to turn from your sin and turn towards Jesus for love, life and liberty. He is waiting for you to move away from darkness into light. He is expending his energy drawing you and cajoling you and urging you to come. He is inordinately patient, as a father is patient for a rebellious toddler.

Next, Peter highlights what some theologians have come to call the *preceptive will of God*. The preceptive will of God expresses his heart's desire for humankind. God's prime passion is that he wishes—he wants—that no one should perish. He does not want judgement to fall on people and for them to be condemned, and thus experience eternal hell without God and without hope. He does not want people to be cut off from him forever. He does not want sin to stand in the way of anyone and prevent anyone from spending eternity with him in life, love and liberty.

While some people *will* experience this darkest of futures, this is not God's *preceptive will*. He wants what is fully the best for us, not some sugar-coated placebic pseudo-life that promises much and gives nothing. That is what the pseudo-teachers have been promoting in the previous chapter—a pretend love, a pretend joy, a pretend hope. God does not wish that for anyone. God wants to be in a relationship with us. This is God's passion. He deeply desires our fulfilment and joy. His preceptive will expresses his heart of love towards people.

Notice that Peter is completely clear about *how* people can avoid building a house of cards with their lives. He describes how people can avoid an otherwise inevitable and just eternal punishment. This punishment, remember, is not a drowning to death in a flood, but a burning judgement. There is only one way to avoid it, and Peter is crystal clear what it is: repentance.

This is how we avoid judgement. We turn from sin. We turn away from the decaying trinkets of this material life. We turn away from society's shattered promises of happiness and hopefulness. We turn away from the western relationship philosophy with its hopeless, convictionless and commitmentless grope for satisfaction. We turn away from the idolatry of self.

Instead, we turn towards the One who gave himself. We turn towards Jesus who stepped in to turn aside the wrath of God against sin, who offered himself as our substitute, who paid with his life to ransom us. 'Repent,' Peter demands again. Turn away from sin towards the Saviour. That is the only route by which we may avoid perishing.

There seems to be an increasing cultural desire to keep our options open. No one wants to commit to anything just in case a better offer comes along. But Peter could not be clearer: The only way to avoid perishing eternally is to come in repentance to the God who created you and sustains you.

You will get all kinds of different offers from the world, but none of them will do anything to rescue you from the hellish eternity that awaits. Instead, they will each slowly harden and shore up your heart against the call of God for you to submit. Each will calcify and petrify your heart until it is as rock, unyielding to any of the things of God until it is too late and your heart is shattered by that final judgement: 'I never knew you; depart from me' (Matthew 7:23).

God is patient, but as we will discover in the final few verses, his patience does not last forever. Judgement will come, like it did for the people of Noah's day. God's Passion is that we recognize his promise, come to him in repentance, and so live. The scoffers are scoffing, seeming to have a good time, but they are heading for destruction. Reject that way of being and *live*.

'What is man's chief end?' asks the *Westminster Shorter Catechism*. The answer? 'Man's chief end is to glorify God and enjoy him forever.'[3] That is what Peter is writing here, too. 'Repent and be baptized every one of you in the name of Jesus Christ for the forgiveness of your sins' (Acts 2:38). God makes the same demand of us every day. The passion of Almighty God is that we repent, because there alone lies hope.

Notes

1 *The Westminster Shorter Catechism*, 1647, Question 1: 'What is the chief end of man?' https://www.apuritansmind.com/westminster-standards/shorter-catechism/

2 For Peter's readers, they had available perhaps Luke, Acts, James, and all the writings of Paul except perhaps for 1 & 2 Timothy and Titus.

3 *The Westminster Shorter Catechism*, 1647, Answer to question 1: 'What is the chief end of man?' https://www.apuritansmind.com/westminster-standards/shorter-catechism/

16 Now and then

2 Peter 3:10-18

On Boxing Day 2004, 230,000 people died in a tsunami in the southern Far East. On thinking back to that day in Thailand, one survivor wrote:

The first thing we knew was when people came running into the café where we were having breakfast, knocking things over: tables, chairs, people. Everyone was panicking. Outside, there was chaos. People were running in all directions. There was a lot of screaming. It was like being in a horror movie; and we had no idea what was going on. Ahead of us, the shoreline was bubbling and boiling. There was a growing roar in the air. And suddenly it was really, really windy. The last thing I remember was the shouted words, 'Find somewhere high up ...' And then came the water.

Here in the final verses of his second letter, Peter looks forward to the 'Day of the Lord'. Like the Boxing Day tsunami, it will be a sudden and unexpected day. For many, unbeknown to them, it will be a day that heralds disaster. Peter first explains what happens on that 'Day of the Lord', before finishing by answering the question, 'In the light of that future, how, then, should we live?' To put it another way, he begins with the 'then' and ends with the 'now'.

Then (vv. 10-13)

'The day of the Lord will come like a thief,' Peter writes (2 Peter 3:10). Before considering the unexpected suddenness of it, though, it would make sense to remember what the phrase, 'Day of the Lord', means in the Bible.

Zephaniah wrote: 'The great Day of the Lord is near ... A day of wrath is that day, a day of distress and anguish, a day of ruin and devastation, a day of darkness and gloom, a day of clouds and thick darkness ...' (Zephaniah 1:14–15). Ezekiel put it this way: 'The day of the Lord is near; it will be a day of clouds, a time of doom for the nations ...' (Ezekiel 30:3). Joel wrote: 'The day of the Lord is near; and as destruction from the Almighty, it comes' (Joel 1:15).

In other words, in the Old Testament, the 'Day of the Lord' is a day of distress, trouble, ruin, darkness, anguish and disaster. In the New Testament, the phrase, 'Day of the Lord', describes the return of Jesus. At Jesus' first coming, his focus was on bearing sin and taking the punishment we deserve. But at his second coming, he will come to judge the living and the dead. Jesus' return is the arrival of judgement day, and that is why it is a day of distress, trouble, ruin, anguish, and disaster.

Notice, though, that Peter begins verse 10 with the word 'but'. In the previous verse, he has asserted that 'the Lord is not slow to fulfil his promise, as some count slowness, but is patient toward you, not wishing that any should perish, but that all should reach repentance.' Then, 'BUT, the day of the Lord will come like a thief.' In other words, God *is* patient, yes. Preaching of the truth will go on right up until the last moment, just as Noah preached for year after year after year after year right up until the rain began to fall. People had every opportunity to repent. *But*—verse 10—God's patience will not last forever.

God shut the door to the ark in Genesis 7, so that no one else could come in. Similarly, God will one day shut the door to eternal life and no one else will be able to come in. As a thief comes unexpectedly, suddenly, unannounced, so that 'Day' will come. As the Boxing Day tsunami came unexpectedly, suddenly, unannounced, so Jesus will come unexpectedly, suddenly, and unannounced. Judgement will follow inevitably. There will be no more delay. God's patience will be spent.

Those who have submitted to Jesus will enter into eternal perfect joy with him, but those who have not submitted, those who have not repented—those who have not turned to Jesus but rather remained against him—their destiny will be exposed. For them, the future is dark, joyless, loveless, fruitless, and empty. Only hell awaits.

An obvious question as we approach the idea of the 'Day of the Lord', though, is to wonder what it will be like. Here, Peter gives us a glimpse *through the keyhole* as it were. He writes, 'The heavens will pass away with a roar' (3:10). Like a coming tsunami, it will be loud! He continues: 'The elements will be destroyed by fire' (NIV), or to translate it another way, 'the heavenly bodies will be burned up and dissolved' (ESV). In our day, of course, we know that the stars are already burning, but on that 'Day of the Lord', the day of Jesus' return, the stars will burn out. Peter finishes: 'And the earth and everything done in it will be laid bare' (NIV), or more literally, 'the earth and the works that are done on it will be exposed' (ESV).

In other words, the God who created all things at the beginning, who sustains all things and upholds all things and keeps all things going, will sustain things no longer. Instead, he will execute his final judgement on all people and all of the cosmos. Think of the terror of that. Think of the finality of that. Think of the horror of that!

We might be tempted to think this *burning up of the stars* (which includes the sun) would mean that the world is plunged into utter darkness, but that is not the case. Look at the final phrase in verse 10: 'The earth and the works that are done on it will be exposed.' Yes—the stars will be gone; even the sun will be gone. But instead of darkness there will be a blinding light. This is the 'Day of the Lord', the day of the second coming of Jesus, who is the Light of the World. The radiant, glorious, overwhelming light of perfect holiness, love and justice will finally and fully be here. In his light, all things will be made known.

It would be tempting to think that only physical things will be made known. But the original language suggests that it is the *works* done on the earth that will be exposed. All of your acts, your deeds, all that you have thought and said, will be laid bare and made known as judgement comes. People who love darkness rather than light will crave hiding places and darkness and shrouding, but there will be none, because Jesus the Light of the World has come, and all sin is finally exposed for what it is.

We know that this exposure of our sinful acts is what sits in Peter's mind here because of what he says next: 'Since all these things are thus to be dissolved, what sort of people ought you to be in lives of holiness and godliness, waiting for and hastening the coming of the day of God ...' (2 Peter 3:11–12). In other words, because this day is coming, so you should live holy and godly lives. Such living will make judgement easier for you.

I find it surprising the way that Peter ends this part—'waiting for and hastening the coming of the day of God ...'. If this is the day when all our sin is laid bare before the world and before Almighty God, why would anyone ever look forward to that day? It seems insane, does it not? When I think of all the sin that lies hidden in my heart—when you think of all the sin that lies hidden in your heart— why in the world would we ever look forward to the day when that sin is exposed? Why would we ever want anyone else to see it? And most importantly, why would we ever want it laid before God, the great Judge of all things?

In fact, Peter makes it even worse by writing that in that day, 'The heavens will be set on fire and dissolved, and the heavenly bodies will melt as they burn' (3:12, ESV) or 'That day will bring about the destruction of the heavens by fire, and the elements will melt in the heat' (NIV). Preternatural things will happen on that day. Elemental things will happen on that day. Terrifying things will happen that are harbingers of death. So why would I ever look forward to that Day and, more, why would I ever wish to speed its coming? Surely, I want that day to be as far away as possible, as far in the future as possible, sometime so far ahead that I can dull my mind and not think about it from day to day. I want it to be so far ahead, perhaps, that I can commission myself to be a better person so that I can be less embarrassed and horrified on that day. Why would I want to speed its coming?

Friends, if you are not a Christian, then you do not want this day to come. This is a day of reckoning. If you continue to hold on to your sin, to reject the authority of God, to live as your own master, and to try and deal with your own mess, then that day will indeed be agonizing. It will be a day for you that provides full exposure of all your sinfulness; a day for you that stretches beyond into punishment and loneliness and despair and eternal darkness.

But it is different for Christians. Remember: Peter is writing primarily to Christians here. In fact, he has already explained this difference, because he began this second letter with the key reason why we should look forward to that day if we are Christians. We have received our faith *because of* the righteousness of Jesus; and because you belong to Jesus, the Holy Spirit lives within you. His job is to prepare you in godliness for that final day. If you are a Christian, then when Jesus returns on that great 'Day of the Lord', your sins — all of them — are covered and paid for and expunged and dealt with and ransomed and obliterated by Jesus. The one who comes to judge the world on that day is the very one who has *already* dealt with your sin. As far as the east is from the west, that is how far he has removed our transgressions from us (Psalm 103:12).

So, for the Christian, that Day is a glorious one. Jesus is returning. Judgement will happen. Justice will be done. All wrongs will be righted. All injustices will be exposed and resolved. An eternal future without sin or pain or trouble or blemish will begin on that day, as we spend all of the forever with our fellow Christians in the presence of our Lord Jesus. It will be a glorious and wonderful day indeed.

The writer to the Hebrews makes the same point: 'Just as it is appointed for man to die once, and after that comes judgement, so Christ, having been offered once to bear the sins of many, will appear a second time, not to deal with sin but to save those [bring salvation to] who are eagerly waiting for him' (Hebrews 9:27–28). Yes, the Day of the Lord is the coming of Jesus as judge. But it is also the coming of Jesus as final Saviour for all those who belong to him.

So, Christian, how should we live as we yearn for that day — how should we 'speed its coming' as Peter puts it? What kind of people ought we to be? Peter answers the question: We ought to live holy and godly lives. We are to live this way, not because if you live a holy and godly life then maybe you can cancel out some of the dirt and mess and horror of your own sinfulness. Neither is it because somehow a holy and godly life can earn acceptance by this grand Judge of all things. Rather, we are to live holy and godly lives because the grand judge of all things has already paid the price for our sin, dealt with it, and given us a joyful future. We seek to live godly and holy lives day by day because we are looking forward to a new heaven and a new earth, the home of righteousness (2 Peter 3:13). We are to live God's way because we are practising for heaven!

Peter tells us that, when Jesus returns, he is going to make everything new. John makes the same point: 'Then I saw a new heaven and a new earth, for the first heaven and the first earth had passed away' (Revelation 21:1–5a). Something new is coming. This word 'new' is also used by Paul: 'If anyone is in Christ, he is a *new* creation. The old has passed away; behold, the *new* has come' (2 Corinthians 5:17). Obviously, Paul is not saying that when we become Christians we morph into a completely different and unrecognizable body, or that our personality is utterly changed. Some things remain the same—if I had knobbly knees before, perhaps I will have them after—I'll just be happy with them then!

Remember Jesus after his resurrection? Mary thought he was the gardener until he said her name. On the road to Emmaus, the two disciples did not recognize him until he broke bread in their home. He was new, different, and yet he was somehow the same as well. He was different and yet he was still recognizable. He had a resurrection body (which was different from his previous body), but there were things about him that were not changed. The tomb was *empty* because his old body had been made new—perhaps 'renewed' would be a better word.

After the flood, sin had not been dealt with and neither was it eradicated. But the 'new heavens and a new earth', Peter is describing, will be a renewed and refreshed and perfected world, sin-free and pain-free and worry-free and regret-free and guilt-free. It will be a world in which we will live in perfection forevermore. Thus, for the Christian, the 'Day of the Lord' is the gateway to a glorious eternal future.

Having considered the 'then' in the last few sentences, Peter moves to talk about the 'now'. In the light of this glorious future, how should we live now?

Now (vv. 14–18)

Since all of us, Christian or otherwise, are waiting for the new heavens and the new earth, we should be 'diligent to be found by him without spot or blemish and at peace' (2 Peter 3:14). In Luke 15, Jesus tells three parables: The lost sheep, the lost coin, and the lost son. In each case, joy is expressed as a result of something being *found*. 'Rejoice with me, for I have *found* my lost sheep' (Luke 15:6), says the farmer. 'Rejoice with me, for I have *found* the coin that I had lost' (Luke 15:9), says the woman. 'It was fitting to celebrate and be glad, for this your brother was dead, and is alive; he was lost and is *found*' (Luke 15:32), says the father. Each one rejoices because something lost is found.

Peter writes here in the NIV, 'make every effort to be *found* spotless, blameless and at peace with him' (2 Peter 3:14b), but I think the ESV puts it more accurately: 'Be diligent to be *found by him*, without spot or blemish and at peace.' In other words, the only way to be without spot or blemish and at peace is to be *found* by Jesus.

If you are not *found*, then you are lost. You are spotted, blemished and without peace. You continue to clutch your sinful way of life, like an orphan preferring to clutch an old dirty blanket than to accept the offer of adoption into the royal family. You grasp your sin tightly, enjoying the pleasure of its momentary comforts, not understanding that it is dripping with acid which slowly destroys your soul. As a result, you stand guilty of your sin. You stand scarred and disfigured by your sin. You stand shamed by your sin. You stand severed from the one person who truly loves you. And you have no peace, no lasting settled-ness in the presence of your Creator, and no serenity in the storms of life. The judgement to come will be terrible for you and will result in your eternal condemnation. Your future will be full of pain and anger and loneliness and hopelessness and despair. So how do you move from this point in life?

Back in Luke 15, the word for 'found' is on a par with repentance. Luke makes this clear himself: 'Rejoice with me, for I have found the coin that I had lost. Just so, I tell you, there is joy before the angels of God over one sinner who *repents*' (15:9–10). Peter has already made the same point, which we considered earlier: God 'is patient toward you, not wishing that any should perish, but that all should reach repentance' (2 Peter 3:9).

How, then, do we come to be without spot or blemish? There is only one way. Only through the salvation that Peter has been explaining throughout his second letter. Only through the work of Jesus on the cross. We cannot make ourselves sinless, and a new start is not enough, as the flood demonstrates. Only Jesus at work in us through the Holy Spirit can cover over our sins, pay for our sins (past, present and future), buy us back, and bring us to Father God without spot or blemish and at peace.

You may wonder, 'To what extent does God *want* me?' The phrase, 'spot/blot or blemish', Peter has already used to describe the pseudo-believers (2 Peter 2:13). It means, 'dirty scabs'. Perhaps you may feel a bit like a scab. Perhaps you would say, 'I know something of the length and breadth and height and depth of my own sin and wickedness and rebellion against God. I know only too well my failure to do what I should. I know my dark and sin-fuelled thought-life, and my regular practice of doing and saying what I should not. In the light of how bad I am, God would not want anything to do with me.'

Peter responds with the reminder that Jesus has not yet returned, reflecting the patience of God. 'Count the patience of our Lord as salvation' (2 Peter 3:15). God *does* want something to do with you. In fact, he wants everything to do with you. His passion—remember from the previous verses—is not for you to perish but that you too should reach repentance. 'Count the patience of our Lord as salvation.' Peter has described God's passion for you, and he has urged you to come to repentance. That is what is required. Nothing more. Nothing less.

Next, though, Peter changes direction a bit. He wonders whether his own lack of education may mean that his readers fail to take his words seriously. In light of this, he points to the apostle Paul. Paul has been described as the *Einstein of his day*. He was *the* top thinker of the first century. Perhaps, then, Peter is expressing: 'This is not just my idea, friends. No—these are words Paul also wrote to you according to the wisdom given him. He is really clever and knows way more than I do about pretty much everything ... (apart from fishing), and he says the same things. If you won't accept my words, accept his.'

Note Peter's assertion about Paul, here in verse 15: 'Paul also wrote to you according to the wisdom given him ...'. The implication is that the wisdom God gave Paul is not the same as the wisdom God gave Peter. This is borne out by what follows—'There are some things in them [Paul's letters] that are hard to understand, which the ignorant and unstable twist to their own destruction, as they do the other Scriptures.'

Peter is affirming that he and Paul are different. He admits that, for him at least (and for most of us too, I suspect!), Paul's letters have some parts that are difficult to understand. Just because you are a Christian does not mean you will automatically get your head around everything that the Bible says. I can identify with Peter. Some of what Paul writes, I find hard to understand. I remember talking to a university chaplain once. He was arguing that we do not have to accept all of the Bible as true. He said, 'For example, Paul's thinking is a bit woolly and confused, isn't it ...?' No, chaplain, it is not. Paul's logic is incisive, direct, deep and profound, and on a human level, the reason you and I find it hard to understand is simply that we are not as clever as Paul. This is what Peter is saying here in chapter 3: 'I am not as clever as Paul.' Thankfully, as we grow nearer to Jesus, so the Holy Spirit continues to open our minds to the truth and we understand more and more, so that not being as clever as Paul does not bar us from understanding things.

On a different note, I cannot imagine Peter wrote this without remembering the strong words Paul spoke to him earlier. When in Galatia, Paul opposed Peter *to his face* in an open, public disagreement, because Peter had begun a practice at odds with the freedom of the gospel (Galatians 2:11–14). Notwithstanding, look how he describes Paul here in his letter: 'Our beloved brother!' (2 Peter 3:15). There is no animosity here. There is no envy here. For the fourth time in this chapter, Peter uses the word, 'beloved', and he uses it to describe Paul. While recognizing and being open about the differences between them, Peter displays a unity in which God's people have the same Lord and therefore the same purpose, despite their differences and disagreements and differing ideas.

This unity is about following the Lord together, recognizing that we do not all agree on every single thing, but being committed nonetheless to the common cause of the gospel of Jesus. This unity includes talking through our differences with openness and love, sometimes in a public setting. This unity recognizes our beloved brothers and sisters who have a different wisdom given to them than the wisdom given to us and accepts that we can learn from them. This unity refuses to allow people to twist the words of others to suit their own ends, even when we are not quite sure what the original words meant!

So, the first thing Peter teaches us here is *togetherness*. Acceptance and openness about our differences can happen in a context of love for one another.

Secondly, Peter writes that *twisting* the words of Paul is ignorant, unstable and leads to destruction. Peter is clear—hold on to Paul's words and do not twist them, even if you do not understand them.

For example, somehow all of our actions are under the authority and rule and direction and management and control of Almighty God. And somehow, at the same time, we have some free will and we are responsible for how we think, what we say and do not say, and what we do and do not do. Those two things: divine sovereignty and human responsibility, are both true. Hard to understand and hard to hold together, but true. They are not to be twisted.

Thirdly, Peter points his readers to *truth*. Peter is abundantly clear here that Paul's letters are Scripture. Peter was a Jew who was brought up on the Old Testament with a great reverence for it, so for him to emphasize that Paul's writing is new, authoritative revelation was hardly a natural step for him. Yet Peter is clear—the Old Testament is God's Word, and the writings of Paul hold the same authority—they are God's Word also. Right here we have not just a recognition but also an assertion that at least some of the New Testament writings are to be regarded as Scripture.

Peter has spent some time in this second letter not just urging people to consider coming to faith in Jesus and growing in their faith, but also campaigning for his readers to take the Scriptures seriously. He has said this about the Old Testament Scriptures. He has said this about much of the New Testament also. Likewise, we are to take them seriously—we are to pay attention to them (2 Peter 1:19)—because they lead us to Jesus over and over and over and over again. This is exactly what we all need. Rejecting or twisting—rewriting, if you will—God's Word means that you are doomed to destruction (2 Peter 3:16).

I remember a conversation with a young person about a debate with an atheist who read from Luke 19:27. Jesus is speaking and, in that verse, he says: 'But as for these enemies of mine, who did not want me to reign over them – bring them here and slaughter them before me.' Reading out this verse, the atheist scoffed, 'See—at the very least, Jesus was a tyrant, and I want nothing to do with him.'

So, the young person and I looked up the passage. We discovered that the atheist read it correctly. But we realized, too, that he had ignored the context. In fact, these words are the last part of a parable Jesus has been telling. A man of noble birth goes to a far-off country to be made king, and when he had gone, we read that his subjects hated him and sent a message ahead of him to say, 'We don't want this man to be our king.' The noble had given different amounts of money to three of his servants to put the money to work while he was away. After his return, the third servant had done nothing at all with the money and criticized the noble for his way of conducting business. The final comment from the noble is to those who hated him and said they did not want him to be king. The noble said, 'But as for these enemies of mine who did not want me to reign over them – bring them here and slaughter them before me.'

The very next verses in Luke describe Jesus entering Jerusalem on a donkey's foal, being proclaimed king. The point of the parable is that many do not want Jesus to be king. And while he goes to the royal city to be made king, they will come against him. His immediate coronation turns out to be with a crown of thorns, not a crown of gold, and Jesus died at the hands of his subjects who hated him. A little later, Jesus is raised from the dead, and now he reigns as king over all. One day he is returning—the *Day of the Lord* is coming—and on that day, those who continue in rebellion against him will face condemnation. For those who are against Jesus, on that day judgement will come and they will face condemnation. That is the purpose of the parable. Just as the noble demanded justice of those who rejected him as king, so God will bring justice against those who reject Jesus as king. Unsurprisingly, the atheist took the words of the parable out of context and twisted them.

On an initial reading, we might expect Peter to write, 'Some things ... are hard to understand, which the ignorant and unstable twist to their own *advantage*, as they do the other Scriptures.' Why do they twist things? To gain an *advantage* for themselves, or over others? So, this is what we would expect Peter to say. But he does not write this way. Instead, he writes that people, who twist the Scriptures, do so to their own *destruction*.

When the atheist pulled a verse out of context and thus twisted it to mean something it does not mean at all, he may think he has twisted to his own advantage, so that he need not bow the knee to Jesus. But that is definitely *not* to his advantage. Quite the opposite. Refusing to bow the knee to Jesus is to secure our eventual destruction. We must never twist the words of God because to do so is to press the self-destruct button. Rather we are to submit to God's Word.

Peter continues with the same line of thought: 'take care that you are not carried away with the error of lawless people ...' (2 Peter 3:17). He is describing those who twist the Word of God.

How are we to take care we are not carried away with the error of lawless people? It is simple: be a Bible addict. Note that Peter is not arguing that if you misunderstand the Bible, or fail to read it often enough, then you will lose your salvation. Rather, if you misunderstand the Bible or fail to read it often enough and get carried away by error, you will lose your own *stability*. Stability involves standing on the truth. It is what the NIV translates as a 'secure position'.

We can only stand on the truth if we know the truth. Jesus *is* the truth. Thus, we need to get further and further into his Word, the Scriptures, in order to know him better and better. That is the only way to avoid being carried away by the error of lawless people.

And what is the result of sticking to the truth? Peter tells us: We 'grow in the grace and knowledge of our Lord and Saviour Jesus Christ' (2 Peter 3:18). There is a deep and essential connection between immersing ourselves increasingly in God's Word and growing in grace and knowledge of Jesus. As we read and study and think, so we love Jesus more, and we grow in grace. Growing in the grace of Jesus and growing in the knowledge of Jesus are inseparable.

Conclusion

Thus, Peter has considered the '*then*' and the '*now*'. We know what is next (what is coming), namely the *Day of the Lord* in all its terror and judgement and glory and salvation. As a result, '*now*' we work diligently to live more and more as Jesus calls us to live, and he works in us to grow more and more like him—this happens as we immerse ourselves increasingly in the truth of God's Word. The thief comes suddenly, unexpectedly, but we can be prepared for his arrival. A baby, likewise, comes suddenly, but a parent will prepare for the arrival. Noah knew God's judgement was coming, but he prepared for its arrival with God's help by doing as God directed him. That terrible Boxing Day tsunami came suddenly, unexpectedly and terrifyingly. But we can be prepared by getting to higher ground—standing on the truth.

Peter tells us: That great 'Day of the Lord' is coming. Are you prepared? For you, will that day be a day of great joy or will it be the day of disaster? God is patient, waiting for you to come to repentance, but his patience will not last forever. Are you prepared?